Reader's Guide to ALEXANDER POPE

Reader's Guide to ALEXANDER POPE

W. Cormier

CENTRUM PRESS
NEW DELHI-110002 (INDIA)

CENTRUM PRESS
H.O.: 4360/4, Ansari Road, Daryaganj,
New Delhi-110 002 (India)
Ph.: 23278000, 23261597

B.O.: No. 1015, Ist Main Road, BSK IIIrd Stage
IIIrd Phase, IIIrd Block,
Bangalore - 560 085 (India)
Tel.: 080-41723429
Visit us at: www.centrumpress.com

Reader's Guide to Alexander Pope

First Edition, 2009

ISBN 978-93-80106-80-9

PRINTED IN INDIA

Printed at Balaji Offset, Delhi.

Contents

Preface

Pope was born 21 May, 1688, in London. His father was a cloth merchant living in the City (a part of London); both his parents were Catholic. It was a period of intense anti-Catholic sentiment in England, and at some point (ca. 1700) in Alexander's childhood, the Pope family was forced to relocate to be in compliance with a statute forbidding Catholics from living within ten miles of London or Westminster. They moved to Binfield.

Pope's early education was affected by his Catholicism: Catholic schools, although illegal, were allowed to survive in some places. Prior to the move to Binfield Pope spent a year at Twyford, where he wrote "a satire on some faults of his master," which led to his being "whipped and ill-used and taken from thence on that account." From Twyford Alexander went to study with Thomas Deane, a convert to Catholicism (who lost his position at Oxford as a result of his religious beliefs). After the Pope family moved to Binfield Alexander became self-taught.

Pope's disease—apparently tuberculosis of the bone—became evident when he was about twelve. Later in Pope's life, Sir Joshua Reynolds described him as "about four feet six high; very humpbacked and deformed." A more recent biographer (Maynard Mack 155-6) has written that Pope was "afflicted with constant headaches, sometimes so severe that he could barely see the paper he wrote upon, frequent violent pain at bone and muscle joints...shortness of breath, increasing inability to ride horseback or even walk for exercise...."

Author

Chapter 1

Introduction

Alexander Pope (21 May 1688 – 30 May 1744) is generally regarded as the greatest English poet of the eighteenth century, best known for his satirical verse and for his translation of Homer. He is the third most frequently quoted writer in the English language, after Shakespeare and Tennyson. Pope was a master of the heroic couplet.

EARLY LIFE

Pope was born in the City of London to Alexander (senior, a linen merchant) and Edith Pope (née Turner), who were both Roman Catholic. Pope's education was affected by the laws in force at the time upholding the status of the established Church of England, which banned Catholics from teaching on pain of perpetual imprisonment. Pope was taught to read by his aunt and then sent to two surreptitious Catholic schools, at Twyford and at Hyde Park Corner. Catholic schools, while illegal, were tolerated in some areas. From early childhood he suffered numerous health problems, including Pott's disease (a form of tuberculosis affecting the spine) which deformed his body and stunted his growth, no doubt helping to end his life at the age of 56. He never grew beyond 1.37 metres (4 feet 6 inches) tall. Although he never married, he had many women friends and wrote them witty letters.

In 1700, his family was forced to move to a small estate in Binfield, Berkshire due to strong anti-Catholic sentiment and a statute preventing Catholics from living within 10 miles (16 km) of either London or Westminster. Pope would later describe the countryside around the house in his poem *Windsor*

Forest. With his formal education now at an end, Pope embarked on an extensive campaign of reading. As he later remembered: "In a few years I had dipped into a great number of the English, French, Italian, Latin, and Greek poets. This I did without any design but that of pleasing myself, and got the languages by hunting after the stories...rather than read the books to get the languages." His favourite author was Homer, whom he had first read at age eight in the English translation by John Ogilby. Pope was already writing verse: he claimed he wrote one poem, *Ode to Solitude*, at the age of twelve.

At Binfield, he also began to make many important friends. One of them, John Caryll (the future dedicatee of *The Rape of the Lock*), was two decades older than the poet and had made many acquaintances in the London literary world. He introduced the young Pope to the aging playwright William Wycherley and to William Walsh, a minor poet, who helped Pope revise his first major work, *The Pastorals*. He also met the Blount sisters, Martha and Teresa, who would remain lifelong friends.

EARLY LITERARY CAREER

First published in 1710 in a volume of *Poetical Miscellanies* by Jacob Tonson, *The Pastorals* brought instant fame to the twenty-year-old Pope. They were followed by *An Essay on Criticism* (1711), which was equally well received, although it incurred the wrath of the prominent critic John Dennis, the first of the many literary enmities which would play such a great role in Pope's life and writings.

Windsor Forest (1713) is a topographical poem celebrating the "Tory Peace" at the end of the War of the Spanish Succession. Around 1711, Pope made friends with the Tory writers John Gay, Jonathan Swift and John Arbuthnot, as well as the Whigs Joseph Addison and Richard Steele. Pope's friendship with Addison would later cool and he would satirise him as "Atticus" in his *Epistle to Doctor Arbuthnot*.

Pope, Gay, Swift, Arbuthnot and Thomas Parnell formed the Scriblerus Club in 1712. The aim of the club was to satirise ignorance and pedantry in the form of the fictional scholar Martinus Scriblerus. Pope's major contribution to the club would be *Peri Bathous, or the Art of Sinking in Poetry* (1728), a parodic guide on how to write bad verse. *The Rape of the Lock* (two-canto version, *The Rape of the Locke*, 1712; revised version in five cantos, 1714) is perhaps Pope's most popular poem. It is a mock-heroic epic, written to make fun of a high society quarrel between Arabella Fermor (the "Belinda" of the poem) and Lord Petre, who had snipped a lock of hair from her head without her permission.

In 1714, the political situation worsened with the death of Queen Anne and the disputed succession between the Hanoverians and the Jacobites, leading to the attempted Jacobite invasion of 1715. Though Pope as a Catholic might be expected to have supported the Jacobites, according to Maynard Mack, "where Pope himself stood on these matters can probably never be confidently known". These events led to an immediate downturn in the fortunes of the Tories, and Pope's friend, Henry St John, 1st Viscount Bolingbroke fled to France. The climax of Pope's early career was the publication of his *Works* in 1717. As well as the poems mentioned above, the volume included the first appearance of *Eloisa to Abelard* and *Elegy to the Memory of an Unfortunate Lady*; and several shorter works, of which perhaps the best are the epistles to Martha Blount.

HOMER AND SHAKESPEARE

Pope had been fascinated by Homer since childhood. In 1713, he announced his plans to publish a translation of Homer's *Iliad*. The work would be available by subscription, with one volume appearing every year over the course of six years. Pope secured a revolutionary deal with the publisher Bernard Lintot, which brought him two hundred guineas a volume. The commercial success of his translation made Pope the first English poet who could live off the sales of his work alone, "indebted to no prince or peer alive", as he put it. His translation of the *Iliad* duly appeared between 1715 and 1720. It was later acclaimed by Samuel Johnson as "a performance which no age or nation could hope to equal" (although the classical scholar Richard Bentley wrote: "It is a pretty poem, Mr. Pope, but you must not call it Homer."). The money he made allowed Pope to move to a villa at Twickenham in 1719, where he created a famous grotto and gardens.

The grotto he decorated with alabaster, marbles, ores such as mundic, crystals: Cornish diamonds, stalactites, spars, snakestones and spongestone. Here and there he placed mirrors (very expensive embellishments for those times). He also installed a camera obscura to delight his visitors, of whom there were many.

The serendipitous discovery of a spring during its excavations enabled the subterranean retreat to fill with the relaxing sound of trickling waters, which quietly echoes around its exotic chambers. Pope was said to have remarked that: "Were it to have nymphs as well – it would be complete in everything." Although house and gardens have long since been demolished or destroyed, much of this grotto still survives. It is opened to the public once a year.

Encouraged by the very favourable reception of the *Iliad*, Pope translated the *Odyssey*. The translation appeared in 1726, but this time, confronted with the arduousness of the task, he enlisted the help of William Broome and Elijah Fenton. Pope attempted to conceal the extent of the collaboration (he himself translated only twelve books, Broome eight and Fenton four), but the secret leaked out. It did some damage to Pope's reputation for a time, but not to his profits.

In this period Pope also brought out an edition of Shakespeare, which silently "regularised" his metre and rewrote his verse in several places. Lewis Theobald and other scholars attacked Pope's edition, incurring Pope's wrath and inspiring the first version of his satire *The Dunciad* (1728), the first of the moral and satiric poems of his last period. Alexander Pope became a freemason and member of the Premier Grand Lodge of England.

"AN ESSAY ON MAN" AND SATIRES

Though the *Dunciad* was first published anonymously in

Dublin, its authorship was not in doubt. As well as Theobald, it pilloried a host of other "hacks", "scribblers" and "dunces". Mack called its publication "in many ways the greatest act of folly in Pope's life". Though a masterpiece, "it bore bitter fruit. It brought the poet in his own time the hostility of its victims and their sympathizers, who pursued him implacably from then on with a few damaging truths and a host of slanders and lies...". The threats were physical too. According to his sister, Pope would never go for a walk without the company of his Great Dane, Bounce, and a pair of loaded pistols in his pocket.

In 1731, Pope published his "Epistle to Burlington", on the subject of architecture, the first of four poems which would later be grouped under the title Moral Essays (1731-35). In the epistle, Pope ridiculed the bad taste of the aristocrat "Timon". Pope's enemies claimed he was attacking the Duke of Chandos and his estate, Cannons. Though the charge was untrue, it did Pope a great deal of damage.

Around this time, Pope began to grow discontented with the ministry of Robert Walpole and drew closer to the opposition led by Bolingbroke, who had returned to England in 1725. Inspired by Bolingbroke's philosophical ideas, Pope wrote An Essay on Man (1733-4). He published the first part anonymously, in a cunning and successful ploy to win praise from his fiercest critics and enemies.

The *Imitations of Horace* followed (1733-38). These were written in the popular Augustan form of the "imitation" of a classical poet, not so much a translation of his works as an updating with contemporary references. Pope used the model of Horace to satirise life under George II, especially what he regarded as the widespread corruption tainting the country under Walpole's influence and the poor quality of the court's artistic taste.

Pope also added a wholly original poem, An Epistle to Doctor Arbuthnot, as an introduction to the "Imitations". It reviews his own literary career and includes the famous portraits of Lord Hervey ("Sporus") and Addison ("Atticus"). In 1738 he wrote the *Universal Prayer*.

After 1738, Pope wrote little. He toyed with the idea of composing a patriotic epic in blank verse called *Brutus,* but only the opening lines survive. His major work in these years was revising and expanding his masterpiece *The Dunciad*. Book Four appeared in 1742, and a complete revision of the whole poem in the following year.

In this version, Pope replaced the "hero", Lewis Theobald, with the poet laureate Colley Cibber as "king of dunces". By now Pope's health, which had never been good, was failing, and he died in his villa surrounded by friends on 30 May 1744. On the previous day, 29 May 1744, Pope called for a priest and received the Last Rites of the Catholic Church. He lies buried in the nave of the Church of St Mary the Virgin in Twickenham.

LITERARY LEGACY

The death of Alexander Pope from *Museus,* a threnody by William Mason. Diana holds the dying Pope, and John Milton, Edmund Spenser, and Geoffrey Chaucer prepare to welcome him to heaven.

The poetry of Alexander Pope holds an acknowledged place in the canon of English literature, although his work has gone in and out of fashion. One edition of the *Oxford Dictionary of Quotations* includes no fewer than 212 quotations from Pope.

Some quotations from Pope's work have passed so deeply into the English language that they are often taken as proverbial by those who do not know their source: "A little learning is a dang'rous thing" (from the *Essay on Criticism*); "To err is human, to forgive, divine" (*ibid.*); "For fools rush in where angels fear to tread" (*ibid*); "Hope springs eternal in the human breast" and "The proper study of mankind is man" (*Essay on Man*). This would have greatly pleased Pope, who wrote:

True wit is nature to advantage dress'd;
What oft was thought, but ne'er so well express'd.

Pope dominated his age to an extent few writers before or since have matched. After his death, it was almost inevitable a reaction would set in against his poetry, especially with the first stirrings of Romanticism in the late eighteenth century.

In *An Essay on the Genius and Writings of Pope* (1756 and 1782), Joseph Warton denied Pope was a "true poet", merely a "man of wit" and a "man of sense". In his *Lives of the Poets* Doctor Johnson countered: "...It is surely superfluous to answer the question that has once been asked, whether Pope was a poet, otherwise than by asking in return, if Pope be not a poet, where is poetry to be found?". But he was fighting a losing battle against changing taste.

The Romantics had little time for Pope, with the notable exception of Lord Byron, who acclaimed him as "the great moral poet of all times, of all climes, of all feelings, and all stages of existence". Keats dismissed the style of writers who wrote in heroic couplets, saying:

They sway'd about upon a rocking horse,
And thought it Pegasus. (*Sleep and Poetry*)

In the Victorian era, Matthew Arnold dismissed Pope and Dryden as "classics of our prose". The 19th century considered his diction artificial, his versification too regular, and his satires insufficiently humane. The third charge has been disputed by various 20th century critics including William Empson, and the first does not apply at all to his best work. That Pope was constrained by the demands of "acceptable" diction and prosody is undeniable, but the elegance and flexibility with which Pope used this technique shows that great poetry could be written with these constraints. His expression is concise and forceful, conveying emotion as well as reason and wit.

In his time Pope was famous for his witty satires and aggressive, bitter quarrels with other writers. When his edition of William Shakespeare was attacked, he answered with the savage burlesque *The Dunciad* (1728), which was widened in 1742. It ridiculed bad writers, scientists, and critics: "While pensive poets painful vigils keep, / Sleepless themselves to give their readers sleep." With the growth of Romanticism Pope's poetry was increasingly seen as outdated and the 'Age of Pope' ended. It was not until the 1930s that any serious attempts were made to rediscover the poet's work.

ISAAC NEWTON'S EPITAPH

Pope is known to have written Isaac Newton's epitaph:
"Nature and nature's laws lay hid in night;
God said "Let Newton be" and all was light."

A reference to this epitaph is made in Dan Brown's novel "The Da Vinci Code".

BELIEFS

Pope openly described himself a Roman Catholic at a time when it was still illegal to profess Catholicism in England, and practise of the religion was subject to stiff penalties.

WORKS

Pope's house at Twickenham, showing the grotto. From a watercolour produced soon after his death.

- (1709) *Pastorals*
- (1711) *An Essay on Criticism*
- (1712) *The Rape of the Lock*
- (1713) *Windsor Forest*
- (1715-1720) Translation of the *Iliad*
- (1717) *Eloisa to Abelard*
- (1717) *Elegy to the Memory of an Unfortunate Lady*
- (1725-1726) Translation of the *Odyssey*
- (1728) *The Dunciad*
- (1734) *Essay on Man*
- (1735) *The Prologue to the Satires* (see the *Epistle to Dr Arbuthnot* and *Who breaks a butterfly upon a wheel?*)

Chapter 2

The Rape of the Lock

The following comes from the Twickenham Edition of Pope's poems:

"The families concerned in the *Rape of the Lock*—the Fermors, Petres, and Carylls—were prominent members of that group of great intermarried Roman Catholic families owning land in the home counties, most of whom came within the circle of Pope's friends and acquaintances and to whom Pope considered his own family to belong. Some time before 21 March, 1712, when Pope sold his poem to Lintott, Robert, Lord Petre had cut off a lock of Arabella Fermor's hair, and John Caryll had suggested to Pope that he should write a poem to heal the estrangement that followed between the two families:

The stealing of Miss Belle Fermor's hair, was taken too seriously, and caused an estrangement between the two families, though they had lived so long in great friendship before. A common acquaintance and well-wisher to both, desired me to write a poem to make a jest of it, and laugh them together again. It was with this view that I wrote the Rape of the Lock. The incident behind the poem has never been authoritatively tracked down to place and time. It is improbable, but possible, that it happened, as the poem states, at Hampton Court; and the counter-claims of the houses of the Fermors, Petres, or Carylls have never been substantiated." (Twickenham, Vol II, p. 83)

Was Belinda, as the poem hints, willing to marry the Baron? "Arabella may well have been considered as the possible bride for Lord Petre. The rape of the lock may well have been an incident in the period of circumspection—how thorough such circumspection was likely to be may be gathered from the correspondence of Caryll during 1710-11 when he was choosing a wife for his son. If two such families who 'had lived so long in friendship before' are estranged through a fairly trivial incident, it seems there is thunder in the air. All the fun of the poem read very differently when, less than two months before the poem was published, Lord Petre married Catherine Warmsley, a Lancashire heiress some seven or more years younger than Arabella and much richer." (Twickenham 93)

By the time Pope revised the poem in 1717, Lord Petre had died (of smallpox) and Arabella was married. Whatever the original purpose of the poem may have been, by the time Pope finished revising *The Rape of the Lock* the feud between the families was no longer particularly relevant.

CHRONOLOGY OF EARLY EDITION OF THE POEM

"The first sketch of this Poem was written in less than a fortnight's time, in 1711..."(or so Pope wrote in 1736. The exact fortnight hasn't been identified, although sometime during August and/or September seems most likely.) Copies of the poem were distributed to the Fermor and Petrie families, and as Pope wrote to Joseph Spence: "copies of it got about, and 'twas like to be printed, on which I published the first draught of it (without the machinery)...." Pope sold his 2 canto, 334 line poem to Bernard Lintott (or Lintot) for 7 pounds on 21 March, 1712; it was published in May.

By 1714 the "machinery" had been added, extending the poem to 5 cantos and 794 lines. This time Pope earned 15 pounds, and Linotott arranged to include 6 copper-plate engravings by Du Guernier and Du Bosc. The edition was a huge success. Pope claimed (to John Caryll) "[the poem] has in four days time sold to the number of three thousand," and by July he reported sales of over 6000. Two more printings were needed in 1714, and a new printing was done in each of 1715,1718, and 1723.

The version of the poem available at this site is based on

the 1717 poem found in Pope's *Works*. The only substantial way it differs from the 1714 version is the inclusion of Clarissa's speech at the start of Canto V. Clarissa, Pope tells us, was a "new Character introduced in the subsequent Editions, to open more clearly the MORAL of the Poem...." (Clarissa had in fact made her cameo appearance as provider of the scissors in both the 1712 and 1714 versions of the poem.)

Modern critics consider *The Rape of the Lock* to be the supreme example of mock-heroic verse in the English language. Written in heroic couplets, the poem was most likely composed during the late summer of 1711 and first published in the May edition of *Lintot's Miscellany* in 1712. The original version of the poem contained 334 lines in two cantos.

A more elaborate version appeared two years later, extending the poem to 794 lines in five cantos; a slight final revision was completed for the poem's inclusion in Pope's *Works* (1717). Inspired by an actual event, *The Rape of the Lock* recounts the circumstances surrounding the theft of a lock of a young woman's hair by an impassioned male admirer, which caused a rift between the families involved. The poem was intended to restore harmonious relations between the estranged families.

Subtitled "an heroi-comical poem," *The Rape of the Lock* treats the petty matter in full-blown epic style, which results in a great deal of humour. It uses the elevated heroic language that John Dryden, Pope's literary forebear, had perfected in his translation of Virgil and incorporates amusing parodies of passages from John Milton's *Paradise Lost,* Vergil's *Aeneid,* and Homer's *Iliad,* which Pope was translating at the time. Celebrated as a masterstroke of English originality, *The Rape of the Lock* established Pope as a master of metrics and a sophisticated satirist.

PLOT AND MAJOR CHARACTERS

Although the precise time and place of the incident that occasioned *The Rape of the Lock* have been lost to history, the depilatory theft and ensuing feud between two prominent Catholic families certainly happened, the standard account of which is documented in the Twickenham edition of Pope's complete works. Briefly stated, the poem elaborates upon the events of a day, most likely during the summer of 1711, when Robert, Lord Petre, brazenly snipped off a curl of Arabella Fermor's hair, an act which estranged their families.

Pope's friend John Caryll, to whom the poem is addressed, suggested that Pope write it in order to "laugh them together again." The poem's epigraph (translated by Aubrey Williams as "I was unwilling, Belinda, to ravish your locks; but I rejoice to have conceded this to your prayers") is a slightly altered passage from Martial's *Epigrams,* in which Pope substitutes Belinda for Martial's heroine, Polytimus, with the implication that the original poem was published with Arabella's consent.

Pope set the central action of his poem at Hampton Court—the traditional home of royalty—which, though a possible site, is a highly unlikely one, since both families were mere gentry as well as members of an ostracized religion.

In the original two-canto poem the "gentle *belle,*" Belinda, awakens one morning and joins friends on a river trip up the Thames to play cards and drink coffee at Hampton. As the afternoon wanes, the Baron snips one of Belinda's favourite locks of hair with scissors provided by Clarissa. Great dismay ensues among the guests, devastating Belinda and scandalizing the company. Her angry demands for the return of her purloined lock are futile, since the destined lock of hair floats away as a new star to adorn the night skies.

As in his later satires, Pope substitutes fictional or type names for the specific personalities he has in mind, so that the character of Belinda is based on Arabella, that of the Baron on Lord Petre, and that of Sir Plume, a blithering guest at Hampton, on Sir George Browne, a relative of Arabella's mother. Pope significantly expanded the straightforward story in subsequent editions by simply adding conventional features of epic verse, then called the "machinery," or supernatural dimension, of the poem.

Adapted from the light erotic work *Le Comte de Gabalis* and Rosicrucian lore, the "machinery" of the five-canto version of the poem introduces such supernatural creatures as the earthy gnome Umbriel—a reincarnation of a prude—and the ethereal sylphs—the spirits of dead coquettes. In addition, Pope inserted a detailed account of Belinda's daily routine at her dressing table, a description of the social rituals involved with a lively game of ombre, and an otherworldly visit to the Cave of Spleen.

Clarissa's speech on "good Humour," or common sense, first appeared in the last revision of the poem, which Pope added "to open more clearly the MORAL of the Poem." In the 1712 and 1714 versions of the poem, Clarissa makes a brief appearance as the one who hands the scissors to the Baron.

MAJOR THEMES

Fusing high humour and moralization, *The Rape of the Lock* offers an ironic perspective on contemporary manners combined with a deep appreciation for the vitality of the eighteenth-century *beau monde.* With sensitivity, exquisite taste, high-spirited wit, and gentle satire, the poem forces a continuous comparison between insignificant and significant things, between the mundane and the exotic. In his mock epic, Pope exploits the difference between the grandeur of "heroic" moments depicted in traditional epics and the consciously trivial events in his poem. By treating the latter incidents as matters of great import, their inconsequence is made obvious.

The poem features the devices of traditional epic poetry in abundant allusions to and parodies of incidents, characters, and themes from a range of classical and modern epics, but these themes are proportionately scaled down. In *The Rape of the Lock,* ladies and gentlemen are the heroines and heroes, exchanging repartee with the opposite sex in salons instead of waging war against noble enemies on fields of combat. Rather than gods and goddesses intruding in human affairs, sylphs and gnomes intervene, with tasks appropriate to their natures.

The epic game is ombre played on the "velvet plain" of a card table, the victors feast on gossip between sips of coffee instead of ambrosia and wine, and the epic struggle is determined by clever quips and innuendo, by winks, nods, and frowns, not weapons. The traditional epic journey to the underworld is evoked by a visit to the Cave of Spleen, an emblem of the petty temperaments of privileged women. These actions unfold against an elegantly appointed backdrop of beautiful objects: rich brocades, glowing diamonds, tortoise shell and ivory combs, cosmetics and hair dressings, varnished furniture, silver coffeepots, and dainty china.

Yet for all the evident beauty, charm, and allure these active, shimmering world exhibits, lighthearted raillery pulses throughout its civilized veneer, a reminder of its trite values and the vanities of its inhabitants.

CRITICAL RECEPTION

The original version of *The Rape of the Lock* accomplished its task—since the Fermors and Petres were reconciled—and it immediately received an enthusiastic response from the public and the critics alike. Joseph Addison, who considered the poem perfect as it was first written, advised Pope against revision, but with the addition of the "machinery" and other material, the poem soon was deemed Pope's most brilliant performance as well as one of his most popular and lucrative, going through seven printings by 1723. Throughout the eighteenth century the poem remained a perennial favourite.

Samuel Johnson pronounced it "the most attractive of ludicrous compositions," in which "New things are made familiar and familiar things are made new." Although appreciation of Pope's poetry generally declined throughout the nineteenth century, Victorian readers and critics continued to delight in the ethereal qualities of *The Rape of the Lock.* James Russell Lowell declared, "For wit, fancy, invention, and keeping, it has never been surpassed," and Leslie Stephen observed that Pope's poem "is allowed, even by his bitterest critics, to be a masterpiece of delicate fancy."

Twentieth-century critics have interpreted the poem in a diverse range of contexts, from character analyses and examinations of the poem's extensive allusions to both literary and folklore traditions, to investigations into Pope's political motivations and his understanding of the commercial aspects of the burgeoning publishing industry. A common thread in much twentieth-century criticism of *The Rape of the Lock* has acknowledged the way in which a deep appreciation for English high society meshes with Pope's critique of its weaknesses.

Since the 1980s a number of critics have delved into other areas of Pope's career in relation to the poem, including the nature of Pope's habit of revision and its effect on the poem's meaning as well as the connections between mercantile discourse and Popean aesthetics. In addition, feminist critics have approached the poem in terms of ideological and cultural assumptions about women and their status in Pope's society, uncovering a significant response to the poem by women readers since its publication. Inarguably, Pope's most popularly cherished poem, *The Rape of the Lock,* also is his most conceptually imaginative work.

Chapter 3

The Christian Vindication of God in Alexander Pope's "An Essay on Man"

Some might argue that Alexander Pope's "An Essay on Man" presents the viewpoint of a deist. Others might claim that the poem fails to exhibit Christian concepts of good and evil, especially since the poet concludes his first epistle with the seemingly unchristian claim that "whatever IS, is Right" (I. 1. 294). Yet Pope's arguments actually reflect a traditional Christian perspective, which can be verified by comparing his poem with New Testament teachings.

In his attempt to vindicate God in the face of suffering, he does not, like the pantheist, rule out the existence of evil. Pope knows that men are capable of vice and that suffering is real. Pope does not argue that evil does not exist; rather he argues that its existence does not preclude the justice of God. Like the writers of the New Testament, particularly the apostle Paul, Pope claims that pride and envy leads man to question the justice of God, and he insists that men submit to God, remaining content with their lot in life.

Although Pope claims that "[o]ne truth is clear, `Whatever IS, is Right'" (I. 1.294), he recognizes suffering:

But errs not nature from this gracious end,
From burning suns when livid deaths descend,
When earthquakes swallow, or when tempest sweep
Towns to one grave, whole nations to the deep? (I. ll. 140-143)

Pope does not only acknowledge the existence of evil. He

describes it in vivid detail. In the above passage, he paints a horrid picture of plagues caused by excessive heat, of destructive earthquakes, and of storms that decimate entire towns and nations. He writes too of Ammon, who was turned "loose to scourge mankind" (I. l. 160). He may argue that nature does not err to allow such disasters, but he never claims that they do not exist.

Nor does Pope deny the existence of personal vice. In the tradition of Christian thought, he claims that although nothing is evil in itself, vice and virtue still exist. For instance, neither self-love nor reason are evil, but each has its place in the order, "self love, to urge, and Reason, to restrain" (I. 154). Therefore, neither "this a good nor that a bad we call" (II. l.56). However, Pope insists that this lack of inherent evil does not imply that neither virtue nor vice exist. "Fools!" he cries, "who from hence into the notion fall, / That Vice or Virtue there is none at all" (II. 210-211). Vice and virtue still exist, even if something as seemingly negative as self-love can be made a virtue. "If white and black bend, soften, and unite / A thousand ways, is there no black or white?" (II. ll. 212-213). Although black and white may mix to form gray, and although vices can be made into virtues and virtues into vices, absolute right and wrong remain.

Pope then anticipates the question: "This light and darkness in our chaos join'd, / What shall divide?" He replies: "The God within the mind" (II. ll. 202-203). Conscience will tell whether a certain quality is a virtue or a vice. For it is not the quality itself, but rather how the quality is applied, that determines whether it is right or wrong.

Indeed, "Nero reigns a Titus if he will" (II. l. 198). Both Titus and Nero possessed the same power, but they applied it differently. Rumor blamed Nero for the great fire in Rome, whereas Titus rebuilt much of the city, including the colosseum and the baths. So Nero used his power to destroy, while Titus used his to rebuild. Both dealt with fires in Rome, but Nero reportedly fiddled, while Titus did everything he could to alleviate the suffering of his people.

Pope's thoughts are hardly unchristian. In fact, they

coincide with the teachings of the apostle Paul. He, too, claimed that "nothing is unclean in itself" (Romans 14:14). Paul also emphasizes the importance of application. "The man who eats does so to honour the Lord...the man who does not eat abstains to honour the Lord" (Romans 14:6).

Just as power is in itself neither good nor bad, the eating of meat is neither good nor bad. It becomes a virtue if a man eats to honour the Lord. If, however, his conscience prevents him from eating (because the meat had once been sacrificed to an idol), eating becomes a vice and abstaining becomes a virtue. As in "An Essay on Man," the deciding factor is conscience. Paul says that "each should be certain of his own conscience" (Romans 14:5). It will divide virtue from vice; it will separate the light and the darkness.

If Pope does not deny the existence of evil, then why does he maintain that whatever is is right? He even says that "respecting Man, whatever wrong we call, / May, must be right, as relative to all" (I. ll. 51-52). When Pope makes these claims, he does not imply that there is no vice. Rather, he implies that God is correct to *allow* imperfection in man, and that whatsoever God's wisdom ordains is right. Whatever we call imperfection in man can not be attributed to God's injustice. For "'tis but a part we see, and not a whole" (I. l.60). If man could relate his imperfection to God's intricate order, if he could see the whole and not just the part, he would understand that he had not been wronged by God.

Pope admits that evil exists, but he refuses to allow his readers to attribute its existence to the injustice of God. Instead, he attributes these complaints to the pride of man: "Ask for what end the heav'nly bodies shine, / Earth for whose use? Pride answers, 'Tis for mine'" (I. ll. 131-132). Men claim that God's creation is imperfect because they mistakenly believe that everything was created specifically for them. Pope admits that "if the great end be human Happiness, / Then Nature deviates" (I. 1. 149-150). He does not believe, however, that God created the world solely for man's happiness. Pride persuades men to consider their present felicity the core purpose of creation. "If Man alone engross not Heav'n's high care," (I. l. 119), if his pride is not satisfied by the fulfillment of every desire, he will enviously cry: "If Man's unhappy, God's unjust" (I. l. 118).

These complaints, besides being prideful, are also ridiculous. Pope writes that men are, in effect, considering themselves to be wiser than God. Pope demonstrates the absurdity of this attitude when he writes: "Snatch from the hand the balance and the rod, / Rejudge his justice, be the God of God!" (I. ll. 121-122). Man, by passing judgement on God's creation, elevates himself to a level of authority higher than that of God Himself. "Aspiring to be Angels," writes Pope, "Men rebel" (I. l. 128). Man refuses to accept that God has wisely placed him in the present order. He aspires first to be an angel, but his aspiration does not end there. Man mutinies against God Himself, snatching from His hand the rod of justice.

Pope emphasizes the absurdity of this rebellion when he asks: "What if the foot, ordained the dust to tread, / Or hand to toil, aspir'd to be the head?" (I. l. 259-260). God has placed each man wisely; if the individual were to succeed in acquiring a different place, then he would pervert the order, because "all are but parts of one stupendous whole" (I. l. 267). Man's envy leads him to wish that he were some other part, "and who but wishes to invert the laws / Of ORDER, sins against th' Eternal Cause" (I. ll. 129-130). Man's very desire is envious and therefore sinful, and his attempt, could it ever succeed, would prove disastrous. For, "from Nature's chain whatever link you strike, / Tenth or ten thousandth, breaks the chain alike" (I. ll.245-246). Fortunately, all rebellion is futile, as Pope's analogy of the body implies.

This analogy provides further evidence that Pope's philosophy is Christian. In fact, the mention of men as parts of one body should remind the Christian reader of Paul's claim that "just as each of us has one body with many members, and not all the members have the same function, so too we, though many, are one body in Christ" (Romans 12:4-5). As in "An Essay on Man," all are parts of the whole. And all should accept the role to which God has assigned them. "If the foot should say, 'Because I am not a hand I do not belong to the body,' would it no longer belong to the body?" (I. Corinthians 12:15). The foot is part of the whole, and it has its role to play. Pope asks what would happen if the foot aspired to be the head. Similarly, Paul asks, "If the body were all eye, what would happen to our hearing?" (I. Corinthians 12:17). Pope probably chooses his analogy to recall this passage. The congregation of the church at Corinth was having many struggles. Prod by envy, people were complaining that they had not been given all the gifts, talents, and positions they wanted, just as the people of Pope's time complained that God had made them imperfect.

Pope asserts that God has wisely placed each man in His great order. "Then say not Man's imperfect, Heav'n in fault; / Say rather, Man's as perfect as he ought" (I. 69-70). Pope does not imply that man has no faults, or that he is incapable of sin. He means only that God should not be criticized merely because He has not endowed men with everything they desire. "Who finds not Providence all good and wise," Pope asks, "alike in what it gives, and what denies?" (I. 1.205-206) Although man may not understand why, God is correct to deny him certain blessings.

Ultimately, Pope insists that men stop complaining that God is unjust and instead submit to His wisdom. Man may not understand why he lacks certain abilities. Even more baffling is the existence of suffering and evil. But rather than seek for an answer, and rather than blame God for evil's existence, men should simply trust God, knowing that one day all will be explained: "Hope humbly then...Wait the great teacher Death, and God adore!" (I. 11.91-92). This hope requires patience. As Paul writes, "hoping for what we cannot see means awaiting it with patient endurance" (Romans 8:25). Both Paul and Pope know that one day evil will be explained, because "there is nothing covered, that shall not be revealed; nether hid, that shall not be known" (Luke 12:2).

Nor is man left without some sense of the future. Pope tells the reader that although "what future bliss, he gives not thee to know," God at least "gives that hope to be thy blessing now" (I. ll. 95-96). The author of Hebrews calls this hope "an anchor of the soul" (Hebrews 6:19). Man may be left without understanding, but God does not leave him without the hope of one day understanding. Even though he may think he suffers now, man has the hope of future bliss, and it, like an anchor, will steady him. Man cannot blame God for evil. Instead, he must adore his Creator, humbly await an explanation, and submit to his present station in life.

Pope's emphasis on submission is decidedly Christian. "Submit-" he writes, "In this, or any other sphere, / Secure to be as blest as thou canst bear" (I. ll. 285-286). Paul writes something similar to Timothy: "And having food and raiment let us therewith be content" (Timothy 6:8). Man is to submit and remain content with what blessings he has been given. Paul would probably agree with Pope's claim that "to reason right is to submit" (I. l. 164). The Christian is constantly called to submission. "Wives should be submissive to their husbands" just "as the church submits to Christ" (Ephesians 5:22-24). Young men should submit to their elders, and all should "obey [their] leaders and submit to them" (Hebrews 13:17). Christ Himself offered this humble prayer of submission: "Thy will be done."

Pope has already shown that the failure to submit is a result of pride, and that it creates ridiculous envyings which threaten, in vain, to upset God's order. Therefore, Pope concludes that the only answer is to stop seeking for answers and to submit to the wisdom of God. "Cease then, nor ORDER Imperfection name: / Our proper bliss depends on what we blame" (I.ll.281-282). If man questions God, or blames Him for injustice, he can never be happy. But if he submits, he may remain "safe in the hand of one disposing Pow'r" (I. l. 287). Nor is God an indifferent power, who does not know of the suffering or the evil in His creation. He is a creator "who sees with equal eye, as God of all, / A hero perish, or a sparrow fall" (I. ll. 87-88). No doubt Pope intends this verse to remind the reader of the passage in Matthew in which Jesus says:

Not a single sparrow falls to the ground without your Father's consent. As for you, every hair of your head has been counted; so do not be afraid of anything. You are worth more than an entire flock of sparrows. (Matthew 10:29-31)

Man can confidently submit to the wisdom of God, because He assures people that He values them. He knows that suffering and evil exist, and nothing occurs without His permission, not even the death of a sparrow. He keeps careful watch over His creation, numbering even the hairs of a man's head. And if man suffers any evil, it is only because God must allow it to preserve His order, not because He is indifferent.

Pope insists on submission, because it alone can bring happiness, but he fails to follow his own advice. He does not wait humbly for death the teacher but attempts to explain evil immediately, in his own poem. He even claims from the very beginning that his object is not to remain quietly submissive, but to "vindicate the ways of God to Man" (I. l. 15). Indeed, this task exhibits the arrogance of refusing to submit, because Pope attempts to explain the ways of a God who has said: "My thoughts are not your thoughts, neither are your ways my ways. For as the heavens are higher than the earth, so are my ways higher than your ways" (Isaiah 55:8). Pope, in supposed humility, asks, "What can we reason, but from what we know?" (I. l. 17). Yet, soon after he asks the question, he proceeds to reason about things he could not possibly know. "So man, who here seems principal alone," he writes, "perhaps acts second to some sphere unknown / Touches some wheel, or verges to some goal" (I. ll. 57-59). Pope, determined to vindicate the ways of God to man, speculates on possibilities and offers tentative explanations for the problem of evil.

A prime example of Pope's failure to follow his own advice appears in the first epistle:

Better for Us, perhaps, it might appear,
Were there all harmony, all virtue here...
But ALL subsists by elemental strife;
And Passions are the elements of Life. (I. ll. 165-168)

If Pope were reasoning from what he knows, he could only conclude that suffering and imperfection were senseless, because it appears that harmony and virtue would be better for man. Yet, Pope does not confess that discord and vice are beyond his comprehension. Nor does he respond to their existence by insisting that men submit to God's wisdom, trusting that He has reasons, however incomprehensible to man, for what He does.

Instead, Pope tries to explain the reason. He argues that we are not surrounded with all harmony and virtue because strife is necessary for anything to exist. Tension between good and evil is essential to creation, and life can not endure without varying passions. Pope's explanation, however, proves inadequate. One could easily ask why God did not create the world so that it could exist just as well without strife. Certainly He is capable of creating a world with both order and harmony.

Surprisingly, Pope's failure to follow his own advice does not injure his argument. In fact, the very inadequacy of Pope's explanations demonstrates the necessity of submitting. Man should not struggle for answers, because any answer he can produce will prove insufficient. He can only trust that God is just, and that whatever evil He permits, He permits for a valid reason.

Perhaps Pope realizes this himself for a moment at the end of the second epistle. For he does not conclude by attempting to explain the existence of evil. Rather, he says only that "one comfort still must rise, / 'Tis this, Tho' Man's a fool, yet God is Wise" (II. ll. 292-293). In the end, it is better to believe that every man (including Pope) is a fool for failing to explain evil than to believe that God is not wise for allowing it. This couplet is one further proof of the Christian influence in Pope's "An Essay on Man." In the Epistle to the Romans, Paul writes: "Let God be true, but every man a liar" (Romans 3:4).

Chapter 4

His Translation of Homer's Iliad (1715)

HOMER is universally allowed to have had the greatest Invention of any Writer whatever. The Praise of Judgment *Virgil* has justly contested with him, and others may have their Pretensions as to particular Excellencies; but his Invention remains yet unrivaled. Nor is it a Wonder if he has ever been acknowledged the greatest of Poets, who most excelled in that which is the very Foundation of Poetry. It is the Invention that in different degrees distinguishes all great Genius's: The utmost Stretch of human Study, Learning, and Industry, which masters every thing besides, can never attain to this.

It furnishes Art with all her Materials, and without it Judgment itself can at best but *steal wisely:* For Art is only like a prudent Steward that lives on managing the Riches of Nature. Whatever Praises may be given to Works of Judgment, there is not even a single Beauty in them but is owing to the Invention. As in the most regular Gardens, however Art may carry the greatest Appearance, there is not a Plant or Flower but is the Gift of Nature.

The first can only reduce the Beauties of the latter into a more obvious Figure, which the common Eye may better take in, and is therefore more entertained with. And perhaps the reason why most Critics are inclined to prefer a judicious and methodical Genius to a great and fruitful one is, because they find it easier for themselves to pursue their Observations through an uniform and bounded Walk of Art, than to comprehend the vast and various Extent of Nature. Our

Author's Work is a wild Paradise, where if we cannot see all the Beauties so distinctly as in an ordered Garden, it is only because the Number of them is infinitely greater.

like a copious Nursery which contains the Seeds and first Productions of every kind, out of which those who followed him have but selected some particular Plants, each according to his Fancy, to cultivate and beautify. If some things are too luxuriant, it is owing to the Richness of the Soil; and if others are not arrived to Perfection or Maturity, it is only because they are over-run and oppress by those of a stronger Nature.

It is to the Strength of this amazing Invention we are to attribute that unequaled Fire and Rapture, which is so forcible in *Homer,* that no Man of a true Poetical Spirit is Master of himself while he reads him. What he writes is of the most animated Nature imaginable; every thing moves, every thing lives, and is put in Action.

If a Council be called, or a Battle fought, you are not coldly informed of what was said or done as from a third Person; the Reader is hurried out of himself by the Force of the Poet's Imagination, and turns in one place to a Hearer, in another to a Spectator. The Course of his Verses resembles that of the Army he describes.

OI D AR ISAG, {O}SEI TE PURI CHTH{O}N PASA GEMOITO

They pour along like a Fire that sweeps the whole Earth before it. It's however remarkable that his Fancy, which is every where vigorous, is not discovered immediately at the beginning of his Poem in its fullest Splendor: It grows in the progress both upon himself and others, and becomes on Fire like a Chariot-Wheel, by its own Rapidity. Exact Disposition, just Thought, correct Elocution, polish'd Numbers, may have been found in a thousand; but this Poetical *Fire,* this *Vivida vis animi,* in a very few.

Even in Works where all those are imperfect or neglected, this can over-power Criticism, and make us admire even while we disapprove. Nay, where this appears, though' attended with Absurdities, it brightens all the Rubbish about it, 'till we see nothing but its own Splendor. This *Fire* is discerned in *Virgil,* but discerned as through a Glass, reflected, and more shining than warm, but every where equal and constant: In *Lucan* and *Statius,* it bursts out in sudden, short, and interrupted Flashes: In *Milton,* it glows like a Furnace kept up to an uncommon Fierceness by the Force of Art: In *Shakespear,* it strikes before we are aware, like an accidental Fire from Heaven: But in *Homer,* and in him only, it burns every where clearly, and every where irresistibly.

I shall here endeavour to show, how this vast *Invention* exerts itself in a manner superior to that of any Poet, thro' all the main constituent Parts of his Work, as it is the great and peculiar Characteristick which distinguishes him from all other Authors. This strong and ruling Faculty was like a powerful Planet, which in the Violence of its Course, drew all things within its *Vortex.* It seem'd not enough to have taken in the whole Circle of Arts, and the whole Compass of Nature; all the inward Passions and Affections of Mankind to supply this Characters, and all the outward Forms and Images of Things for his Descriptions; but wanting yet an ampler Sphere to expatiate in, he open'd a new and boundless Walk for his Imagination, and created a World for himself in the Invention of *Fable.*

That which *Aristotle* calls the *Soul of Poetry,* was first breath'd into it by *Homer.* I shall begin with considering him in this Part, as it is naturally the first, and I speak of it both as it means the Design of a Poem, and as it is taken for Fiction.

Fable may be divided into the *Probable,* the *Allegorical,* and the *Marvelous.* The *Probable Fable* is the Recital of such Actions as tho' they did not happen, yet might, in the common course of Nature: Or of such as tho' they did , become Fables by the additional Episodes and manner of telling them. Of this sort is the main Story of an Epic Poem, *the Return of* Ulysses, *the Settlement of the* Trojans *in* Italy, or the like. That of the *Iliad* is {{Sig. B3v}} *the Anger of* Achilles, the most short and single Subject that ever was chosen by any Poet. Yet this he has supplied with a vaster Variety of Incidents and Events, and crouded with a greater Number of Councils, Speeches, Battles, and Episodes of all kinds, than are to be found even in those Poems whose Schemes are of the utmost Latitude and Irregularity. The Action is hurried on with the most vehement Spirit, and its whole Duration employs not so much as fifty Days. *Virgil,* for want of so warm a Genius, aided himself by taking in a more extensive Subject, as well as a greater Length of Time, and contracting the Design of both *Homer*'s Poems into one, which is yet but a fourth part as large as his.

The other Epic Poets have used the same Practice, but generally carried it so far as to super induce a Multiplicity of Fables, destroy the Unity of Action, and lose their Readers in an unreasonable Length of Time. Nor is it only in the main Design that they have been unable to add to his Invention, but they have followed him in every Episode and Part of Story. If he has given a regular *Catalogue* of an *Army,* they all draw up their Forces in the same Order. If he has funeral Games for *Patroclus, Virgil* has the same for *Anchises,* and *Statius* (rather than omit them) destroys the Unity of his Action for those of *Archemorus.*

If *Ulysses* visits the Shades, the *Æneas* of *Virgil* and *Scipio* of *Silius* are sent after him. If he be detain'd from his Return by the Allurements of *Calypso, so is Æneas* by *Dido,* and *Rinaldo* by *Armida.* If *Achilles* be absent from the Army on the Score of a Quarrel thro' half the Poem , *Rinaldo* must absent himself just as long , on the like account. If he gives his Heroe a Suit of celestial Armour, *Virgil* and *Tasso* make the same Present to theirs. *Virgil* has not only observ'd this close Imitation of *Homer* , but where he had not led the way, supply'd the Want from other *Greek* Authors. Thus the Story of *Sinon* and the *Taking of Troy* was copied (says *Macrobius*) almost word for word from *Pisánder* , as the Loves of *Dido* and *Æneas* are taken from those of *Medæa* and *Jason* in *Apollonius* , and several others in the same manner.

To proceed to the *Allegorical Fable:* If we reflect upon those innumerable Knowledges, those Secrets of Nature and Physical Philosophy which *Homer* is generally suppos'd to have wrapt up in his *Allegories* , what a new and ample Scene of Wonder may this Consideration afford us? How fertile will that

Imagination appear, which was able to cloath all the Properties of Elements, the Qualifications of the Mind, the Virtues and Vices, in Forms and Persons; and to introduce them into Actions agreeable to the Nature of the Things they shadow'd?

This is a Field in which no succeeding Poets could dispute with *Homer*; and whatever Commendations have been allow'd them on this Head, are by no means for their Invention in having enlarg'd his Circle, but for their Judgment in having contracted it. For when the Mode of Learning chang'd in following Ages, and Science was deliver'd in a plainer manner, it then became as reasonable in the more modern Poets to lay it aside, as it was in *Homer* to make use of it. And perhaps it was no unhappy Circumstance for *Virgil* , that there was not in his Time that Demand upon him of so great an Invention, as might be capable of furnishing all those Allegorical Parts of a Poem.

The *Marvelous Fable* includes whatever is supernatural, and especially the Machines of the Gods. If *Homer* was not the first who introduc'd the Deities (as *Herodotus* imagines) into the Religion of *Greece*, he seems the first who brought them into a System of *Machinery* for Poetry, and such an one as makes its greatest Importance and Dignity. For we find those Authors who have been offended at the literal Notion of the Gods, constantly laying their Accusation against *Homer* as the undoubted Inventor of them.

But whatever cause there might be to blame his *Machines* in a Philosophical or Religious View, they are so perfect in the Poetick, that Mankind have been ever since contented to follow them: None have been able to enlarge the Sphere of Poetry beyond the Limits he has set: Every Attempt of this Nature has prov'd unsuccessful; and after all the various Changes of Times and Religions, his Gods continue to this Day the Gods of Poetry.

We come now to the *Characters* of his Persons, and here we shall find no Author has ever drawn so many with so visible and surprizing a Variety, or given us such lively and affecting Impressions of them. Every one has something so singularly his own, that no Painter could have distinguished them more by their Features, than the Poet has by their Manners. Nothing can be more exact than the Distinctions he has observ'd in the different degrees of Virtues and Vices. The single Quality of *Courage* is wonderfully diversify'd in the several Characters of the *Iliad*. That of *Achilles* is furious and intractable; that of *Diomede* forward, yet list'ning to Advice and subject to Command: We see in *Ajax* an heavy and self-considering Valour, in *Hector* an active and vigilant one: The Courage of *Agamemnon* is inspirited by Love of Empire and Ambition, that of *Menelaus* mix'd with Softness and Tenderness for his People: We find in *Idomeneus* a plain direct Soldier, in *Sarpedon* a gallant and generous one.

Nor is this judicious and astonishing Diversity to be found only in the principal Quality which constitutes the Main of each Character, but even in the Under-parts of it, to which he takes care to give a Tincture of that principal one. For Example, the main Characters of *Ulysses* and *Nestor* consist in *Wisdom*, and they are distinct in this; the Wisdom of one is *artificial* and *various*, of the other *natural, open*, and *regular*. But they have, besides, Characters of *Courage*; and this Quality also takes a different Turn in each from the difference of his Prudence: For one in the War depends still upon *Caution*, the other upon *Experience*. It would be endless to produce Instances of these Kinds. The Characters of *Virgil* are far from striking us in this open manner; they lie in a great degree hidden and undistinguish'd , and where they are mark'd most evidently, affect us not in proportion to those of *Homer*.

His Characters of Valour are much alike; even that of *Turnus* seems no way peculiar but as it is in a superior degree; and we see nothing that differences the Courage of *Mnestheus* from that of *Sergesthus, Cloanthus*, or the rest. In like manner it may be remark'd of *Statius*'s Heroes, that an Air of Impetuosity runs thro' them all; the same horrid and savage Courage appears in his *Capaneus, Tydeus, Hippomedon*, | *&c.* | They have a Parity of Character which makes them seem Brothers of one Family. I believe when the Reader is led into this Track of Reflection, if he will pursue it through the *Epic* and *Tragic* Writers, he will be convinced how infinitely superior in this

Point the Invention of *Homer* was to that of all others. The *Speeches* are to be consider'd as they flow from the Characters, being perfect or defective as they agree or disagree with the Manners of those who utter them.

As there is more variety of Characters in the *Iliad*, so there is of Speeches, than in any other Poem. *Every thing in it has Manners* (as *Aristotle* expresses it) that is, every thing is acted or spoken. It is hardly credible in a Work of such length, how small a Number of Lines are employ'd in Narration. In *Virgil* the Dramatic Part is less in proportion to the Narrative; and the Speeches often consist of general Reflections or Thoughts, which might be equally just in any Person's Mouth upon the same Occasion. As many of his Persons have no apparent Characters, so many of his Speeches escape being apply'd and judg'd by the Rule of Propriety. We oftner think of the Author himself when we read *Virgil*, than when we are engag'd in *Homer*: All which are the Effects of a colder Invention, that interests us less in the Action describ'd: *Homer* makes us Hearers, and *Virgil* leaves us Readers.

If in the next place we take a View of the *Sentiments*, the same presiding Faculty is eminent in the Sublimity and Spirit of his Thoughts. *Longinus* has given his Opinion, that it was in this Part *Homer* principally excell'd. What were alone sufficient to prove the Grandeur and Excellence of his Sentiments in general, is that they have so remarkable a Parity with those of the Scripture: *Duport*, in his *Gnomologia Homerica*, has collected innumerable Instances of this sort. And it is with Justice an excellent modern Writer allows, that if *Virgil* has not so many Thoughts that are low and vulgar, he has not so many that are sublime and noble; and that the *Roman* Author seldom rises into very astonishing Sentiments where he is not fired by the *Iliad*.

If we observe his *Descriptions*, *Images*, and *Similes*, we shall find the Invention still predominant. To what else can we ascribe that vast Comprehension of Images of every sort , where we see each Circumstance and Individual of Nature summon'd together by the Extent and Fecundity of his Imagination; to which all things, in their various Views, presented themselves in an Instant, and had their Impressions taken off to Perfection at a Heat?

Nay, he not only gives us the full Prospects of Things, but several unexpected Peculiarities and Side-Views, unobserv'd by any Painter but *Homer*. Nothing is so surprizing as the Descriptions of his Battels, which take up no less than half the *Iliad*, and are supply'd with so vast a Variety of Incidents, that no one bears a Likeness to another; such different Kinds of Deaths, that no two Heroes are wounded in the same manner and such a Profusion of noble Ideas, that every Battel rises above the last in Greatness, Horror, and Confusion. It is certain there is not near that Number of Images and Descriptions in any Epic Poet; tho' every one has assisted himself with a great Quantity out of him: And it is evident of *Virgil* especially, that he has scarce any Comparisons which are not drawn from his Master.

If we descend from hence to the *Expression*, we see the bright Imagination of *Homer* shining out in the most enliven'd Forms of it. We acknowledge him the Father of Poetical Diction, the first who taught that *Language of the Gods* to Men. His Expression is like the colouring of some great Masters, which discovers itself to be laid on boldly, and executed with Rapidity. It is indeed the strongest and most glowing imaginable, and touch'd with the greatest Spirit. *Aristotle* had reason to say, He was the only Poet who had found out *Living Words*; there are in him more daring Figures and Metaphors than in any good Author whatever.

An Arrow is *impatient* to be on the Wing, a Weapon *thirsts* to drink the Blood of an Enemy, and the like. Yet his Expression is never too big for the Sense, but justly great in proportion to it: 'Tis the Sentiment that swells and fills out the Diction, which rises with it, and forms itself about it. For in the same degree that a *Thought* is warmer, an *Expression* will be brighter; and as That is more strong, This will become more perspicuous: Like Glass in the Furnace which grows to a greater Magnitude , and refines to a greater Clearness , only as the *Breath* within is more powerful, and the *Heat* more intense.

To throw his Language more out of Prose, *Homer* seems

to have affected the *Compound-Epithets*. This was a sort of Composition peculiarly proper to Poetry, not only as it heighten'd the *Diction*, but as it assisted and fill'd the *Numbers* with greater Sound and Pomp, and likewise conduced in some measure to thicken the *Images*. On this last Consideration I cannot but attribute these to the Fruitfulness of his Invention, since (as he has manag'd them) they are a sort of supernumerary Pictures of the Persons or Things they are join'd to. We see the Motion of *Hector*'s Plumes in the Epithet Kornthaiolos, the Landscape of Mount *Neritus* in that of Einosiphullos, and so of others; which particular Images could not have been insisted upon so long as to express them in a Description (though' but of a single Line) without diverting the Reader too much from the principal Action or Figure. As a Metaphor is a short Simile, one of these Epithets is a short Description.

Lastly, if we consider his *Versification*, we shall be sensible what a Share of Praise is due to his Invention in that also. He was not satisfied with his Language as he found it settled in any one Part of *Greece*, but searched thro' its differing *Dialects* with this particular View, to beautify and perfect his Numbers: He consider'd these as they had a greater Mixture of Vowels or Consonants, and accordingly employ'd them as the Verse requir'd either a greater Smoothness or Strength. What he most affected was the *Ionic* , which has a peculiar Sweetness from its never using Contractions, and from its Custom of resolving the Diphthongs into two Syllables; so as to make the Words open themselves with a more spreading and sonorous Fluency.

With this he mingled the *Attic* Contractions, the broader *Doric*, and the feebler *Æolic*, which often rejects its Aspirate, or takes off its Accent; and compleated this Variety by altering some Letters with the License of Poetry. Thus his Measures, instead of being Fetters to his Sense, were always in readiness to run along with the Warmth of his Rapture; and even to give a farther Representation of his Notions, in the Correspondence of their Sounds to what they signify'd. Out of all these he has deriv'd that Harmony, which makes us confess he had not only the richest Head, but the finest Ear in the World.

This is so great a Truth, that whoever will but consult the Tune of his Verses even without understanding them (with the same sort of Diligence as we daily see practis'd in the Case of *Italian Opera's*) will find more Sweetness, Variety, and Majesty of Sound , than in any other Language or Poetry. The Beauty of his Numbers is allow'd by the Criticks to be copied but faintly by *Virgil* himself, tho' they are so just to ascribe it to the Nature of the *Latine* Tongue. Indeed the *Greek* has some Advantages both from the natural *Sound* of its *Words,* and the Turn and *Cadence* of its *Verse,* which agree with the Genius of no other Language. *Virgil* was very sensible of this, and used the utmost Diligence in working up a more intractable Language to whatsoever Graces it was capable of, and in particular never fail'd to bring the Sound of his Line to a beautiful Agreement with its Sense.

If the *Grecian* Poet has not been so frequently celebrated on this Account as the *Roman,* the only reason is, that fewer Criticks have understood one Language than the other. *Dionysius* of *Halicarnassus* has pointed out many of our Author's Beauties in this kind, in his Treatise of the *Composition of Words,* and others will be taken notice of in the Course of the Notes. It suffices at present to observe of his Numbers, that they flow with so much ease, as to make one imagine *Homer* had no other care than to transcribe as fast as the *Muses* dictated; and at the same time with so much Force and inspiriting Vigour, that they awaken and raise us like the Sound of a Trumpet. They roll along as a plentiful River, always in motion, and always full; while we are born away by a Tide of Verse, the most rapid and yet the most smooth imaginable.

Thus on whatever side we contemplate *Homer,* what principally strikes us is his *Invention.* It is that which forms the Character of each Part of his Work; and accordingly we find it to have made his Fable more *extensive* and *copious* than any other, his Manners more *lively* and *strongly marked,* his Speeches more *affecting* and *transported,* his Sentiments more *warm* and *sublime,* his Images and Descriptions more *full* and *animated,* his Expression more *rais'd* and *daring,* and his

Numbers more *rapid* and *various*. I hope in what has been said of *Virgil* with regard to any of these Heads, I have no way derogated from his Character.

Nothing is more absurd or endless, than the common Method of comparing eminent Writers by an Opposition of particular Passages in them, and forming a Judgment from thence of their Merit upon the whole. We ought to have a certain Knowledge of the principal Character and distinguishing Excellence of each: It is in *that* we are to consider him, and in proportion to his Degree in *that* we are to admire him.

No Author or Man ever excell'd all the World in more than one Faculty, and as *Homer* has done this in Invention, *Virgil* has in Judgment. Not that we are to think Homer wanted Judgment, because *Virgil* had it in a more eminent degree; or that *Virgil* wanted Invention, because Homer possest a larger share of it: Each of these great Authors had more of both than perhaps any Man besides, and are only said to have less in Comparison with one another. *Homer* was the greater Genius, *Virgil* the better Artist.

In one we most admire the *Man*, in the other the *Work*. *Homer* hurries and transports us with a commanding Impetuosity, *Virgil* leads us with an attractive Majesty: *Homer* scatters with a generous Profusion, *Virgil* bestows with a careful Magnificence: *Homer* like the *Nile*, pours out his Riches with a sudden Overflow; *Virgil* like a River in its Banks, with a gentle and constant Stream. When we behold their Battels, methinks the two Poets resemble the Heroes they celebrate: *Homer*, boundless and irresistible as *Achilles*, bears all before him, and shines more and more as the Tumult increases; *Virgil* calmly daring like *Æneas*, appears undisturb'd in the midst of the Action, disposes all about him, and conquers with Tranquillity: And when we look upon their Machines, *Homer* seems like his own *Jupiter* in his Terrors, shaking *Olympus*, scattering the Lightnings, and firing the Heavens; *Virgil* like the same Power in his Benevolence, counselling with the Gods, laying Plans for Empires, and regularly ordering his whole Creation.

But after all, it is with great Parts as with great Virtues, they naturally border on some Imperfection; and it is often hard to distinguish exactly where the Virtue ends, or the Fault begins. As Prudence may sometimes sink to Suspicion, so may a great Judgment decline to Coldness; and as Magnanimity may run up to Profusion or Extravagance, so may a great Invention to Redundancy or Wildness. If we look upon *Homer* in this View, we shall perceive the chief *Objections* against him to proceed from so noble a Cause as the Excess of this Faculty.

Among these we may reckon some of his *Marvellous Fictions,* upon which so much Criticism has been spent as surpassing all the Bounds of Probability. Perhaps it may be with great and superior Souls as with gigantick Bodies, which exerting themselves with unusual Strength, exceed what is commonly thought the due Proportion of Parts, to become Miracles in the whole; and like the old Heroes of that Make, commit something near Extravagance amidst a Series of glorious and inimitable Performances. Thus *Homer* has his *speaking Horses,* and *Virgil* his *Myrtles distilling Blood* without so much as contriving the easy Intervention of a Deity to save the Probability.

It is owing to the same vast Invention that his *Similes* have been thought too exuberant and full of Circumstances. The Force of this Faculty is seen in nothing more, than its Inability to confine itself to that single Circumstance upon which the Comparison is grounded: It runs out into Embellishments of additional Images, which however are so manag'd as not to overpower the main one. His Similes are like Pictures, where the principal Figure has not only its proportion given agreeable to the Original, but is also set off with occasional Ornaments and Prospects.

The same will account for his manner of heaping a Number of Comparisons together in one Breath, when his Fancy suggested to him at once so many various and correspondent Images. The Reader will easily extend this Observation to more Objections of the same kind.

If there are others which seem rather to charge him with a Defect or Narrowness of Genius, than an Excess of it; those seeming Defects will be found upon Examination to proceed wholly from the Nature of the Times he liv'd in. Such are his *grosser Representations* of the *Gods,* and the vicious and *imperfect Manners* of his *Heroes,* which will be treated of in the following *Essay*: But I must here speak a word of the latter, as it is a Point generally carry'd into Extreams both by the Censurers and Defenders of *Homer*. It must be a strange Partiality to Antiquity to think with Madam *Dacier,* "that those Times and Manners are so much the more excellent, as they are more contrary to ours." Who can be so prejudiced in their Favour as to magnify the Felicity of those Ages, when a Spirit of Revenge and Cruelty reign'd thro' the World, when no Mercy was shown but for the sake of Lucre, when the greatest Princes were put to the Sword, and their Wives and Daughters made Slaves and Concubines?

On the other side I would not be so delicate as those modern Criticks, who are shock'd at the *servile Offices* and *mean Employments* in which we sometimes see the Heroes of *Homer* engag'd. There is a Pleasure in taking a view of that Simplicity in Opposition to the Luxury of succeeding Ages; in beholding Monarchs without their Guards, Princes tending their Flocks, and Princesses drawing Water from the Springs.

When we read *Homer,* we ought to reflect that we are reading the most ancient Author in the Heathen World; and those who consider him in this Light, will double their Pleasure in the Perusal of him.

Let them think they are growing acquainted with Nations and People that are now no more; that they are stepping almost three thousand Years backward into the remotest Antiquity , and entertaining themselves with a clear and surprizing Vision of Things no where else to be found, and the only authentick Picture of that ancient World. By this means alone their greatest Obstacles will vanish; and what usually creates their Dislike , will become a Satisfaction.

This Consideration may farther serve to answer for the constant Use of the same *Epithets* to his Gods and Heroes, such as the *far-darting Phœbus,* the *blue-ey'd Pallas,* the *swift- footed Achilles,* | *&c.* | which some have censured as impertinent and tediously repeated. Those of the Gods depended upon the Powers and Offices then believ'd to belong to them, and had contracted a Weight and Veneration from the Rites and solemn Devotions in which they were us'd: They were a sort of Attributes that it was a Matter of Religion to salute them with on all Occasions, and an Irreverence to omit.

As for the Epithets of great Men, Mons. *Boileau* is of Opinion; that they were in the Nature of *Sir-Names*, and repeated as such; for the *Greeks* having no Names deriv'd from their Fathers , were oblig'd when they mention'd any one to add some other Distinction; either naming his Parents expressly, or his Place of Birth, Profession, or the like: As *Alexander* Son of *Philip* , *Herodotus* of *Halicarnassus, Diogenes* the *Cynic,* | *&c.* | *Homer* therefore complying with the Custom of his Countrey , us'd such distinctive Additions as better agreed with Poetry. And indeed we have something parallel to these in modern Times, such as the Names of *Harold Harefoot* , *Edmund Ironside* , *Edward Long-shanks* , *Edward* the *black Prince,* | *&c.* | If yet this be thought to account better for the Propriety than for the Repetition, I shall add a farther Conjecture.

Hesiod dividing the World into its Ages, has plac'd a fourth Age between the Brazen and the Iron one, of *Heroes distinct from other Men, a divine Race, who fought at* Thebes *and* Troy, *are called Demi- Gods, and live by the Care of* Jupiter *in the Islands of the Blessed.* Now among the divine Honours which were paid them, they might have this also in common with the Gods, not to be mention'd without the Solemnity of an Epithet, and such as might be acceptable to them by its celebrating their Families, Actions, or Qualities.

What other Cavils have been rais'd against *Homer* are such as hardly deserve a Reply, but will yet be taken notice of as they occur in the Course of the Work. Many have been occasion'd by an injudicious Endeavour to exalt *Virgil*; which is much the same, as if one should think to praise the Superstructure by undermining the Foundation: One would imagine by the whole Course of their Parallels, that these Criticks never so much as heard of *Homer*'s having written first; a Consideration which whoever compares these two Poets ought to have always in his Eye. Some accuse him for the same things which they overlook or praise in the other; as when they prefer the Fable and Moral of the *Æneis* to those of the *Iliad,* for the same Reasons which might set the *Odysses* above the *Æneis*: as that the Heroe is a wiser Man; and the Action of the one more beneficial to his Countrey than that of the other: Or else they blame him for not doing what he never design'd; as because *Achilles* is not as good and perfect a Prince as *Æneas,* when the very Moral of his Poem requir'd a contrary Character.

It is thus that *Rapin* judges in his Comparison of *Homer* and *Virgil.* Others select those particular Passages of *Homer* which are not so labour'd as some that *Virgil* drew out of them: This is the whole Management of *Scaliger* in *his Poetices.* Others quarrel with what they take for low and mean Expressions, sometimes thro' a false Delicacy and Refinement, oftner from an Ignorance of the Graces of the Original; and then triumph in the Aukwardness of their own Translations.

This is the Conduct of *Perault* in his *Parallels.* Lastly, there are others, who pretending to a fairer Proceeding , distinguish between the personal Merit of *Homer,* and that of his *Work;* but when they come to assign the Causes of the great Reputation of the *Iliad,* they found it upon the Ignorance of his Times, and the Prejudice of those that followed. And in pursuance of this Principle, they make those Accidents (such as the Contention of the Cities, |&c.|) to be the Causes of his Fame, which were in Reality the Consequences of his Merit. The same might as well be said of *Virgil,* or any great Author, whose general Character will infallibly raise many casual Additions to their Reputation. This is the Method of Mons. *de la Motte;* who yet confesses upon the whole, that in whatever Age *Homer* had liv'd he must have been the greatest Poet of his Nation, and that he may be said in this Sense to be the Master even of those who surpass'd him.

In all these Objections we see nothing that contradicts his Title to the Honour of the chief *Invention;* and as long as this (which is indeed the Characteristic of Poetry itself) remains unequal'd by his Followers, he still continues superior to them.

A cooler Judgment may commit fewer Faults, and be more approv'd in the Eyes of *One Sort* of Criticks: but that Warmth of Fancy will carry the loudest and most universal Applauses which holds the Heart of a Reader under the strongest Enchantment. *Homer* not only appears the Inventor of Poetry, but excells all the Inventors of other Arts in this, that he has swallow'd up the Honour of those who succeeded him. What he has done admitted no Encrease, it only left room for Contraction or Regulation.

He shew'd all the Stretch of Fancy at once; and if he has fail'd in some of his Flights, it was but because he attempted every thing. A Work of this kind seems like a mighty Tree which rises from the most vigorous Seed, is improv'd with Industry, flourishes, and produces the finest Fruit; Nature and Art have conspir'd to raise it; Pleasure and Profit join'd to make it valuable: and they who find the justest Faults, have only said, that a few Branches (which run luxuriant thro' a Richness of Nature) might be lopp'd into Form to give it a more regular Appearance.

Having now spoken of the Beauties and Defects of the Original, it remains to treat of the Translation, with the same View to the chief Characteristic. As far as that is seen in the main Parts of the Poem, such as the *Fable, Manners,* and *Sentiments,* no Translator can prejudice it but by wilful Omissions or Contractions. As it also breaks out in every particular *Image, Description,* and *Simile;* whoever lessens or too much softens those, takes off from this chief Character. It is the first grand Duty of an Interpreter to give his Author entire and unmaim'd; and for the rest, the *Diction* and *Versification* only are his proper Province; since these must be his own, but the others he is to take as he finds them.

It should then be consider'd what Methods may afford some Equivalent in our Language for the Graces of these in the *Greek.* It is certain no literal Translation can be just to an excellent Original in a superior Language: but it is a great Mistake to imagine (as many have done) that a rash Paraphrase can make amends for this general Defect; which is no less in danger to lose the Spirit of an Ancient, by deviating into the modern Manners of Expression. If there be sometimes a *Darkness*, there is often a *Light* in Antiquity, which nothing better preserves than a Version almost literal I know no Liberties one ought to take, but those which are necessary for transfusing the Spirit of the Original, and supporting the Poetical Style of the Translation: and I will venture to say, there have not been more Men misled in former times by a servile dull Adherence to the Letter, than have been deluded in ours by a chimerical insolent Hope of raising and improving their Author.

It is not to be doubted that the *Fire* of the Poem is what a Translator should principally regard, as it is most likely to expire in his managing: However it is his safest way to be content with preserving this to his utmost in the Whole, without endeavouring to be more than he finds his Author is, in any particular Place. 'Tis a great Secret in Writing to know when to be plain, and when poetical and figurative; and it is what *Homer* will teach us if we will but follow modestly in his Footsteps.

Where his Diction is bold and lofty, let us raise ours as high as we can; but where his is plain and humble, we ought not to be deterr'd from imitating him by the fear of incurring the Censure of a meer *English* Critick. Nothing that belongs to *Homer* seems to have been more commonly mistaken than the just Pitch of his Style: Some of his Translators having swell'd into Fustian in a proud Confidence of the *Sublime*; others sunk into Flatness in a cold and timorous Notion of *Simplicity*.

Methinks I see these different Followers of *Homer*, some sweating and straining after him by violent Leaps and Bounds, (the certain Signs of false Mettle) others slowly and servilely creeping in his Train, while the Poet himself is all the time proceeding with an unaffected and equal Majesty before them. However of the two Extreams one could sooner pardon Frenzy than Frigidity: No Author is to be envy'd for such Commendations as he may gain by that Character of Style, which his Friends must agree together to call *Simplicity*, and the rest of the World will call *Dulness*. There is a *graceful* and *dignify'd* Simplicity, as well as a *bald* and *sordid* one, which differ as much from each other as the Air of a *plain* Man from that of a *Sloven*: 'Tis one thing to be tricked up, and another not to be dress'd at all. Simplicity is the Mean between Ostentation and Rusticity.

This pure and noble Simplicity is no where in such Perfection as in the *Scripture* and our Author. One may affirm with all respect to the inspired Writings, that the *Divine Spirit* made use of no other Words but what were intelligible and common to Men at that Time, and in that Part of the World; and as *Homer* is the Author nearest to those, his Style must of course bear a greater Resemblance to the sacred Books than that of any other Writer.

This Consideration (together with what has been observ'd of the Parity of some of his Thoughts) may methinks induce a Translator on the one hand to give into several of those general Phrases and Manners of Expression, which have attain'd a Veneration even in our Language from their use in the *Old Testament*; as on the other, to avoid those which have been appropriated to the Divinity, and in a manner consign'd to Mystery and Religion.

For a farther Preservation of this Air of Simplicity, a particular Care should be taken to express with all Plainness those *Moral Sentences* and *Proverbial Speeches* which are so numerous in this Poet. They have something Venerable, and as I may say *Oracular*, in that unadorn'd Gravity and Shortness with which they are deliver'd: a Grace which would be utterly lost by endeavouring to give them what we call a more ingenious (that is a more modern) Turn in the Paraphrase.

Perhaps the Mixture of some *Græcisms* and old Words after the manner of *Milton*, if done without too much Affectation, might not have an ill Effect in a Version of this particular Work, which most of any other seems to require a venerable *Antique* Cast. But certainly the use of *modern Terms* of *War* and *Government*, such as *Platoon, Campagne, Junto* , or the like (which some of his Translators have fallen into) cannot be allowable; those only excepted , without which it is impossible to treat the Subjects in any living Language.

There are two Peculiarities in *Homer*'s Diction that are a

sort of *Marks* or *Moles*, by which every common Eye distinguishes him at first sight: Those who are not his greatest Admirers look upon them as Defects, and those who are seem pleased with them as Beauties.

I speak of his *Compound-Epithets* and of his *Repetitions*. Many of the former cannot be done literally into *English* without destroying the Purity of our Language. I believe such should be retain'd as slide easily of themselves into an *English-Compound*, without Violence to the Ear or to the receiv'd Rules of Composition; as well as those which have receiv'd a Sanction from the Authority of our best Poets, and are become familiar thro' their use of them; such as the *Cloud-compelling Jove*, | *&c.* | As for the rest, whenever any can be as fully and significantly exprest in a single word as in a compounded one, the Course to be taken is obvious.

Some that cannot be so turn'd as to preserve their full Image by one or two Words, may have Justice done them by Circumlocution; as the Epithet einosiphullos to a Mountain would appear little or ridiculous translated literally *Leaf-shaking*, but affords a majestic Idea in the *Periphrasis: The lofty Mountains shakes his waving Woods*. Others that admit of differing Significations, may receive an Advantage by a judicious Variation according to the Occasions on which they are introduc'd. For Example, the Epithet of *Apollo*, eknbolos, or *far-shooting*, is capable of two Explications; one literal in respect of the Darts and Bow, the Ensigns of that God; the other allegorical with regard to the Rays of the Sun: Therefore in such Places where *Apollo* is represented as a God in Person, I would use the former Interpretation, and where the Effects of the Sun are describ'd, I would make choice of the latter. Upon the whole, it will be necessary to avoid that perpetual Repetition of the same Epithets which we find in *Homer*, and which, tho' it might be accommodated (as has been already shewn) to the Ear of those Times, is by no means so to ours: But one may wait for Opportunities of placing them, where they derive an additional Beauty from the Occasions on which they are employed; and in doing this properly, a Translator may at once shew his Fancy and his Judgment.

As for *Homer*'s *Repetitions*; we may divide them into three sorts; of whole Narrations and Speeches, of single Sentences, and of one Verse or Hemistich. I hope it is not impossible to have such a Regard to these, as neither to lose so known a Mark of the Author on the one hand, nor to offend the Reader too much on the other. The Repetition is not ungraceful in those Speeches where the Dignity of the Speaker renders it a sort of Insolence to alter his Words; as in the Messages from Gods to Men, or from higher Powers to Inferiors in Concerns of State, or where the Ceremonial of Religion seems to require it, in the solemn Forms of Prayers, Oaths, or the like.

In other Cases, I believe the best Rule is to be guided by the Nearness, or Distance, at which the Repetitions are plac'd in the Original: When they follow too close one may vary the Expression, but it is a Question whether a profess'd Translator be authorized to omit any: If they be tedious, the Author is to answer for it.

It only remains to speak of the *Versification*. *Homer* (as has been said) is perpetually applying the Sound to the Sense, and varying it on every new Subject. This is indeed one of the most exquisite Beauties of Poetry, and attainable by very few: I know only of *Homer* eminent for it in the *Greek*, and *Virgil* in *Latine*. I am sensible it is what may sometimes happen by Chance, when a Writer is warm, and fully possest of his Image: however it may be reasonably believed they design'd this, in whose Verse it so manifestly appears in a superior degree to all others. Few Readers have the Ear to be Judges of it, but those who have will see I have endeavour'd at this Beauty.

Upon the whole, I must confess my self utterly in capable of doing Justice to *Homer*. I attempt him in no other Hope but that which one may entertain without much Vanity, of giving a more tolerable Copy of him than any entire Translation in Verse has yet done. We have only those of *Chapman, Hobbes,* and *Ogilby*. *Chapman* has taken the Advantage of an immeasurable Length of Verse, notwithstanding which there is scarce any Paraphrase more loose and rambling than his. He has frequent Interpolations of four or six Lines, and I remember one in the thirteenth Book of the *Odysses*, where he has spun twenty Verses out of two. He is often mistaken in so bold a manner, that one might think he deviated on purpose, if he did not in other Places of his Notes insist so much upon Verbal Trifles.

He appears to have had a strong Affectation of extracting new Meanings out of his Author, insomuch as to promise in his Rhyming Preface, a Poem of the Mysteries he had revealed in *Homer*; and perhaps he endeavoured to strain the obvious Sense to this End. His Expression is involved in Fustian, a Fault for which he was remarkable in his Original Writings, as in the Tragedy of *Bussy d' Amboise* |*&c.*| In a word, the Nature of the Man may account for his whole Performance; for he appears from his Preface and Remarks to have been of an arrogant Turn, and an Enthusiast in Poetry. His own Boast of having finish'd half the *Iliad* in less than fifteen Weeks, shews with what Negligence his Version was performed. But that which is to be allowed him, and which very much contributed to cover his Defects, is a daring fiery Spirit that animates his Translation, which is something like what one might imagine *Homer* himself would have writ before he arriv'd to Years of Discretion.

Hobbes has given us a correct Explanation of the Sense in general, but for Particulars and Circumstances he continually lopps them, and often omits the most beautiful. As for its being esteem'd a close Translation , I doubt not many have been led into that Error by the Shortness of it, which proceeds not from his following the Original Line by Line, but from the Contractions above-mentioned. He sometimes omits whole Similes and Sentences, and is now and then guilty of Mistakes which no Writer of his Learning could have fallen into, but thro' Carelesness. His Poetry, as well as *Ogilby*'s, is too mean for Criticism.

It is a great Loss to the Poetical World that Mr. *Dryden* did not live to translate the *Iliad*. He has left us only the first Book and a small Part of the sixth; in which if he has in some Places not truly interpreted the Sense, or preserved the Antiquities, it ought to be excused on account of the Haste he was obliged to write in. He seems to have had too much

Regard to *Chapman,* whose Words he sometimes copies, and has unhappily follow'd him in Passages where he wanders from the Original. However had he translated the whole Work, I would no more have attempted *Homer* after him than *Virgil,* his Version of whom (notwithstanding some human Errors) is the most noble and spirited Translation I know in any Language. But the Fate of great Genius's is like that of great Ministers, tho' they are confessedly the first in the Commonwealth of Letters, they must be envy'd and calumniated only for being at the Head of it.

That which in my Opinion ought to be the Endeavour of any one who translates *Homer,* is above all things to keep alive that Spirit and Fire which makes his chief Character. In particular Places, where the Sense can bear any Doubt, to follow the strongest and most Poetical, as most agreeing with that Character. To copy him in all the Variations of his Style, and the different Modulations of his Numbers. To preserve in the more active or descriptive Parts, a Warmth and Elevation; in the more sedate or narrative, a Plainness and Solemnity; in the Speeches a Fulness and Perspicuity; in the Sentences a Shortness and Gravity. Not to neglect even the little Figures and Turns on the Words, nor sometimes the very Cast of the Periods.

Neither to omit or confound any Rites or Customs of Antiquity. Perhaps too he ought to include the whole in a shorter Compass, than has hitherto been done by any Translator who has tolerably preserved either the Sense or Poetry. What I would farther recommend to him, is to study his Author rather from his own Text than from any Commentaries, how learned soever, or whatever Figure they make in the Estimation of the World. To consider him attentively in Comparison with *Virgil* above all the Ancients, and with *Milton* above all the Moderns. Next these the Archbishop of *Cambray*'s *Telemachus* may give him the truest Idea of the Spirit and Turn of our Author, and *Bossu*'s admirable Treatise of the Epic Poem the justest Notion of his Design and Conduct. But after all, with whatever Judgment and Study a Man may proceed, or with whatever Happiness he may perform such a Work; he must hope to please but a few, those only who have at once a Taste of Poetry, and competent Learning. For to satisfy such as want either, is not in the Nature of this Undertaking; since a meer Modern Wit can like nothing that is not *Modern*, and a Pedant nothing that is not *Greek*.

What I have done is submitted to the Public, from whose Opinions I am prepared to learn; tho' I fear no Judges so little as our best Poets, who are most sensible of the Weight of this Task. As for the worst, whatever they shall please to say, they may give me some Concern as they are unhappy Men, but none as they are malignant Writers. I was guided in this Translation by Judgments very different from theirs, and by Persons for whom they can have no Kindness, if an old Observation be true, that the strongest Antipathy in the World is that of Fools to Men of Wit. Mr. *Addison* was the first whose Advice determined me to undertake this Task, who was pleased to write to me upon that Occasion in such Terms as I cannot repeat without Vanity.

I was obliged to Sir *Richard Steele* for a very early Recommendation of my Undertaking to the Public. |Dr.| *Swift* promoted my Interest with that Warmth with which he always serves his Friend. The Humanity and Frankness of Sir *Samuel Garth* are what I never knew wanting on any Occasion. §238 I must also acknowledge with infinite Pleasure the many friendly Offices as well as sincere Criticisms of |Mr.| *Congreve* , who had led me the way in translating some Parts of *Homer* , as I wish for the sake of the World he had prevented me in the rest. I must add the Names of |Mr.| *Rowe* and |Dr.| *Parnell,* tho' I shall take a farther Opportunity of doing Justice to the last, whose Good-nature (to give it a great Panegyrick) is no less extensive than his Learning.

The Favour of these Gentlemen is not entirely undeserved by one who bears them so true an Affection. But what can I say of the Honour so many of the *Great* have done me, while the *First Names* of the Age appear as my Subscribers, and the most distinguish'd Patrons and Ornaments of Learning as my chief Encouragers. Among these it is a particular Pleasure to me to find, that my highest Obligations are to such who have done most Honour to the Name of Poet: That his Grace the *Duke* of *Buckingham* was not displeas'd I should undertake the Author to whom he has given (in his excellent *Essay*) the finest Praise he ever yet receiv'd.

Read Homer *once, and you can read no more;*
For all things else appear so mean and poor,
Verse will seem Prose: yet often *on him look,*
And you will hardly need another Book.

That the Earl of *Halifax* was one of the first to favour me, of whom it is hard to say whether the Advancement of the Polite Arts is more owing to his Generosity or his Example. That such a Genius as my Lord *Bolingbroke,* not more distinguished in the great Scenes of Business than in all the useful and entertaining Parts of Learning , has not refus'd to be the Critick of these Sheets, and the Patron of their Writer. And that so excellent an Imitator of *Homer* as the noble Author of the Tragedy of *Heroic Love,* has continu'd his Partiality to me from my writing Pastorals to my attempting the *Iliad.* I cannot deny my self the Pride of confessing, that I have had the Advantage not only of their Advice for the Conduct in general, but their Correction of several Particulars of this Translation.

I could say a great deal of the Pleasure of being distinguish'd by the *Earl* of *Carnarvon,* but it is almost absurd to particularize any one generous Action in a Person whose whole Life is a continued Series of them. The Right Honourable Mr. *Stanhope,* the present Secretary of State, will pardon my Desire of having it known that he was pleas'd to promote this Affair. The particular Zeal of Mr. *Harcourt* (the Son of the late Lord Chancellor) gave me a Proof how much I am honour'd in a Share of his Friendship. I must attribute to the same Motive that of several others of my Friends, to whom all Acknowledgments are render'd unnecessary by the Privileges of a familiar Correspondence: And I am satisfy'd I can no way better oblige Men of their Turn, than by my Silence.

In short, I have found more Patrons than ever *Homer* wanted. He would have thought himself happy to have met the same Favour at *Athens*, that has been shewn me by its learned Rival, the University of *Oxford*. If my Author had the *Wits* of After-Ages for his Defenders, his Translator has had the *Beauties* of the present for his Advocates; a Pleasure too great to be changed for any Fame in Reversion. And I can hardly envy him those pompous Honours he receiv'd after Death, when I reflect on the Enjoyment of so many agreeable Obligations, and easy Friendships which make the Satisfaction of Life.

This Distinction is the more to be acknowledg'd, as it is shewn to one whose Pen has never gratify'd the Prejudices of particular *Parties*, or the Vanities of particular *Men*. Whatever the Success may prove, I shall never repent of an Undertaking in which I have experienc'd the Candour and Friendship of so many Persons of Merit; and in which I hope to pass some of those Years of Youth that are generally lost in a Circle of Follies, after a manner neither wholly unuseful to others, nor disagreeable to my self.

Chapter 5

Elegy to the Memory of an Unfortunate Lady

"Who is this Pope that I hear so much about?" said George II; "I cannot discover what is his merit. Why will not my subjects write in prose? I hear a great deal, too, of Shakespeare, but I cannot read him, he is such a bombast fellow."

Alexander Pope, an only child, was born in London, on May 21, 1688, the year of the Glorious revolution. His father, a linen-draper, was forty-two, his mother forty-six. Both were Roman Catholics, and his father, Alexander Sr., retired from business after his son's birth, perhaps because a new act of Parliament prohibited Catholics from living within ten miles of London. Between 1696 and 1700 Pope was tutored at home by a priest, and then enrolled in two Catholic schools, but he was largely self-educated. His religion would have made it impossible, at the time, to pursue a career in law or medicine or the Clergy even had he wished to: as a Catholic he was not, for example, permitted to attend a university.

A precocious child, he could read Latin, Greek, French and Italian while still very young, and (according to his own account of the matter) was already, at sixteen, writing the rather sophisticated verse later published as his "Pastorals." Characteristically, however, he would destroy a great deal of his juvenalia, the continued existence of which might have detracted from the image of the poet as child prodigy which he desired, later in life, to propagate.

In 1700 the Pope family moved to Whitehill House at Binfield in Windsor Forest, and there, circa 1705, Pope, until then a healthy child, contracted a tubercular bone disease, attributed at the time to his "perpetual application" to his studies. Attacks of this disease would recur at intervals throughout what he would refer to as "this long Disease, my Life." It left him frail, prone to various other illnesses, humpbacked, and permanently stunted: fully grown, he would attain a height of only four and one half feet.

In his early twenties he made frequent visits to London, and became acquainted with the literati there, including Wycherley and Walsh. In 1709 the "Pastorals," Pope's first published work, appeared in Tonson's Poetical Miscellanies. In 1711 he met the Blount sisters, Teresa and Martha: he became infatuated, briefly, with Teresa, but the amiable Martha remained a close friend for the rest of his life: he had many friendships with women, perhaps because though he admired them greatly he was too diminutive ever to be considered as a possible husband or prospective lover.

His "Essay on Criticism" was published anonymously in 1711, and was furiously attacked in print by John Dennis, a famous literary critic of the day whom Pope had satirized in the poem.

Dennis retaliated by referring to Pope as a "hump-backed toad," but the "Essay" brought him to the attention of Swift, Addison, Gay, Parnell, Oxford, and Steele, all Tory members of the Martinus Scriblerus Club, and in 1712 Steele would published Pope's "Messiah" in the Spectator No. 378. In the same year, at the suggestion of John Caryll, a friend and a member of the circle of prominent Catholics which centered on the Englefields and the Blounts, Pope wrote and published the first version of The Rape of the Lock, ostensibly to reconcile two feuding but prominent Catholic families.

1713 saw the publication of Pope's "Windsor Forest," a poem celebrating the Treaty of Utrecht, which had been negotiated by the Tories. "Windsor Forest" won him a closer friendship with Swift, and in 1714 he published a more complex version of The Rape of the Lock. In 1715 Pope met Lady Mary Wortley Montagu. His letters reveal that he was at least temporarily infatuated with her, though much later he would hold her up to malicious ridicule in his essay Peri Bathous, published much later, in 1728. By now a successful author, he embarked, between 1715 and 1720, on his verse translation of Homer's Iliad (which, with his translation of the Odyssey, written in collaboration with William Broome and Elijah Fenton, would be the great literary labour of his life) and which, published at intervals over the years, in six volumes, was also a great popular and financial success.

His father died in 1717, the year the first volume of his collected Works was published. With the money his Iliad had earned him, Pope (the first author in English history to be able to sustain himself financially entirely on the profits derived from the publication of his own works) was able, in 1718, to lease the villa of Twickenham on the Thames near Richmond, where he moved with his widowed mother: over the years he entertained his friends there, and oversaw the construction of his famous grotto.

In 1725 he published his edition of Shakespeare's Works, and the first three volumes of his translation of the Odyssey also appeared: 1726 saw the appearance of the final three volumes of the same work. In 1727 Swift and Pope published the first two volumes of their Miscellanies, and Pope himself was at work on his Dunciad, which had originated as a scheme of the Scriblerus Club: in this, its earliest incarnation, Lewis Theobald, a Shakespearean scholar who had feuded with Pope (who feuded, during the course of his life, with innumerable critical and literary rivals) had the dubious honour of being its central character.

The final volume of the Swift-Pope Miscellanies appeared in 1728, and included Peri Bathouse, which provides us with a notion of how nasty, on occasion, Pope could be: William Broome, a man of talent if not of genius, had, as we have noted, helped him to write his Odyssey, but Pope offended him not only in Peri Bathous but in these lines which appear in the first version of the Dunciad, which appeared, in three books, during that same year: "Hibernian Politicks, O Swift, thy doom,/ And Pope's, translating three whole years with Broome." Broome commented on Pope's ungenerous malice in a letter: "I often resemble him to an hedgehog; he lies snug and warm, and sets his bristles out against all mankind. Sure he is fond of being hated. I wonder he is not thrashed: but his littleness is his protection; no man shoots a wren." As soon as The Dunciad appeared, the dunces, in their turn, attacked Pope, but he had much the better of the affair. 1729 brought the publication of the Dunciad Variorum. The first three epistles of An Essay on Man were published anonymously in 1733, the year Pope's mother died. The Fourth epistle of the Essay on Man appeared, also anonymously, in 1734.

The colorfully scurrilous Edmund Curll, perhaps (and this is saying a good deal) the most unscrupulous publisher of his day, brought out an expurgated and incomplete edition of Pope's letters in 1735; an edition which appeared to be unauthorized. In fact, however, the devious Pope initiated the work himself, carefully edited all of the letters, and himself put them in Curll's hands. The same year saw the publication of the second volume of Pope's collected Works.

In 1737 the artful Pope produced an "authorized" version of his Letters, and, when his authorship of the Essay on Man was acknowledged, he came under vehement attack for the religious views he had expressed there. The following year his satirical imitations of Horace were published, which attacked the corruption and venality of the Whig government under Sir Robert Walpole, and the indifference of the King, George II, both to the immorality which Walpole tolerated and to all things literary or cultural.

With the help of William Warburton, Pope produced the final version of the Dunciad, which appeared, in four books, in 1743: Colley Cibber, a bad poet who had nevertheless managed to become the poet laureate, replaced Theobald as its hero. Pope's health, which had never been very good, was failing rapidly, and he died at Twickenham on May 30, 1744.

"Elegy to the Memory of an Unfortunate Lady" is a poem in heroic couplets by Alexander Pope, first published in his *Works* of 1717. Though only 82 lines long, it has become one of Pope's most celebrated pieces. The work begins with the poet asking what ghost beckons him onward with its "bleeding bosom gor'd"; it is the spirit of an unnamed woman (the "lady" of the title) who acted "a *Roman's* part" (i.e., committed suicide) due to loving "too well." The speaker eulogizes her sacrifice and then for several lines berates and curses her uncle (who is also her guardian) for being a "mean deserter of [his] brother's blood" and having no compassion on the lady. There follows a description of her foreign burial in a "humble grave" unattended by friends and relatives, which Pope sums up in the striking couplet:

"A heap of dust alone remains of thee;
'Tis all thou art, and all the proud shall be!"
(lines 73-4)

The concluding lines contain the speaker's application of this lesson of mortality to himself: someday he too will die and the last thought of the lady will be torn from him as he passes away.

Readers' reactions to this work have been varied, and some have offered severe criticisms. John Wesley in "Thoughts on the Character and Writings of Mr. Prior" (1782) compared the poet Matthew Prior with Pope, mostly to the detriment of the latter; in this essay, Wesley says of Pope:

"As elegant a piece as he ever wrote was, 'Verses to the Memory of an Unfortunate Lady.' But was ever anything more exquisitely injudicious? First, what a subject! An eulogium on a self-murderer! And the execution is as bad as the design: It is a commendation not only of the person, but the act!"

Most of Wesley's grounds for criticism are moral: since—as he would consider self-evident—suicide is an evil act that affronts God and causes the doer to go to hell, the glorification of the lady's act in this poem is seriously objectionable. (This did not, however, prevent him from quoting the couplet given above in his *Journal* on more than one occasion.) Samuel Johnson in his *Lives of the Poets* also faulted the "Elegy" on similar grounds, referring to "the illaudable singularity of treating suicide with respect."

A different kind of criticism, one on artistic grounds, is made by Maynard Mack in his important biography *Alexander Pope: A Life*. Mack acknowledges that there are beautiful passages in the poem, but also finds that it is marked by a certain incoherence between elements and attitudes which are not fully reconciled, such as the idea of Roman suicide vs. that of Christian burial, or the strange curse on the uncle and all his posterity for his unspecified crimes. Johnson also anticipates some of this artistic censure in judging that "the tale [in the poem] is not skilfully told."

Though Mack's critique is effective and arguably well justified, most critics would not deny the emotional impact of Pope's "Elegy," and even Johnson acknowledges that the poem "must be allowed to be written in some parts with vigorous animation, and in others with gentle tenderness." It is frequently included in antholcgies that include Pope's best-known poems or those of his era, and the "Elegy's" effective phrasing is often remembered and quoted.

Chapter 6

Pope and Eighteenth-century Gender Ideology

Alexander Pope, who assumed a female persona in one of his major works (Eloisa to Abelard) while devoting others—most notably, Epistle II of Epistles to Several Persons, To a Lady—to extended descriptions of women's behaviour and experiences, and who, through The Rape of the Lock, became known for his feminization of the mock-epic poem, is a writer who has regularly been touted by critics for his supposed unique affinity with the female sensibility: typical are Maynard Mack's assertion that "Pope had always a special sympathy for the lot of women" and Alastair Fowler's statement that in The Rape of the Lock "Pope identifies with women to an unusual extent."

At the same time Pope has come to be portrayed by an increasing number of feminist critics as the voice of phallic authority, as a symbol of the oppressive power of patriarchy. Ellen Pollak, for example, argues that in The Rape of the Lock "woman is made to function as the sign not of her own subjectivity but of a male desire of which she is the object," while Ruth Salvaggio cites Pope's poetry as evidence of how Enlightenment England "imprisoned women within representational categories created by men." Underlying these diametrically opposed views are conflicting answers to the question, "For whom (which is also to say, what body of interests) is Pope speaking" in his writings—particularly in those works that claim to be presenting a female voice or perspective?

Contemporary theoretical challenges to traditional notions of representation warn us against the presumption and bad faith involved in the act of speaking for others. Hence Gilles Deleuze's insistence that "only those directly concerned can speak in a practical way on their own behalf" and his invocation of Foucault's prison information group, organized to allow prisoners themselves to be heard, as a model for "teach[ing] us something absolutely fundamental: the indignity of speaking for others."

And yet, Gayatri Chakravorty Spivak's incisive critique of this position, based on the fact that, tacit claims to the contrary, "representation has not withered away" and that only a naive or deluded stance of self-transparency on the part of the speaker can make it appear so is well taken. So too is Linda Alcoff's point that speaking for others can produce positive as well as negative results, since there are times when "we do need a 'messenger' to advocate for our needs." Indeed, it could be argued that Foucault acted as precisely such a "messenger" through his writings on the incarcerated and the mad.

Still, Deleuze's point remains compelling to the extent that it underscores the numerous instances in which speaking for someone else functions as an act of arrogance and appropriation, constituting a form of what Paolo Freire terms "antidialogic actions," whereby one person "names the world" on behalf of others and thereby robs them of their right to speak. This problem is addressed in a particularly suggestive way by Donna Haraway, through her rejection of the politics of representation in favour of a "politics of articulation." Arguing for the speciousness of the claims made by certain would-be defenders of endangered species in remote lands and by anti-abortion activists, both of whom put themselves forward as protectors of entities with which they have no direct involvement, Haraway explains what is wrong with the questions "Who speaks for the jaguar? Who speaks for the fetus?":

> Both questions rely on a political semiotics of representation.

Permanently speechless, forever requiring the services of a ventriloquist, never forcing a recall vote, in each case the object or ground of representation is the realization of the representative's fondest dream.... Both the jaguar and the fetus are carved out of one collective entity and relocated in another, where they are reconstituted as objects of a particular kind—as the ground of a representational practice that forever authorizes the ventriloquist. Tutelage will be eternal. The represented is reduced to the permanent status of the recipient of action, never to be a co-actor in an articulated practice among unlike, but joined, social partners.

It is tempting to consider possible applications of Haraway's conceptual framework to eighteenth-century literature, where we repeatedly find certain groups of beings—slaves, cannibals, children, the poor, hunted animals, satirized fools, and (most obviously and frequently) women—in effect disempowered through their consignment to the category of the "permanently represented," hence forever passive and silent even, perhaps one should say especially, about issues that most directly and vitally affect them.

In a sense it is precisely this situation that is exposed in Swift's A Modest Proposal, which among other things dramatizes how, according to the politics of representation, "the power of life and death [in Haraway's words] must be delegated to the epistemologically most disinterested ventriloquist": in this case, the Modest Proposer, whose credentials for solving the problems of Ireland's mendicant population are based largely on his status as a detached observer rather than on his actual membership in this class; whose claim of being the most appropriate person to devise a scheme for the fate of Irish babies is rooted precisely in the fact that he himself has no babies (his youngest child being nine years old); and who vindicates his right to speak for the interests of Irish parents by pointing to the unlikelihood of his ever again becoming one himself (his wife being past childbearing age).

The Proposer's act of "speaking for the fetus"—to the extent that his scheme is designed, among other things, to "prevent those voluntary Abortions, and that horrid Practice of Women murdering their Bastard Children; alas! too frequent among us"—here reveals itself, with gruesome irony, as but the first step toward organized infanticide: a fact which becomes less incomprehensible when we consider that the act of objectifying mothers as mere "Breeders" is logically continuous with the act of objectifying the end product of their "breeding" as saleable, consumable items.

The inverse relationship between the speaker's lofty non-involvement and the presumed authority of his representations of and for others, which includes making life-and-death decisions about their future, is shown to shape all aspects of the relationship between England and Ireland, so that the politics of representation is exposed in this context as an expression, on the semiotic level, of colonialist subjugation and devourment.

In Swift's verse, The Petition of Frances Harris, the act of a lower-class Irishwoman presuming to voice her own concerns by formally petitioning the (emphatically non-female, non-Irish, and non-working-class) Lord Justices constitutes a shocking if also comic reversal that subverts our "normal" expectations about who gets to speak to—and for—others.

However much we may feel moved to laugh at the verbal inelegancies of Harris's petition and at the absurdity of her endeavor to communicate with the highest colonial officials (save one) in the land, we can scarcely ignore the no-less-absurd fact that these same officials were authorized to communicate with and speak for the Irish people without even knowing their native language. In this case, the irony is even more pronounced given that one of the two Lord Justices petitioned by Harris was the Earl of Galway (nee Henri de Massue, Marquis de Ruvigny), a French expatriate whose command of even the English language would no doubt have been more equivocal than Harris's.

Although of course Harris isn't literally expressing her own thoughts in her own words since the poet is "speaking for" her, in this instance the usual hierarchic and appropriative implications of such an act are substantially mitigated, not only by the poet's concern for the persona's idiomatic and colloquial speech (i.e., Harris is allowed her own mode of discourse and hence doesn't speak like Swift in the way that, say, Eloisa speaks like Pope), but also by the way in which the poet presents himself in the verse through Harris's eyes, as the lecherous and mercenary chaplain working for Lord Justice Berkeley: an object of satiric deflation incapable of speaking for anyone with any credibility or authority, even though he is technically a member (however lowly) of the "spokesmen class" of English (or part-English) Anglicans in Ireland.

In Pope's writings the problematic of representation, the act of one person or group portraying, legislating, and/or speaking for another, manifests itself in a very different way. Whereas Swift's writings offer a continuing critique of the political implications of representation, Pope's linguistically and aesthetically exploit the latter while mystifying or naturalizing the consequences of its operations in terms of power relationships. Hence in much of his verse about women he occupies the position of coolly detached observer and "ventriloquist," but without any Swiftian irony to undercut it.

In the few instances where this distance is diminished by Pope's adoption of a female voice, this act tends to function as a rhetorical tactic for negating other perspectives through co-optation—ultimately, for subsuming the other into oneself. I am arguing, in other words, that Pope's writings are characterized on the whole by impulses toward and strategies of appropriation vis-a-vis women. At the same time, I wish to suggest that these strategies take on a special coloration, and produce a special set of ironies, as a result of Pope's peculiar brand of marginality, which rendered his position within the sexual hierarchy and the patriarchal structure of eighteenth-century society highly equivocal.

Deformed, dwarfish, sickly, and probably impotent as a result of having contracted spinal tuberculosis in infancy, Pope was someone whose "manhood" was continually being called into question both by his enemies in print and by the women in his life, not to mention by his own ironic perceptions of himself. As Helen Deutsch succinctly notes, "Pope's body is above all a body of contradictions, and Pope a figure of personal and historical liminality."

The contradictory and liminal conditions of his existence were likewise exemplified in his status as a self-proclaimed "manly" bard who, in his enforced confinement and inactivity (as well as occasional silence in response to both personal and public forms of intimidation) lived out his society's prescribed role for women.

Moreover, however committed in theory and temperament he may have been to a conservative ideology upholding the idea that "whatever is, is right," existing political and social institutions were largely unresponsive to his needs, in various ways inimical to his basic interests and ambitions as a Roman Catholic Tory with Jacobite sympathies in a Whig-dominated society who spent much of his life both on the fringes of the law (which threatened him with prosecution on several occasions) and just outside the geographical boundaries of London, to which he was relegated as a member of a religious group with restricted legal and property rights.

Pope's ambiguous and contradictory position in society affords us the opportunity to explore the dialectical interaction between the voices of marginality and dominance as these vye, not only among different groups in society, but also within a single personality and consciousness. At the same time, it serves to remind us that ideological generalizations must not be allowed to stray very far from the particularities of person and place, nor from the bodily realities, that helped to shape them.

We might recall Sartre's observation that "Valery is a petit bourgeois intellectual, no doubt about it. But not every petit bourgeois intellectual is Valery." By the same token, even if it can be argued that Pope is a bourgeois misogynist in terms of his sexual ideology, not every bourgeois misogynist—not even every early eighteenth-century English bourgeois misogynist—is Pope. To recognize the uniqueness of his perspective and situation—which is also to insist upon the crucial role played by individual expressions and mediations of any given social or political outlook—is not to deny the validity of broader ideological categories but, on the contrary, to make these categories more precise and meaningful.

Pope's marginality affected on some level all of his attitudes toward sexuality and the institutions designed to contain it. Physically, as Dennis Todd has recently argued, Pope was widely viewed by his contemporaries—and on occasion by himself—as the very "monster" he continually attacked in his satires. This fact had profound ideological as well as psychological consequences, ensuring a certain degree of estrangement from societal norms.

As the self-described "little Alexander the women laugh at," as one of those "Ugliest fellows" whom only the women of India could appreciate because they "look upon Deformities as the Signatures of divine Favour," and as one who could declare that the only offspring he would ever have would be those begot upon his muse, Pope recognized from an early age that a masculine identity and a place in the patriarchal order, to the extent that he would be able to construct and maintain these, would not be founded on the traditional roles of husband and father, which in turn produced an awareness of the at least partial inadequacy of public institutions to fulfill private needs.

This awareness created certain tensions in his advocacy of social convention which complicate his articulation of bourgeois sexual myths. In his Elegy to the Memory of an Unfortunate Lady, for example, he portrays the "Lady" of the title as heroic victim of a familial system in which an uncle-guardian has power over the life and fate of his niece-ward, including the right to decide who should be her husband. And despite Pope's well-known invocations of marriage as a symbolic ideal and as woman's "proper" destiny in some of his most celebrated works, he could on occasion expose its role as an instrument of oppression:

Marriage may all those petty Tyrants chace,
But sets up One, a greater, in their Place;
Well might you wish for Change, by those accurst,

But the last Tyrant ever proves the worst.
(Epistle to Miss Blount, With the Works of Voiture, 37-40)

The variations in Pope's particular brand of social conformism include, moreover, a somewhat ironically detached perspective toward traditional gender definitions, along with a vantage point from which he could playfully question their claims to absolute validity on one level while reaffirming what we might call their political authority on another. Although clearcut distinctions are central to Pope's outlook, we find a curious confounding and intermingling of the sexes in certain of his writings, along with a fascination with sexual possibilities beyond the officially reinforced categories of male and female.

There is, for example, a trying on of different sexual roles in his personal correspondence, including the roles of both husband and wife, lover and mistress vis-a-vis male friends and associates. Writing to Lord Peterborough while the latter was abroad, Pope declares, "These are my Merits as a Man, but as a Woman (for you know I am abhominably Epicoene) what merits have I not, that can remember and preserve my duty to my Husband after a Whole Fortnight's absence?.... [I]s it my unhappy fate in particular, that I can no sooner learn to love, but I must be banishd from what I love? Even when the mercy of the Government has excused you from that Sentence of Exile, will you impose it on yourself?

only to make your poor Wife unhappy?" Pope characterizes his friendship with the painter Jervas in similarly connubial terms: "'Tis not unlike the happy Friendship of a stay'd man and his wife, who are seldom so fond as to hinder the business of the house from going on all day, or so indolent as not to find consolation in each other every evening". He reminisces to Jervas of past intimacies and expresses his longing "to renew our old intercourse and conversation, our morning Conferences in bed in the same Room, our evening Walks in the Park, our amusing Voyages on the Water, our philosophical Suppers, our Lectures, our Dissertations, our Gravities, our Reveries, our Fooleries, our what not?" Later in life he was to write to Lord Bathurst, "But dull as I am, I wake a little at the thought of you, I dream of you still, & you are the object of my Dotings; like an old Woman that loves the man that had her Maidenhead: You animated my Youth, my Lord, Comfort my age!"

It is important to keep in mind that for Pope, letters were as much a public as a private mode of expression, designed to disseminate a carefully crafted image of himself for posterity. Hence we can assume that, in the epistolary examples just cited, Pope is remaining safely within the bounds of accepted conventions governing male relationships and their expression in the eighteenth century. And indeed, in (for example) the letter to Bathurst cited above, Pope is careful to situate his address within the context of a pure and exalted friendship by assuring his correspondent, "I know you to be so much a better friend to me than myself," and by quoting a couplet adapted from Dryden's Epistle to Congreve ("Let not th' insulting foe my fame pursue, / But shade those Laurels that were raisd by You").

Yet the overall picture is more complicated than this. For in likening himself not only to the "old Woman that loves the man that had her Maidenhead" but also to "a Child that comes to complain to its best friend who has humoured it always," Pope seems to be using his epistolary communications to act out an entire range of relations based on differences of age and worldly position as well as gender. The metaphorical acknowledgments of his "lesser" status (as an old woman, a young deflowered girl, and a child in need of humoring), while on one level affirming Pope's social inferiority to Bathurst, on another level seem to allow him a greater latitude to test—even to give a playful hint of flouting—the boundaries separating them in society.

Pope's representation of his "connubial" relationship with Jervas in terms of an equality of status, while obviously contrasting with his self-portrayal vis-a-vis Bathurst, similarly stretches the limits of the conventional without actually transgressing them. It is interesting (and not a little ironic) to note that the picture he draws of his friendship with Jervas seems to approximate more closely the ideal of "companionate marriage" claimed for the eighteenth century by Lawrence Stone than do the officially recognized, legally constituted marriages invoked to support Stone's thesis. Several rather different conclusions can be drawn from this observation. One might be that the problems surrounding Pope's highly self-conscious romanticizations of himself and his friendships in his letters, which concealed the darker realities of his life and his relationships with others, find a telling counterpart in Stone's idealizations of eighteenth-century family life, which have the effect of eliding the continuing hardships and inequalities characterizing women's position in society.

A somewhat different (though not necessarily incompatible) conclusion might be that the flaws in Stone's argument can be redressed, not only through the more sustained and careful investigation of contemporary women's lives that various feminist critics have called for, but also via a broader consideration of the range of ways in which people in the eighteenth century organized (and expressed) their affections, their desire for connection and community, outside of as well as within the dominant structures of society (as symbolized by Stone's triumvirate, "Family, Sex and Marriage"—institutional categories largely or wholly irrelevant to Pope's mode of existence).

In this regard, Pope's letters to his male friends can offer an important perspective for understanding relationships that defy neat, either-or labels, seeming to skirt the borders of the conventional by at once functioning to shore up and to reveal slippages in the patriarchal order.

Pope's fascination with a world of gender reversal and sexual possibility is highlighted in a curious letter he wrote, ostensibly "To a Lady from her Brother" (though addressed to Teresa Blount), which describes in detail his visit to a hermaphrodite, in the company of a physician and a divine, with a view to determining the creature's sex. The account stresses the relativity of perception and judgment characterizing the process of making this kind of determination; gender, it is suggested, resides in the eye of the beholder. Hence the widely divergent explanations for the creature's condition, ranging from the opinion that it is a sinister aberration of nature to the view that it is entirely normal and wholly unexceptional (C 1:278). A similar divergence of viewpoint emerges among Pope and his fellow inspectors, each of whom comes to a different conclusion as to the hermaphrodite's "true" nature.

The priest opts for its being a male; the doctor, for its being a female; and Pope himself (or at least the Popeian persona), for its being a happy combination of the two: "As for this Party's temper of mind, it appears to be a most even disposition, partaking of the good qualities of both sexes: for she is neither so inaccessible as other Ladies, nor is he so impudent as other Gentlemen. Of how obliging and complaisant a turn appears by this, that he tells the Ladies he has the Inclinations of a Gentleman, and that she tells the Gentlemen she has the Tendre of a Lady". It is interesting that this fantasy of hermaphroditical monstrosity concludes with the affirmation of an androgynous ideal reminiscent of the final stanzas of To a Lady, in which heaven is said to "Pic[k] from each sex, to make its Fav'rite blest", and of the portrayal of the sylphs in The Rape of the Lock: "Spirits, freed from mortal Laws," who can "with ease / Assume what Sexes and what Shapes they please" (I:6970).

In his extended description of the sylphs' delicate shapes and equivocal natures (II:61-62), Pope is able to indulge his ambisexual fantasies, even place them in an appealing and seductive light, while at the same time censuring them through satiric subversion and association with Milton's fallen angels.

The scenario depicted in Pope's letter both reflects and anticipates changing ideas about sexual identity throughout the eighteenth century, by the end of which, according to Foucault, "when confronted with a hermaphrodite, the doctor was no longer concerned with recognizing the presence of the two sexes, but rather with deciphering the true sex that was hidden beneath ambiguous appearances." Ann Rosalind Jones and Peter Stallybrass argue a similar shift in the eighteenth century from earlier views about hermaphroditism in particular and gender in general: "The problem with most existing attempts to understand this ambivalence [toward the hermaphrodite in the Renaissance] is that they assume either the fixity of a binary logic or its dissolution.

Against both these views, we argue that the hermaphrodite in Renaissance discourses enables us to interrogate the eighteenth-century establishment of gender as a fetish which misrecognizes itself, masquerading as the 'real.'" Pope's letter seems to function as a kind of threshold document, shuttling comically but uneasily between Renaissance and late eighteenth-century conceptions of gender, and poised on the boundary between a potentially liberating ambiguity and a seemingly repressive demand for fixed definition. While dramatizing the impulse to inspect and clarify, to establish the creature's "true" sex, the letter constitutes at the same time a mocking of this whole enterprise through its satiric comment on self-proclaimed "experts" (whose judgments are clearly revealed as biased and irrational) purporting to be able to determine another's "real" gender—and underlying this an acknowledgment of the possibility that there might exist a sexual doubleness irreducible to clearcut, either-or categories.

Of further interest in Pope's epistolary account of his visit to the hermaphrodite is the way he conceives of the latter in social and sartorial as well as biological terms, thereby conveying a sense of the provisional and arbitrary nature of gender identification, and indirectly underscoring the latter's fetishistic aspect—what Jones and Stallybrass term the "prosthetic" character of all attempts to fix gender through various forms of exchange, substitution, or displacement designed to supply an imagined deficiency. The creature, we are told, came into the room "drest in that habit in which the Ladies affect an Hermaphroditical imitation of Men" —this is explained to mean a riding habit—and we learn that the hermaphrodite "formerly receiv'd visits of the fair sex in their masques, till an impertinent fellow in a female disguise mingled with a party of ladies, and impudently overheard their improving Speculations".

The social and sartorial practices reinforcing sexual ambiguity alluded to in this letter—i.e., cross-dressing and masquerades, with their sanctioning of disguise and a potentially liberating role-playing—are mentioned elsewhere in Pope's letters, in a similar tone of furtive attraction and curiosity about the forbidden. In one instance he reports that he almost persuaded Teresa Blount to "go a Rakeing with [him] in Man's Cloathes," fantasizing about the adventures they would be able to recount to her sister upon their return, and in another he tells Martha Blount, "May you have all possible success both at your Devotions this week, & your Masquerade the next: Whether you repent or Sin, may you do all you wish".

Pope is generally viewed as a staunch opponent of masquerade in all its implications. Terry Castle, for example, numbers Pope among the eighteenth-century moralists and satirists who, in condemning it as "a foolish, irrational, and corrupt activity," were expressing "a fear of ontological promiscuity and a desire for firm conceptual boundaries." But Pope's position in this matter was more complicated than Castle's statements would have us believe; for there are, as I've been indicating, hints in Pope's writings of a very different kind of insight, one a good deal more congenial to the view of masquerade as, in Castle's words, "a charismatic meditation on human possibility" and an intimation of "a new and sympathetic realm of the imagination."

The question is how this insight relates to the more conservative, hierarchic world of moral and institutional constraints that we usually associate with Pope. It would seem on the face of it to represent an alternative to this world: a realm briefly flirted with but ultimately repressed for the sake of social orthodoxy. Yet in many ways the gender ambiguities discussed above appear to have fit in easily enough with the prevailing system of patriarchal relationships and lines of authority.

In the Epistle to Dr. Arbuthnot, for example, Pope's presentation of himself in various feminized postures and roles—as a figure in need of protection because vulnerable to penetration ("They pierce my Thickets, thro' my Grot they glide"); as a sickly, fragile creature falling far short of the physical standards of masculinity ("The Muse but serv'd to ease some Friend, not Wife, / To help me thro' this long Disease, my Life" [131-32]); and as a maternal caretaker nursing a mother-turned-infant ("Me, let the tender Office long engage / To rock the Cradle of reposing Age" —in no way interferes with his aim to celebrate the manly virtues of his father (392-403) while proudly affirming his own place in the familial lineage as a follower in paternal footsteps: "O grant me thus to live, and thus to die! / Who sprung from Kings shall know less joy than I" (404-5).

And in the Epistles to Several Persons and the Imitations of Horace, Pope metaphorically transforms his Twickenham villa into an idealized, all-male community where the noblest and most virtuous (not to mention the exceptionally rich and powerful) gather to landscape his gardens and devise strategies for restoring England to her former greatness:

> *There, my Retreat the best Companions grace, Chiefs, out of War, and Statesmen, out of Place. There St. John mingles with my friendly Bowl, The Feast of Reason and the Flow of Soul: And He, whose Lightning pierc'd th' Iberian Lines, Now, forms my Quincunx, and now ranks my Vines, Or tames the Genius of the stubborn Plain, Almost as quickly, as he conquer'd Spain.*
> *(Imit. Hor., Sat. II.i, 125-32)*

Here, the homosociality of Pope's world blends into a politically reactionary vision rooted in elitism, militarism, imperialism, and a general elision not only of women but of all values traditionally coded as feminine. That the great war hero exalted in the final four lines of the passage is the same Lord Peterborough whom Pope addresses (in the letter cited earlier) as his sorely missed "Husband" only serves to underscore the compatibility between Pope's seemingly transgressive gender play and his embrace of a conservative patriarchal ideology.

Not that I mean to simply collapse the two into a single perspective or to suggest that this kind of gender play is always and automatically recuperable by hegemonic forces. Undoubtedly there are instances and contexts in which such play can meaningfully be said to challenge established structures of authority. In Pope's case, however, it seems to me more appropriate to acknowledge the gender ambiguities and accord them their due—as occasionally unconventional expressions that intriguingly hint at certain ideological slippages—but without exaggerating their influence or imbuing them with a misleading political (i.e., fashionably "subversive") significance.

A different form of gender play is evident in Pope's letters to women, where we find a sexual role-playing calculated to create a masculine identity, clearly distinguished from the feminine identity he constructs for his female correspondents. In place of the roles of husband and family patriarch, Pope acts out other roles that function to define his relationships with women: rake, courtly lover, protector, heroic rescuer. His early libertine pose, for example—what James A.

Winn terms Pope's "playing the rake"—allowed Pope to carry on epistolary flirtations, occasionally marked by erotic fantasies and slightly lewd innuendoes, with young women such as the Blount sisters. In these letters he tells them, "I love no meat but Ortolans and no women but you.... For to love you, is as if one should wish to Eat Angels, or drink Cherubim-Broath" (C 1:428) and teases, "Do, keep your own secrets, that such fellows as I may laugh at ye in the valley of Jehosaphat, where Cunning will be the foolishest thing in nature, & those white Bums which I dye to see, will be shown to all the world".

He playfully suggests the analogy between his epistolary correspondence with the opposite sex and illicit intercourse with them: a sexual interaction, it is intimated, they secretly desire even if they don't openly admit it. Thus he warns Teresa Blount that her reputation cannot remain unblemished, nor her hands kept pure, "while [her] heart consents to encourage [a male correspondent] in this lewd liberty of writing", insinuating a guilty connection between them cemented by what he describes as the "stain" of ink, of the pen's—and, implicitly, the body's—secretions. These passages exemplify what James Grantham Turner terms "Pope's transgressive play with the boundaries of decorum." More to the point, these epistolary forays into the interrelated realms of verbal and erotic play simultaneously mocked and upheld the sexual myths which were becoming increasingly powerful as instruments for regulating women's conduct in society. Pope's rakish role shared important characteristics with the more formalized and legally sanctioned roles of suitor and husband: in relation to all three, woman was made to serve a function, to act out a particular part, in a drama or institution not of her own making, created to fulfill the desires and interests of another.

Viewed in this light, the lines that Pope addresses to Teresa Blount in his Epistle to Miss Blount, with the Works of Voiture—"Ah quit not the free Innocence of Life! / For the dull Glory of a virtuous Wife!" —are less an instance of Pope's championing women's rights than of his trying to "protect" Blount from subsumption into one male scenario so that she would be free to play a role in another: his own. The "freedom" Pope envisages here is the freedom to be addressed and played with—in words if not in physical deeds—by Pope himself.

Both Teresa Blount and Lady Mary Wortley Montagu pose particularly interesting examples of the demands made upon others by his masculine role-playing proclivities and the kinds of resistance these demands occasionally encountered—a resistance more easily subdued in art than in life. Pope was clearly drawn to each woman by her special brand of energy and assertiveness, even as he felt impelled to encompass each within his own imaginative constructs. With Blount these took the form of projected adventures such as the fantasized cross-dressing exploit cited earlier, and schemes to bestow an annuity upon her on the condition that she remain unmarried for at least six years.

Pope was subsequently quick to respond with moral outrage to news of her affair with a married man: that is, when her rakishness was no longer available to fulfill a role in his own self-titillating scenarios. Of course, by this time Pope had transformed the sisters into antithetical but interdependent stereotypes of womanhood, one bad, the other good beyond measure: an analogue to the division between the ridiculed and the idealized portraits of women we find in his satiric verse.

In the case of Montagu the initial attraction was more powerful; the subsequent rejection, considerably more obsessive and virulent. The basic tenor of Pope's letters to her in 1716 and 1717, while she was travelling on the Continent with her husband, may be gleaned from the opening to one of them: "After having dream'd of you severall nights, besides a hundred Reveries by day, I find it necessary to relieve myself by writing". The remainder of this letter and those that follow bear out their erotic and masturbatory function as suggested here, but what is perhaps even more revealing about them is the singlemindedness with which they strive to pull Montagu into the vortex of Pope's imagination and assign her a role in the elaborate fiction he weaves throughout them.

Portraying himself as a devoted, lovesick worshipper at the shrine of Montagu's exalted femininity, Pope fantasizes about meeting her in Lombardy to share both pleasure and danger with her; assures her, "I lye dreaming of you in Moonshiny Nights exactly in the posture of Endymion gaping for Cynthia in a Picture"; and dramatizes himself as the unrequited lover of courtly love tradition, reduced to "imitating in my ravings the dreams of Spleenatic [sic] Enthusiasts and Solitaires, who fall in love with Saints, and fancy themselves in the favour of Angels, and Spirits, whom they can never see, or touch".

Direct contact between mere mortals and goddesses being forbidden, Pope petitions Montagu to send him an intermediary—in effect, a surrogate sex object, described as a "fair Circassian Slave to whom my Imagination had drawn more amiable than Angels, as beautiful as the Lady who was to chuse her by a resemblance to so divine a face".

Montagu, for her part, judging from her epistolary responses, was unmoved by Pope's romantic and erotic fantasies about her, as well as unimpressed by his strenuous efforts to elevate her to saintly status. Politely sidestepping them, or even ignoring them altogether, her letters quietly insist on a connection of friendship rather than romance between herself and her correspondent, in the process revealing their author's determination to avoid having her character and experiences appropriated to satisfy the dictates of someone else's story about her.

Coolly and matter-of-factly she regales Pope with detailed accounts of the landscape she has traversed, the villas and monuments she has visited, and the exotic social customs and rituals that have especially captured her attention on her sojourns in Hungary and Turkey. Her letters are anecdotal, informative, highly descriptive; above all, they are focused outward, on external phenomena and happenings, in sharp contrast to the inward-directed, self-centered and self-obsessed epistolary effusions of Pope's.

One might be tempted to argue that their correspondence represents yet another example of gender reversal, with Pope performing a conventionally defined feminine role by writing primarily about his feelings and inner thoughts, while Montagu fixes her attention almost exclusively on the "masculine" domain of worldly realities and events. This is true up to a point—and seems reinforced by Pope's metaphorical identification with decidedly non-"macho" lovers like the beautiful, poetically sensitive Endymion and with explicitly female ones such as the "Spouse in the Song of Solomon".

But as I read Pope's letters there is also something traditionally and symbolically "masculine" about his emotional outpourings in the way they make demands upon their audience for immediate and total recognition, as well as in the way they assert their own priority over the thoughts and feelings of the one to whom they are being communicated. The expression of the writer's subjectivity is only one half of the story of Pope's letters to Montagu. The other half is the intrusiveness and imposition of this subjectivity on another, the negation or absorption of the other voice trying to express a subjectivity of its own: in short, a kind of imaginative and emotional imperialism whose opening up to others constitutes a form of taking them over. Pope's fantasies about slave girls and Turkish concubine add a special resonance to the colonialist implications of his epistolary stance.

Some recent critics have responded negatively to Montagu's letters, blaming (for example) her "habitual refusal to exhibit sympathy, here perfectly exemplified" for the later ugly rupture between her and Pope, and sternly declaring that "the detachment of her replies comes as a shock." There is, however, another way of understanding Montagu's epistolary responses to Pope, as Patricia Meyer Spacks suggests when she observes, "Lady Mary reveals not callousness but only the kind of self-assertion she had gradually evolved—the assertion of her refusals.... [S]he claims her control of written language to insist on the value of an imagination different from Pope's." The way in which the authority of literary tradition and convention supported Pope's epistolary project while it impeded Montagu's efforts at autonomous self-expression points beyond Pope's letters to the successful strategies of appropriation and control evident in his major poems dealing with women.

Pope's satires abound in examples of such appropriation, of enclosure of the female voice within his own structures of thought and expression: the Goddess Dulness in The Dunciad, who ostensibly has her say but whose words are satirically framed and subverted by the epic machinery and (especially) the voice of the epic poet, representing the authority of tradition and high culture; Clarissa in The Rape of the Lock, who is first recruited into the service of the Baron, to supply the "weapon" that enables him to perpetrate the "rape," and later promoted to the higher service of Pope, given the exalted task of "open[ing] more clearly the moral of the Poem" (see note to Canto V, 7f.) by in effect counseling Belinda to act in conformance to male interests (i.e., to take the rape "like a woman" by accepting both her violation and her wifely destiny with grace); and Martha Blount in To a Lady, whose supposed words opening the verse are voiced, in effect mediated and authorized, by Pope himself ("Nothing so true as what you once let fall, / 'Most Women have no Characters at all'") and whose attempt to insert her own viewpoint into the poem ("'Yet Cloe sure was form'd without a spot—'") is immediately interrupted by the poet, who converts her diffident objection into a springboard for his own peremptory thoughts on the matter ("Nature in her then err'd not, but forgot"). Blount is thus transformed into a kind of "straight woman" for Pope, supplying him with lines—or one and one-half lines, to be exact, since she is silent for the remainder of the poem—that help set up his witty repartee and tendentious observations on women.

It is telling that in To Cobham and To Bathurst, Epistles I and III of the Epistles to Several Persons, the male addressees are allowed far more of an independent voice and perspective than is Martha Blount in To a Lady, even though there is no presence of a dialogue taking place in the former poems. The first eight lines of To Cobham, for example, present Richard Temple's views concerning the relative merits of empirical study versus book learning.

The poet's subsequent observations acknowledge the validity of Temple's argument even as they proceed to qualify, dispute, and/or build upon it. In To Bathurst, the first fourteen lines are devoted to setting out the ostensibly divergent views of Bathurst and Pope himself concerning the role of riches in human affairs. Although the views are finally revealed to be harmonious—"Like Doctors thus, when much dispute has past, / We find our tenets just the same at last" (15-16)—the effect is to affirm a reconciliation of separately held views rather than to create a specious unity or a homogenized outlook achieved through the absorption of all potentially different perspectives into one (i.e., the poet's).

By contrast, any independent views Martha Blount might have are absent from To a Lady. Apparently incapable of answering her own question or completing her own thought, not to mention of filling out her own heroic couplet, without the intervention of a male authority, Blount is shown to be fundamentally dependent on Pope throughout the entire course of the poem, no less than she is at the very end for the poetic immortality he wittily, magnanimously confers on her. Thus, although To a Lady purports to be a dialogue, and has traditionally been discussed as such by critics, what we in fact hear is a monologue: a strictly one-way conversation which depends on the illusion of a female voice and presence to support its own authority and self-sufficiency.

That a poem so insistently univocal could be interpreted by so many as dialogic underscores the validity of Judith Butler's observation that "The very notion of `dialogue' is culturally specific and historically bound, and while one speaker may feel secure that a conversation is happening, another may be sure it is not. The power relations that condition and limit dialogic possibilities need first to be interrogated." In other words, like the question of who is speaking for whom, the question of whether or not a dialogue is taking place cannot be answered without considering precisely those issues of domination and control that poems such as To a Lady serve variously to mystify or translate into other (e.g., "aesthetic") terms.

The strategies of domination and containment evident in Pope's treatment of women bear an interesting—if complex and highly mediated—relationship to the modes of imperial self-assertion and control characterizing England's new role in eighteenth-century world affairs. As indicated in the earlier-cited passage from Satire II.i of the Imitations of Horace describing the congregation of male companions at Pope's Twickenham retreat, figures such as Lord Peterborough assume symbolic identities that bring together manly virtue, military conquest, and the "taming" of what for Pope (as well as others in his milieu) is an invariably feminized landscape:

Here waving Groves a checquer'd Scene display,
And part admit and part exclude the Day;
As some coy Nymph her Lover's warm Address,
Nor quite indulges, nor can quite repress.
(Windsor-Forest, 17-20)

These specifically masculine-coded attributes assumed growing prominence over the course of Pope's career through his increasing preoccupation with patriotism—through the exaltation of his own role and that of his friends (including "Cobham's Cubs" or the "Boy Patriots" of the Whig Opposition) as potential saviors of the realm. Like the other virtues he extolled, patriotism encompassed a wide range of views, about gender as well as politics, economics, and foreign policy.

My aim here is not to argue that Pope was a producer of "imperialist poems" per se, since I have reservations regarding the notion of Pope as a "poet of empire" that are similar to my earlier-noted reservations about assigning him the label of bourgeois patriarchal writer: that is, I don't so much reject the argument as find it insufficiently attentive to the individual mediations that made Pope's treatment of imperialist issues both complicated and distinctive. Rather, my particular concern here is with the psychological and epistemological (though also, inevitably, ideological) implications of Pope's depictions of women within the context of poems that are variously involved with national identity, foreign trade, and the "discovery" of new lands, along with the display or appropriation of their exotic inhabitants and treasures.

If we accept Laura Brown's proposition that "eighteenth-century aesthetics provides an ideal context in which to observe the functional relationship of gender and empire," we might ask ourselves what Pope's frequent use of the female figure as a simultaneous marker for difference and sameness can tell us about his attitudes vis-a-vis questions of colonialism. In the simplest terms, what light does Pope's treatment of the relationship between men and women—between himself and the female figures he celebrates or degrades in his writings—shed on his conception of the relationship between the English and the natives of lands that were falling under the British sphere of influence?

How does Pope alternately assimilate and reject a variety of sexual and racial or cultural others as part of his mechanism for defining a distinct and unique self, enriched by certain external associations while refined by a much larger body of external exclusions? I believe that a significant part of the answer to these questions is suggested in Tzvetan Todorov's description of the seemingly opposite but ultimately identical poles of Columbus's attitude toward the Indians in the New World:

Either he conceives the Indians as human beings altogether, having the same rights as himself; but then he sees them not only as equals but also as identical, and this behaviour leads to assimilationism, the projection of his own values on the others. Or else he starts from the difference, but the latter is immediately translated into terms of superiority and inferiority. What is denied is the existence of a human substance truly other, something capable of being not merely an imperfect state of oneself. These two elementary figures of the experience of alterity are both grounded in egocentrism, in the identification of our own values with values in general, of our I with the universe—in the conviction that the world is one.

Because of the distortions and willed blindness resulting from this mindset, Todorov concludes that "Columbus has discovered America but not the Americans."

One might say of Pope too that on the whole his poetry suggests he has discovered a woman's world—the world of female portraiture and feminized mock-epic and feminine "Gothic" sensibility—but not women. He acknowledges the presence of the Other, of others clearly not himself, but his ideological and rhetorical strategies for dealing with them are not unlike Columbus's vis-a-vis the Indians: they must either (as in what critics tend to see as his glowing tributes to women) be rendered basically identical with himself—versions of the "softer man" into which Martha Blount is transformed in To a Lady—hence capable of reflecting back his own image in a self-validating hall of mirrors; or (as in his more frequent and memorable satires on women) they must be conceived of as irreducibly separate and different, thus automatically inferior to himself on the Great Chain of Being that underlies so much of his verse.

This mindset, with its rootedness in the binary oppositions of elevated and debased, is underscored by Montagu's remark, "What a goddess [Pope] made of me in [his letters], though he makes such a devil of me in his writings afterwards."

Pope may never have directly encountered the New World, but as we've seen, he did vicariously encounter the exotic through Montagu's meticulously recounted travels abroad, especially in Turkey. A letter of his written to her shortly after her return to England suggests his mode of perceiving a racial and cultural other, as well as its close connection with his manner of treating the sexual other: "You have no way of making me amends [for having gone abroad with your husband], but by continuing an Asiatic when you return to me, whatever English Airs you may put on to other people.... I long for nothing so much as your Oriental Self. You must of necessity be advanced so far Back into true nature & simplicity of manners, by these 3 years residence in the East, that I shall look upon you as so many Years younger than you was, so much nearer Innocence and Infancy" (C 1:493-94).

What we see here is Pope's desire to translate the other into terms that preserve just enough of the exotic to tantalize and titillate while at the same time fitting into familiar imagistic and ideological categories. Through this act of translation, Pope is able to subsume the other into his own mental and linguistic system, much as he does with the "painted Chiefs" and the "Feather'd People crowd[ing England's] wealthy Side" in Windsor-Forest and the "poor [untutor'd] Indian" appearing in An Essay on Man (I:99).

In the case of Montagu, Pope performs a double conversion, projecting both the mysteries of the Orient and the mysteries of femaleness onto a familiar canvas receptive to his own defining brush strokes. Tellingly, as the letter goes on Montagu is increasingly described in physical terms, with references to her "Soul stark naked the prettiest kind in the universe," and praise of the twinkle in her eye and the dimple in her cheek (C 1:494). Thus Montagu, "Oriental Self" and all, becomes transformed into one more very English—not to mention very feminine—portrait; and indeed, upon her return Pope commissioned Sir Godfrey Kneller to paint her picture to hang in his bedroom, thereby capturing her on canvas and symbolically confining her within his own sphere long after she had in fact taken flight from him.

The foregoing discussion suggests both the contradictions of Pope's identity and the various ways that he attempted to "resolve" them. It was an identity that continually strained the narrow limits of a selfhood defined by Christian and neoclassical essentialist assumptions —assumptions that were themselves coming under increasing challenge during this period, most notably from Lockean influences. The variety of literary roles and voices that Pope adopted has given rise to Bakhtinian analyses of his work—not without some justification. But in the end, concepts like "heteroglossia" and "dialogism" can only give a misleading picture of Pope's poetic world, the multiplicity of which Pope continually strove to contain and hierarchize in his attempts to construct a "purer," more unified identity for himself.

Often this was accomplished by suppressing or disavowing, while at the same time projecting onto others, disturbing elements incapable of being integrated into his idealized self-image. A telling example occurs in the Epistle to Dr. Arbuthnot, in his attack on Sporus—i.e., the bisexual Lord Hervey—who in effect becomes the picture for Pope's Dorian Gray, acting out (and being condemned for) the sexual doubleness that Pope himself expressed elsewhere: "His Wit all see-saw between that and this, / Now high, now low, now Master up, now Miss, / Fop at the Toilet, Flatt'rer at the Board, / Now trips a Lady, and now struts a Lord" (323-24; 328-29).

This process of projection and denial can be seen as closely bound up with broader cultural movements of the period, as described by Peter Stallybrass and Allon White:

[Augustan poetry] nourished and replenished its refined formalisms from the symbolic repertoire of the grotesque body in the very name of exclusion. It took the grotesque within itself so as to reject it, but this meant only that the grotesque was now an unpalatable and interiorized phobic set of representations associated with avoidance and with others. It could never be owned. It was always someone else who was possessed by the grotesque, never the self. In this way the bourgeois public sphere, that "idealist" realm of judgment, refinement, wit and rationalism was dependent upon disavowal, denial, and projection.

Pope's persistent (if ultimately doomed) struggle to "clean

up" the realms of both personal identity and art, to purge both of all heterogeneous matter that would prevent the creation of a "pure," clearly defined self as well as an exalted sphere of "high" culture, highlights both the triumphs and the failures of what has come to be known as English Augustanism. It was a struggle that revealed Pope's complicity in the very things—e.g., the "gross" materiality of his satiric projections, as well as their "debased" world of commercialism—that his poems attack most forcefully.

Complicity there is—but reciprocity is another matter. Among other things, I want to argue here that there is a crucial difference between the tendency to see the other in and through oneself, and the ability to see oneself in, and in relation to, the other. We might try to understand this difference in light of Todorov's distinction between the comparatist and the ethnologist: "The comparatist puts certain objects, all of which are external to him, on the same level, and he himself remains the sole subject. The ethnologist, on the other hand, contributes to the reciprocal illumination of one culture by another, to 'making us look into the other's face,' according to the splendid phrase already devised in the sixteenth century by Urbain Chauveton: we know the other by the self, but also the self by the other."

What seems to me lacking in Pope is precisely this kind of reciprocal illumination, precisely this capacity to "look into the other's face" and through that act learn new and unsuspected, perhaps even disturbing things about oneself. It is just such an act as this that Swift dramatizes when he has Gulliver stare with horror at the Yahoo and suddenly recognize himself, in all his appalling humanity—thereby satirically staging a version of Swift's own moments of anxiety-ridden self-revelation when (for example), after years of living in Ireland and taking the advice he gives to others, to "ride round the Kingdom, and observe the Faces of the Natives," he is forced to come to terms with the realization that he too is "a Teague, or an Irishman, or what people please."

By contrast, Pope's act of examining and judging the portraits of women in a picture gallery, or painting a series of women while moralizing on their character (or lack of it), tacitly affirms his confident possession of unchanging knowledge and places Pope in a position of unquestionable power, as a scrutinizing and judging subject vis-a-vis a scrutinized and judged object. There is no risk-taking involved in this act, no possibility of self-exposure or self-revelation. We might recall in this context Pope's fervent declaration to Montagu while she was still abroad: "I can't express how I long to see you, face to face"; but what this translated into upon her return was Pope's commissioning Kneller to paint her portrait while explaining to her, "I have made a perfect Passion of preferring your present Face to your past".

Once finished, the portrait hung on the wall of Pope's room, constituting in effect a travesty of what it means to come together with another person "face to face." To a Lady is filled with the faces of others, but no mutual or mutually illuminating look is possible between them and the poet. It is strictly a one-way gaze exhibited here: a gaze that can expose "Sappho at her toilet's greazy task" or spotlight "a Pimple on [Silia's] nose", but that refuses to examine, although it unwittingly reveals, its own egocentric and authoritarian assumptions; a gaze that projects onto blank canvas a set of a priori assumptions and stereotypes not open to revision or modification as a result of its collision with the eye of the other.

The poem's one-way gaze is the visual equivalent of the one-sided conversation, the monologue disguised as a dialogue, which structures the work. Both strategies are designed to keep the beast—and woman—at bay, thereby preserving an uncontaminated self capable of "pleas[ing] by manly ways" (Epistle to Dr. Arbuthnot, 337).

I am reminded of the conclusion to Sartre's study of Genet, where he calls for "the courage to go to the limits of ourselves in both directions [subjective and objective] at once" and declares, "At the present time, we must bring to light the subject, the guilty one, that monstrous and wretched bug which we are likely to become at any moment. Genet holds the mirror up to us: we must look at it and see ourselves." Pope was not unfamiliar with that "monstrous and wretched bug" that just might turn out to bear an uncanny resemblance to oneself. In The Guardian, no. 92 he had described the "little poet, Dick Distich"—clearly in part a self-portrait—as "a lively little Creature with long Arms and Legs: A Spider is no ill Emblem of him," and he was later to observe to Hugh Bethel that his numerous physical woes forced him to "live like an Insect, in hope of reviving with the Spring" (C 4:499).

But, as he had done in the case of the woman he saw in himself, Pope used his verse to exorcise the insect by projecting it onto a satirized other: Sporus, "this Bug with gilded wings, / This painted Child of Dirt that stinks and stings" (Epistle to Dr. Arbuthnot, 309-10); the scribbler who, after his cobweb is broken through, "spins the slight, self-pleasing thread anew" (Epistle to Dr. Arbuthnot, 89-90); and Timon, "A puny insect, shiv'ring at a breeze!" (To Burlington, 108). It is thus perhaps only fitting that the two images, of woman and insect, should merge in To a Lady, following reflection upon Rufa's and Sappho's inconsistencies: "So morning Insects that in muck begun, / Shine, buzz, and fly-blow in the setting-sun".

Through this kind of satiric objectification—by employing ideological and rhetorical strategies that function to keep the "vermin of nature" in their "proper" place at the bottom of the cosmic and moral hierarchy, safely distant from man ("Vast chain of being, that from God began"), Pope attempted to ensure against the possibility that he could ever "become at any moment" either the "monstrous and wretched bug" or the indeterminate feminine being that lurked at the corners of his psyche and threatened to destabilize his identity. He produced as a result a more elegant and controlled kind of poetry, but at a cost: for it is also a poetry that is less emotionally powerful and less politically liberating than it might have been.

Chapter 7

Bakhtin, Dialogism and Pope's Essay on Criticism

Alexander Pope's Essay on Criticism, first published in 1711, constituted a young poet's bold first foray into an often-acrimonious critical environment, a "learned world," Pope later wrote, that threatened authors with such a "dangerous fate" that they "must have the constancy of a martyr"(Twick. 6). Based on this rhetorical context and on characteristics of the text, the Essay has often been treated as an attempt to reconcile or transcend opposing critical doctrines—Aristotelian decorum and Longinian sublimity, for example (Fairer 33), or extreme eighteenth-century notions of "authority" and "taste" (Morris, Alexander Pope 49-50).

At the same time, the Essay as a poem has inspired many contradictory critical and aesthetic assessments. On the one hand, some critics have described it as a loose collection of aphorisms, a "potpourri of Augustan cliches" (Hooker 185),while on the other hand, David Morris calls the poem an "original and significant contribution" to literary theory (AP 48). DeQuincey dismissed the Essay for having "no natural order or logical dependency" (qtd. in Morris, AP47), but New Critics such as Arthur Fenner have noticed considerable unity achieved through, among other things, the theme of pride (236-37). Even Maynard Mack, in his admiration for Pope, admits that the Essay's argument is not completely "tidy".

Recently, suspecting perhaps that a search for textual unity or rhetorical coherence may be beside the point, some scholars have questioned the usefulness of approaching Pope's

Essay as a homogeneous, self-contained whole. Morris acknowledges generally that we "are beginning to recognize...how much in Pope's life and art proves unreconciled, unresolved, implicitly resisting or disrupting the closed circle of harmony and synthesis" ("Bootstrap" 107). Ironically, some New Critical efforts to find unity in the Essay not only call attention to its very "looseness," but also hint that the poem may be less the pronouncement of a clear, unchanged, and universal voice than discourse engaged in dialogue with itself and with other voices.

Thus Fenner, for example, articulates the poem's inherent tensions as "a dialectical zig-zag across the golden mean" and concludes that the poem is an "act of speech" by a "partisan, but conciliatory" voice. The terms speech and voice, as well as the very tension and struggle evident in the Essay's reputation, irresistibly suggest Mikhail Bakhtin's concept of dialogism as a way to elaborate on the poem's "loose," discursive quality in the framework of contemporary literary theory.

Of course, the conversational quality of much Augustan verse has not gone unnoticed, and some Pope scholarship actually anticipates Bakhtin's thinking and some of his terminology. In a study of what he designates Pope's "conversational poems," William Bowman Piper attributes those texts' conversational richness to such phenomena as "awareness", "responsiveness", and "sensitivity", terms all suggestive of Bakhtinian dialogism. Bakhtin's work, by showing that these qualities are inherent in rather than incidental to language, can provide us with a theoretical vocabulary for examining them in An Essay on Criticism and other poems.

For his part, Piper perceives a relative dearth of "'conversational" qualities in An Essay on Criticism compared to Pope's later works, arguing that this poem is conversationally "timid", merely "an elegant compendium of Augustan literary opinion rather than a living conversation about literature". However, by carefully listening to the Essay on Bakhtin's wavelength we can fine-tune our sensitivity to the poem's dialogical signals and discern more resemblances to "living conversation" than are obvious on first hearing. A Bakhtinian approach, in other words, can, among other services, considerably amplify earlier work on Augustan conversational verse.

Reading Pope's poetry, or any poetry, as dialogical requires confrontation with Bakhtin's own reluctance to regard most poetry in this way. In Discourse in the Novel, Bakhtin flatly dismisses poetry "in the narrow sense" as possessing dialogical properties; in most poetic genres, he says, "the natural dialogization of the word is not put to artistic use, the word is sufficient unto itself and does not presume alien utterances beyond its own boundaries". The well-wrought, organically unified lyric poem achieves its formal coherence by excluding what Bakhtin would call other, "alien" voices.

But Bakhtin's almost categorical dismissal of poetry from the dialogic imagination seems itself too dogmatic and authoritarian, and not impervious to challenge; accordingly, scholars have begun to see considerable applicability of Bakhtinian dialogism to poetry of various sorts. Don H. Bialostosky has outlined a number of Bakhtinian approaches to the poetry of Wordsworth and Coleridge; his own study of Wordsworth uses Bakhtin's work fruitfully not only to treat the Romantic writer's individual poems as "dialogic art," but also to pursue a much more ambitious mission: to accommodate the many competing voices of contemporary Wordsworth criticism in a dialogue that "does not reduce the situation to a struggle against the supposed hegemony of a dominant voice or to a despair at the 'chaos' of divergent voices".

If some poetry can be shown to be dialogical, though, eighteenth-century English poetry may seem especially resistant to dialogical reading. In its impulse to emulate the privileged models of antiquity and to maintain decorum of expression, neoclassical poetry may be considered more akin to Bakhtin's "unitary language," which seeks to "crystalize" discourse into "literary language, 'correct language'" (Discourse 270). Pope may seem particularly dubious as a candidate for a dialogical poet; after all, An Essay on Criticism urges others to learn "for Ancient Rules a just Esteem" and issues precepts in away that Bakhtin might regard as "authoritarian, dogmatic and conservative" Discourse 287).

In an essay considering the work of Robert Burns in light of Bakhtin's theories, David Morris mentions factors that he says tended to discourage dialogism in eighteenth-century poetry, and he compares Pope unfavorably with Burns in terms of dialogic possibility ("Burns" 12). Pope, Morris states, "in Bakhtin's terms is...a strongly monological poet" who "maintains...dialogical relations" chiefly with classical texts and political rhetoric. But at least one scholar, Ronald Schleifer, does find a Bakhtinian approach pertinent to Pope's work, having discussed in an essay on The Rape of the Lock as mock-epic as "a kind of hybrid genre that is, in its very intention, 'double-voiced'".

And Morris himself allows that Pope does find "diverse uses for the discourse of the other," if in a limited way ("Burns" 22); Morris observes, for instance, that An Essay on Man "includes numerous, distinct voices and modulations of style, [although] its range is still comparatively narrow" next to, say, the "polyglot" eighteenth-century novel. Indeed, it is that very "range" of possibility for dialogism, whether narrow or broad, that calls for a closer look in An Essay on Criticism; after all, a poem that wittily and chattily begins "'Tis hard to say, if greater Want of Skill/Appear in Writing or in Judging ill" (1-2, emphasis added) invites us, not to say teases us, into an exploration of its dialogic potential.

Pope's Essay reflects Bakhtinian dialogism in several key respects: its variously shifting voices anticipating the response of their audience(s); its representation of competing impulses within the consciousness of Pope the poet/critic; its participation in the fractious public debate that was Augustan literary criticism; and its engagement of ancient texts in a search for ways to appropriate classical tradition without making it into a poetic straitjacket. To begin, we can sense in the Essay a "multiplicity" of voices, to borrow Bakhtin's term (Discourse 263), that speak while inclining their ears toward a gallery of audiences and prompting their response. Like Bakhtin's "word in living conversation," the Popean utterance is "oriented toward a future answer-word: it provokes an answer, anticipates it and structures itself in the answer's direction". The several implied audiences from which the Essay expects this answering are distinguished from each other by whether Pope identifies himself with or distances himself from them, as signaled grammatically by verb moods and implied subjects.

One of these voices, which we may justifiably call authoritative or authoritarian, imparts the Essay's major neoclassical precepts. Often employing the imperative mood, this voice instructs an audience explicitly or implicitly identified as "you":

First follow Nature, and your Judgment frame By her just Standard, which is still the same[.]

You then whose Judgment the right Course wou'd steer, Know well each Ancient's proper Character[.] (118-19)

Learn hence for Ancient Rules a just Esteem; To copy Nature is to copy Them. (139-40)

Detached, confident in the self-evident authority of "Nature" and the "Ancients," the voice hands out instruction to an audience ("You then") that it fully expects to share in its deference to classical example.

A different voice, for which we might borrow Fenner's term "conciliatory," mitigates the first voice's authoritarian tone with a more diplomatic mission. It speaks to an implied audience of "all of you," the squabbling critics whom the voice would persuade to resolve their differences. More friendly, though still detached, this voice of the peacemaker adopts an informal, discursive tone for a presumably receptive, teachable audience:

A perfect Judge will read each Work of Wit With the same Spirit that its Author writ, Survey the Whole, nor seek slight Faults to find, Where Nature moves, and Rapture warms the Mind[.] Whoever thinks a faultless Piece to see, Thinks what ne'er was, nor is, nor e'er shall be.

This voice does not simply set out principles, as does the

authoritative voice; it seeks to coax warring critics to adopt more humane and tolerant attitudes. When it uses the imperative mood, its tone is not so much imperious as persuasive, following its commands with reasons for their rightness:

Be thou the first true Merit to befriend; His Praise is lost, who stays till All commend[.]

Ah ne'er so dire a Thirst of Glory boast, Nor in the Critick let the Man be lost! Good-Nature and Good-Sense must ever join; To Err is Humane; to Forgive, Divine.

Waxing expansive, the conciliatory voice uses its own good nature and generous example to cajole its audience into burying, or at least blunting, the critical hatchet.

A third type of voice, which is allied with, not detached from, its audience, is identifiable by its use of "we," "us," and "our." Commiserating with its listeners about human failings, as if to say "You and I know how things are," this voice admits complicity in the foibles it laments. Thus it discusses the "Limits" which "Nature to all things fix'd", including the mind, and sighs over the limits of human wisdom:

Like Kings we lose the Conquests gain'd before, By vain Ambition still to make them more[.]

We think our Father Fools, so wise we grow; Our Wiser Sons, no doubt, will think us so.

Fondly we think we honour Merit then, When we but praise Our selves in Other Men.

This voice acknowledges that everyone, including the poet, is liable to error.

Not so sympathetic to the excessive or less excusable errors of "some" or "other" poets and critics is yet another voice that identifies itself with an implied "we," an audience of apparently savvy poets and critics. This voice directs the attention of the in-crowd to another group, cataloguing its mistakes:

Some have at first for Wits, then Poets past, Turn'd Criticks next, and prov'd plain Fools at last; Some neither can for Wits nor Criticks pass, As heavy Mules are neither Horse nor Ass. Some to Conceit alone their Taste confine, And glitt'ring Thoughts struck out at ev'ry Line; Pleas'd with a Work where nothing's just or fit; One glaring Chaos and wild Heap of Wit[.]

Following the latter passage is an extended discussion about mistaken emphasis on the superficialities of versification: "Others for Language all their Care express"; "Some by Old Words to Fame have made Pretence"; and "most by Numbers judge a Poet's Song". As solutions to these problems the voice offers practical wisdom—e.g., true expression is appropriate to the subject and occasion, like proper dress; the poem's sound should be an echo to the sense—and expects its audience to discern and affirm these maxims' rightness. By displacing the errors onto a detached group of "them," Pope saves his audience from shame or embarrassment in case the errors are in fact its own, nudging and winking while instructing on how to avoid being one of "them." Thus he practices a version of the diplomatic didacticism he espouses for critics: "Men must be taught as if you taught them not;/And Things unknown propos'd as Things forgot".

Pontificating, cajoling, reasoning, Pope's varying voices experiment with degrees of detachment and involvement, authority and conciliation, seeking (or claiming) to offer advice, chide foolishness, and restore grace and tolerance to criticism. Ultimately, though, the collective Popean voice is not detached from but entangled with the audience as it participates in the very follies it purports to criticize. "Fear most to tax an Honourable Fool," the poem advises, immediately after poking fun at John Dennis, the Appius who "reddens at each Word you speak,/And stares, Tremendous! with a threatning Eye".

The poem is not above making fun of "half-learn'd Witlings", "tuneful Fools", and the "Bookful Blockhead, ignorantly read,/With Loads of Learned Lumber in his Head". Does Pope follow his own advice of speaking, "tho' sure, with seeming Diffidence"? Evidently not, and so he seeks to make amends by adopting a final voice in the concluding apostrophe to William Walsh; this is the young poet who offers "humble

Praise" to the "lamented Shade" of his mentor and suggests that his "tender Wing" is among those that need to be "prun'd"—at the same time disingenuously claiming with a final wink that his wing "no more attempts to rise". In surprisingly Bakhtinian fashion, then, the Essay presents us with an elaborately jumbled utterance in which no one voice prevails. The humane peacemaker and the indignant judge of bad writing, Pope the poet's apologist and Pope the sensible critic—all anticipate the "answer-words" (Bakhtin, Discourse 280) of their variously-construed audiences.

But the voices do not talk solely to their listeners; they also talk among themselves, and in this way Pope's Essay exemplifies its second dialogic characteristic: Bakhtin's "alien voices" that "enter into the struggle for influence within an individual's consciousness (just as they struggle with one another in surrounding social reality)" (Discourse 348). Pope's shifting attitudes of authoritative confidence and generous conciliation are reminiscent of the Bakhtinian consciousness trying to find "one's own voice" by "experimentally objectifying another's discourse" in artistic representation. As Bakhtin says, an author

> utilizes now one language, now another, in order to avoid giving himself up wholly to either of them; he makes use of this verbal give-and-take, this dialogue of languages at every point in his work, in order that he himself might remain as it were neutral with regard to language, a third party in a quarrel between two people (although he might be a biased third party). (Discourse 314)

This process in the Essay is subtle but unmistakable the Popean consciousness, learned, precocious, a skilled poet, yet no more than twenty-three years old, weighs a variety of possible stances as it strives to shape its own critical voice and express as "ne'er so well" what "oft was Thought".

Likewise, Bakhtin's concept of "alien voices" helps to account for the apparent contradictions in the Essay's critical precepts and offers a theoretical explanation for what many scholars characterize as an attempt to come to terms with those perceived opposites. In these scholars' view, the poem seeks to take account of disparate poetic values and suggest a new, workable, poet-friendly theory. Thus Fairer, for example, explains that the Essay "negotiates" between Aristotelian imitation and decorum on the one hand and Longinian sublimity and inspiration on the other. Similarly, Morris notes Pope's rejection of the extremes of "authority," in the form of "petrified" quasi-classical dramatic unities, and "taste," defined as "anarchic" individual preference (Alexander Pope 49-50).

Reading the Essay as internal dialogue can accommodate these polarities without the necessity of either choosing between them or forcing them into synthesis, but more than that, dialogism can give a name to the very process by which the poem's speaking consciousness wrangles with authority and taste, decorum and inspiration. In Pope's text, furthermore, conflicting or complementary mental faculties seesaw in Bakhtinian fashion just as those competing doctrines do. Here Pope explores, for example, the tidal ebb and flow of sense in every mind: "Pride, where Wit fails, steps in to our Defence,/And fills up all the mighty Void of Sense!": He represents as domestic battling the conflict between wit and judgment, which "often are at strife,/Tho' meant each other's Aid, like Man and Wife". And he parcels out territory to contrasting but equally valuable traits in the mind of the ideal critic, who is

Unbiass'd, or by Favour or by Spite; Not dully prepossest, nor blindly right; Tho' Learn'd, well-bred; and tho' well-bred, sincere; Modestly bold, and Humanly severe[,] Who to a Friend his Faults can freely show, And gladly praise the Merit of a Foe[.]

Read dialogically, the poem represents a consciousness coming to terms with the conflicting demands of good sense and tolerance for human error, of poetic (or critical) justice and mercy.

An essentially public utterance, Pope's Essay evidences its dialogic quality not only in its internal "voices" but in its participation in eighteenth-century literary criticism, itself a dialogue with the classical tradition that, as Maynard Mack asserts, Pope sought to reinvigorate. Thus the Essay manifests a third Bakhtinian characteristic: its availability for being turned over, taken apart, argued with by its contentious first readers. The poem takes part in what Bakhtin calls "the social life of discourse outside the artist's study, discourse in the open spaces of public squares, streets, cities and villages, of social groups, generations and epochs" (Discourse 259).

John Barnard reminds us of the relentlessly social nature of Pope's writing in general when he says, "More than any other major English poet, [Pope's] work is rooted in the immediate facts, personalities, and literary tastes of his time". In Pope's world, "another's word, another's utterance," as Bakhtin phrases it, was indeed "the subject of passionate communication, an object of interpretation, discussion, evaluation, rebuttal, support, further development and so on" (Discourse 337). No product of an isolated garret artist fearing to go unnoticed, the Essay became a contestant as well as a would-be mediator in the debate over writing and judging ill—a poem about criticism that itself became an object of critical discourse, both praised by Addison as "a Master-piece in its kind" (spectator 483) and vilified by John Dennis as "A most notorious Instance of...Depravity of Genius and Tast".

Pope participated in the dialogical discourse surrounding his Essay by continually revising it in light of others' opinions, and in his own zeal for improvement and consciousness of public perception. The attention he devoted to revising all of his works, both in manuscript and after publication, has been called "compulsive" (Hammond 4). Numerous revisions of the Essay—some minor, some substantive—through four published editions (Twick. 234-35) exemplify, as do any writer's revisions, a Bakhtinian dialogue with himself, a debate of competing inner voices over the relative merits of this or that word or phrase. Similarly, Pope's reflection on others' criticisms indicates an ability to maintain a dialogical give-and-take with his critical world.

At least one revision in the Essay's second edition of 1713 was apparently prompted by objections from Roman Catholics to the poem's comparison of wit with faith (Twick. 203-05);

Pope wrote to John Caryll, somewhat condescendingly, "I promise you, Sir, if the alteration of a word or two will gratify any man of sound faith tho' of weak understanding, I will, (tho' it were from no other principle than that of common good nature) comply with it" (corresp. I.118).An even more telling instance is the well-documented feud with John Dennis. This furious flurry of answer-words and counter-answer-words, beginning with Dennis's attack in Reflections Critical and Satyrical, Upon a Late Rhapsody, Call'd, An Essay Upon Criticism, resembles guerrilla warfare more than dialogue; yet Pope appears to have taken some of Dennis's objections seriously. "[T]o give this man his due," Pope writes, again to Caryll, "he has objected to one or two lines with reason, and I will alter them in case of another edition: I will make my enemy do me a kindness where he meant an injury, and so serve instead of a friend".

Notes appended to the manuscript list a number of lines and couplets for reconsideration, some explicitly keyed to page numbers in Dennis's Reflections (Twick. 482-84), and three passages that Dennis criticized were changed, although it is not clear that his remarks were the deciding factor in all three cases (206, 312-13n.). To be sure, the revisions are more subtle than sweeping, and not all of the lines reconsidered were finally revised; some are marked with such notations as "not to be alterd" and "stet sic" (Twick. 483, 484). Still, Pope's willingness to sift serious arguments from personal abuse represents an ability to listen to the voices of others, even when those voices could be intensely hostile and insulting.

That hostility—Dennis calls the disabled Pope a "hunch-back'd Toad" and a "Monkey" (415, 417)—reminds us that the "passionate communication" Bakhtin celebrates is often, in reality, far from charitable. Indeed, critical nitpicking is one of the very occasions for Pope's Essay. John Oldmixon, tapping a drum also beaten by Addison, Swift, Dryden, and others, observes that English criticism of his day "is generally mistaken to be an Effect of Envy, Jealousy, and Spleen; an invidious Desire to find Faults only to discredit the Author, and build a Reputation on the Ruin of his". The chatty volubility of Bakhtin's dialogic imagination should not lull us into forgetting the snarls and sniping that led Pope to sigh that "the life of a Wit is a warfare upon earth" (Twick. 6). The "naively appealing benevolence" of dialogism, which Morson and Emerson call its main limitation and "most vulnerable side", fails to take into account the Pope-Dennis rivalries of the world:

even a cursory reading of Bakhtin reveals that the implied potential other in his dialogues lives on friendly boundaries and continuums.... Bakhtin presumes no absolute conflict between an organism and its surroundings, just as he presumes no conflict in principle between self and society.

Nor should we forget Pope's power to strike back at his enemies, which he does not hesitate to use, or the deliberateness of the ambitious young author who is perhaps not more interested in moderating a gentlemanly forum on literary criticism than he is in orchestrating his own burgeoning career. As Paul Hammond illustrates, Pope self-consciously deploys an array of strategies to fashion a public image through his writings, strategies that include the "compulsive" revision, close attention to all phases of publication, meticulously crafted rhetoric ranging from "careful sleight of hand" to "outrageous mendacity", and a variety of poses adopted for effect. Pope's self-marketing and promotion certainly caution against imputing too much innocence to the dialogism we posit in his work.

The internal and external dialogues of composition and revision, anticipating and answering readers' responses, all take place in still a larger dialogical framework, the neoclassical concern with finding a desirable relation to the models of antiquity. Despite the Essay 5 firmly rooted temporality, it also sought to give eighteenth-century poets and critics ways to engage in dialogue with ancient discourse, to fully test it and integrate it in what Bakhtin calls the "assimilation...of others' words" (Speech Genres 89).

Modeled after Horace's Ars Poetica and Boileau's Art Poetique, packed with the inherited wisdom of similar treatises both ancient and modern, Pope's Essay at once built upon, subsumed, and reshaped classical ideas for consideration by his contemporaries. Having made earlier texts his own, Pope offers his version for possible assimilation by readers, acting out the phenomenon Bakhtin describes by which both our speech and artistic representations are "filled with others' words, varying degrees of otherness or varying degrees of 'our-own-ness" (Speech Genres 89).

The precursor texts may present themselves as "authoritative" discourse, which Bakhtin says "demands our unconditional allegiance" (Discourse 343), but through assimilation these texts become "internally persuasive " discourse, which is "half ours and half someone else's". More than a slavish duplication of ancient sententiae, then, the Essay stands in "truly dialogic relation" to classical tradition because "to agree with a discourse is already to have tested it, deprived it of unconditional allegiance, and integrated it into one's own framework" (Morson and Emerson 220). Maynard Mack puts the point another way that captures the resonance of dialogue:

To keep the great voices sounding behind [Pope's] own was to identify his poem with the collective classical tradition, and thus with the sensibility of the society formed by that tradition, whose spokesman in this work he was offering to become. (171; emphasis added)

Far from rising "urbanely" above the fray, as Fenner suggests, the Essay rather bounded provocatively into its midst, energizing the dialogue that extended centuries into the past and would continue for centuries afterwards.

The work of Bakhtin enables us to recognize salient features of An Essay on Criticism—its conversational style, its anticipatory responsiveness to its audience, its shuttling between judgmental and conciliatory stances—as characteristic of discourse in all times and places. Pope's Essay demonstrates that even a somewhat authoritative discourse can exhibit more dialogic fluidity than is obvious at first glance.

In its experimentation with various voices—internal and external, past and present—and in its subtle evolution through revision, the Essay engaged in dialogue with both the ancient critical tradition and the "passionate communication" of

Pope's day. Neither homogeneous reconciliation nor eternal opposition is the issue in the Essay; rather, by weighing and mediating among conflicting ideas the poem seeks to introduce into critical discourse more of the "humanity" and "compassion" for which Pope earnestly, if self-consciously, pleads in the preface to his 1717 Works (Twick. 4, 8).

We might even say that Pope's Essay has entered the internal discourse of (English-) "speaking persons," Bakhtin's sine qua non (Discourse 338), through its most famous aphorisms, for who has not heard or said that to err is human, to forgive divine Perhaps the ongoing scholarly "dialogue on Pope" that David Morris seeks in a tercentenary reflection—a dialogue that "demands other voices and other visions" ("Bootstrap" 118)—can include a new examination of dialogue in Pope's work as well.

Chapter 8

Necessary Desolation in Pope's Eloisa to Abelard

Walk in faith even though Heaven seems out of reach. Think how good it would be if you could write that. MOTHER Mary Joseph's words to Sister John of the Cross near the conclusion of Mark Salzman's recent novel, Lying Awake, capture the central impulse of Alexander Pope's 1717 poem, Eloisa to Abelard. Like Sister John who faces a devastating choice between living with a small brain tumor that provides moments of spiritual ecstasy and surgery that could potentially lead her back to the aridity of her prior monastic existence, Eloisa too faces a crisis of faith, here described as a choice between her unruly passion for Abelard and her spiritual love for God. Just as Mother Mary Joseph understands the power of language to console the fainthearted on their journeys to Heaven, so too does Pope realise that his poem creates both a painful dissonance and a compelling resolution that encourages and heartens others on their sometimes wayward walks to God.

Traditionally, much of the criticism that touches upon Eloisa's spiritual crisis-a crisis that seems to put "Heaven just out of reach" centers on the extensive interpretive debate about the struggle between "grace and nature, virtue and passion" that Alexander Pope articulates in "The Argument" to Eloisa to Abelard:

It was many years after this separation, that a letter of Abelard's to a Friend which contain'd the history of his misfortune, fell into the hands of Eloisa. This awakening all her tenderness, occasion'd those celebrated letters (out of which the following is partly extracted) which give so lively a picture of the struggles of grace and nature, virtue and passion.'

As this debate is typically formulated, it raises opposing questions concerning Eloisa's spiritual status in the poem. According to the dialectic Pope seems to have established in "The Argument," critics either emphasize her redemption through the saving power of God's grace, or they alert readers to her failure as a religious woman because of her inability to free herself from her idolatry of Abelard.2 Instead of taking sides in this debate, which grounds its arguments in the dialectic that Pope's "Argument" seems to suggest, I propose that we focus on another key concept presented in "The Argument"; that is, the idea of struggle.

Pope's Eloisa rejects an easy conventional conversion narrative, seeking instead, as Linda Georgianna has written, "a new spiritual model that can adequately describe and account for her complex spiritual state". Eloisa wishes to account for the gap between her unruly inner life and a static monastic life that she professes in order to help herself and others "do good and avoid evil, for the love of God, requirements that entail an ongoing interior struggle with one's motives, memories and desires".

If we focus on Eloisa's ongoing interior struggle rather than on the irreconcilable tension between "grace and nature, virtue and passion," we can more fully appreciate the poem's deeply complex spiritual, monastic and Catholic dimensions. My aim in this essay is to historicize Pope's poem in several ways, first by closely analyzing Pope's representation of Eloisa in light of his own Catholicity and contemporary depictions of her, and then by showing how some understanding of the Benedictine monastic context which underwrites the poem serves to deepen the poem's pathos and increase our appreciation of Eloisa's sacrifice and pain.

Further, within this fuller historical account, I will suggest that Eloisa remains an exemplary religious woman because she participates whole— heartedly in the ongoing interior struggle between desolation and consolation. These movements, which Pope painstakingly delineates in his poem, effectively mirror the sometimes slow and painful spiritual process whose success is always in question. Finally, I will consider how Pope's introduction of the creator-poet at the poem's conclusion, just at the moment when Eloisa seems to recognize the futility of seeking spiritual perfection, points to a compelling paradox. Eloisa's consolation seems dependent upon a grace that falls to the poet, who, by retelling her story, may offer consolation and guidance to those who might, like Eloisa, "fear God's judgment even as they seek God's love" (Georgianna 202).

In his study of Alexander Pope's poem, Eloisa to Abelard, James Wellington describes in detail the processes by which Pope extrapolated material for his poem from an unfaithful English translation of the letters of Abelard and Heloise (Wellington 19-25). At one point in the analysis, Wellington notices that Pope's material is drawn mainly from the second, fourth, and fifth letters in this version, known as the Hughes translation, which was published in 1713. Furthermore, Wellington makes the point that "Hughes's French precursor completely suppressed the original third letter of Heloise, with its searching theological questions and its final acquiescence in the religious life and replaced it with a far more impassioned utterance of his own devising".

In its place, the anonymous authors included a "wholly fictitious" third letter which represents Heloise as "far more amorous than the real one and debases the dignity and piercing eloquence of the historical Heloise into the coquetry of a salon flirt". As another part of my goal in this essay I would like to suggest that Pope was sufficiently well-versed in the Catholic tradition to recreate in his poem what was missing from the Hughes translation from which he worked: the sentiments of the historical Heloise's third letter in which she expresses her experience of both desolation and consolation in her religious life. In doing so, Pope not only acted like many early eighteenth-century writers who used their imaginations to bridge the gap between history and fiction, but he manifested his life-long need to be correct in his poetry, "to put the image straight" (Mack 660). With Pope, correctness meant "an exquisite weighing of sound, of textures, of rhythm, as well as an adaptation of metre to the idea, the congruence of feeling with form, and, one need hardly add, appropriate diction" as well as constant devotion to the craft of poetry (Dobree 188).

Given Pope's startling poetic integrity, then, it is not inconceivable to suggest that Pope wrote Eloisa to Abelard to "correct" the misrepresentation of her in the Hughes translation of the letters by recreating her spiritual anxieties. Pope's knowledge and experience as a Roman Catholic find their way into the poem to emphasize the magnitude of Eloisa's genuine spiritual crisis, a crisis he recognizes as absent from his source for the poem.

ALEXANDER Pope had never seen the original, unromanticized version of Abelard's and Heloise's letters. The Latin text of the letters and Abelard's major works were published in Paris by Nicholas Buon in 1616. This edition, known as the Duchesne-d'Amboise edition, became the basis for a highly romanticized version in French of Heloise's two love letters and Abelard's reply to the first. This version was created by Roger de Rabutin, Comte de Bussy in 1687. In 1695 an expanded French version was published at the Hague by an unidentified author or authors. The whole of these letters, paraphrased by F N. Du Bois, ran into many editions, and it generally made the couple's romance known in England (Radice 50-51). John Hughes, Whig poet, dramatist, journalist and friend of Pope's, produced an English translation in 1713. The Hughes translation, which inherited the aberrations of the Du Bois version, became the source for Pope's poem (Wellington 20-21).

Maynard Mack, in his biography of Pope, suggests several possibilities for Pope's interest in the Heloise-Abelard story (326-31). First, he speculates that because of turmoil among his co-religionists, Pope wrote Eloisa to Abelard to reveal his solidarity with the old faith, although Mack thinks the representation of monastic life much too severe to warrant warm praise for its adherence to Catholic precepts. Next, he explores at some length the possibility that Pope identified with both Abelard and Heloise. Like Abelard, Pope was brilliant but frail, given his dwarfish stature and deformity. Like Heloise, Pope was prone to suppress his emotions, especially in the realm of love, and he was acutely sensitive to ridicule.

Through her he could articulate his longing to love and be loved, and his need to express his anger and despair at his own physical and emotional imprisonment, something he had no control over. Finally, Mack concludes that while there is a danger in connecting the poem with Pope's life, the poem nonetheless opens "a window on Pope's sense of his situation at the time, and marks, perhaps, a personal urge to come to terms, imaginatively, poetically, dramatically, by means of an objective correlative, with the austere future that lay ahead". Pope's identification with the psychological dimensions of the Heloise-Abelard story, a story made popular in England by the Hughes translation, and his acute Catholic sensibilities, which prompted him to recognize his source's misapprehension of Heloise's situation, serve to produce a poem unique in his canon, for he never wrote another poem with such passionate and melancholic content.

To appreciate Pope's sharply focused conflict between Eloisa's religious vows and her love for Abelard-a perspective the Hughes translation effaces-we must know something of the story's historical roots. In approximately 1119, Peter Abelard, the brilliant twelfth-century theologian, was asked by one of the canons at Notre Dame in Paris, Fulbert, to tutor his niece Heloise, "already known throughout France for her love of learning" (Mack 320).

She was about sixteen or seventeen, Abelard in his late thirties. To facilitate the task of educating Heloise, Abelard lived in Fulbert's house; Abelard and Heloise soon found themselves passionately in love and she became pregnant. To avoid embarrassment, Abelard arranged for Heloise to live with his sister in Brittany, where a son was born. Recognizing that a secret marriage to Abelard would not satisfy Fulbert if the scandal broke and also influenced by classical writers who believed a woman was a hindrance to a man, especially a man of great mind like Abelard, Heloise offered to remain Abelard's mistress rather than his wife. However, despite Heloise's protests, she and Abelard were secretly married in Paris. In an effort to protect Abelard from any further embarrassment, Heloise denied to Fulbert that they were married. Further, to escape Fulbert's wrath, Abelard arranged for Heloise to move to the Benedictine convent at Argenteuil where she lived as a lay woman and where Abelard visited her as her husband.

Fulbert, for his part, wrongly assumed that Abelard had sent Heloise to the convent in order to get rid of her. To take revenge, Fulbert hired two men to enter Abelard's quarters and emasculate him. To resolve their marital crisis, Abelard requested that Heloise become a Benedictine nun at Argenteuil and he a Benedictine monk. Eventually, Abelard was allowed by the order to build a retreat near Nogent-sur-Seine, which he named the Paraclete in honour of the third person of the Trinity.

Later he was named abbot of St. Gildas on the Brittany coast and left the Paraclete to Heloise, who moved there in 1129 with a group of sisters over whom she was abbess. The Paraclete, under Heloise's leadership, became one of the most distinguished houses in France, with six daughter houses founded in her lifetime (Radice 43). While she was abbess at the Paraclete, mysteriously, a copy of Abelard's autobiography, "which contain'd the history of his misfortune," fell into her hands and it is at this point that Pope's poem begins.

EVEN a cursory reading of the poem reveals Pope's familiarity with Catholic spirituality of the time. Although he was quite ambiguous about his religious education-necessarily so given the increasing anti— Catholic sentiment after 1688 and the stringency of the penal laws-Pope remarked to Joseph Spence, Pope's first biographer, that four priests played a part in his education (Thornton 31). Interestingly, and useful to my argument here, one of these priests, according to Francis Thornton, was a Benedictine, John Anselm Mannock, O.S.B., whose brother, William, was also a priest and tutor to Pope.

Both brothers were intimate friends of the Pope family. Pope's education, in addition to his quiet religious training under the Mannocks and later with Fathers Thomas Phillips and Richard Caryll, S.J., was surely informed by his voracious reading at home. Marilyn Francus, who reports that Pope had read the Metaphysical poets, Donne and Crashaw in particular, as early as 1706, argues that Eloisa to Abelard manifests the characteristics of the Metaphysical devotional poem: the conflict between human and divine love, which, after much vacillation, is resolved by creating a divine lover, namely Abelard. Along with the Metaphysical poets, another singular literary influence on Pope was Milton, whose picture he kept in his "chamber round about me, that the constant remembrance of [him] may keep me always humble" (Mack 107).

Milton's L'Allegro and II Penseroso are poems that testify to the necessary co-existence of Mirth and Melancholy and shape Pope's conception of Eloisa as someone who experiences both desolation and consolation in the course of her religious life. Not only does the "brooding darkness" which "spreads his jealous wings" over "ebon shades and low— browed rocks" in Milton's scene at the beginning of L'Allegro anticipate Eloisa's "Black Melancholy," but Milton's sense that a person's peace seems dependent upon the capacity to sustain the vicissitudes of Melancholy at the end of II Penseroso resembles Pope's emphasis on Eloisa's desolation as a necessary condition to the reconciliation of her very human dilemma.

Eloisa to Abelard suggests that Pope was also familiar with various structures of devotional meditation, exercises recommended to struggling souls by Counter-Reformation handbooks (Mack 326-27). Eloisa's visions and thoughts resemble key concepts in the mode of meditation advocated by St. Ignatius of Loyola in his Spiritual Exercises (1539—1540), namely "composition of place," a particular mental image of a scene, usually from the New Testament, and the "application of the senses," an exercise designed to arouse the emotions that, in turn, move the will. Moreover, Eloisa, as Pope represents her, experiences the excruciating movements between spiritual desolation and consolation. According to St. Ignatius, in his Spiritual Exercises, desolation is [the] darkness of soul, [the] disturbance in it, movement to things low and earthly, the unquiet of different agitations and temptations, moving to want of confidence, without hope, without love, when one finds oneself lazy, tepid, sad, and as if separated from [the] Creator and Lord. Because, as consolation is contrary to desolation, in the same way the thoughts which come from consolation are contrary to the thoughts which come from desolation. (Fleming 206)

By way of contrast, Ignatius describes the movement of the soul toward God as consolation. In other words, "neither anything nor anyone presents itself in competition with a total gift of self to God in love". These Ignatian categories frame Eloisa's experience, her inability to recognize "the different movements which are caused in the soul". For Ignatius assumes that Christians experience both desolation and consolation in the course of their lives, and they need guidelines in order to distinguish the "evil spirit" from the "good spirit." In order to follow God more closely, the person must learn to accept that both movements constitute the heart of the spiritual life and to discern the different movements within the soul.

Pope reveals Eloisa's desolation by having her project her spiritual paralysis onto the landscape:

Black Melancholy [that] sits, and round her throws
A death-like silence, and a dread repose:
Her gloomy presence saddens all the scene,
Shades ev'ry flow'r, and darkens ev'ry green,
Deepens the murmur of falling floods,
And breathes a browner horror on the woods.

Eloisa finds herself enmeshed in turmoil and weighed down by a heavy darkness that impedes her ability to see that, in Ignatius' words, "all the things in this world are gifts of God, created for us, to be the means by which we come to know him better, to love him more surely, and serve him more faithfully" (Fleming 23). Thus her environment becomes fragmented and she feels like a prisoner in the very convent that is intended to offer her freedom in prayer:

In these deep solitudes and awful cells,
Where heav'nly pensive, contemplation dwells,
And ever-musing melancholy reigns;
What means this tumult in a Vestal's veins?

This despair and intense restlessness that stem from Eloisa's continuous carnal desire for Abelard force Eloisa to project the split between her body and soul onto the landscape. Her attention to her body and its desires for Abelard places her in a hostile environment where she is unable to adore God as the ultimate good and to consider "all other things as a means to attaining that goal" (Sena 450). By contrast, her description of a deeply contemplative state suggests perfect innocence and harmony, concord between body and soul:

How happy is the blameless Vestal's lot!
The world forgetting, by the world forgot.
Eternal sun-shine of the spotless mind!
Each pray'r accepted, and each wish resign'd;
Labour and rest, that equal periods keep;
'Obedient slumbers that can wake and weep';
Desires compos'd, affections ever ev'n,
Tears that delight, and sighs that waft to heav'n.
Grace shines around her with serenest beams,
And whisp'ring Angels prompt her golden dreams.
For her th' unfading rose of Eden blooms,
And wings of Seraphs shed divine perfumes;
For her white virgins Hymenaeals sing;
To sounds of heav'nly harps, she dies away,
And melts in visions of eternal day.

Unfortunately, Eloisa's vision of peace and heavenly harmony cannot be sustained throughout the poem, in part, because she experiences such difficulty in her meditatio, "a kind of study, but not in the modern sense; it [is] confined to sacred texts, principally Scripture, and its goal [is] not purely intellectual but an existential appropriation of the word in view of forming [one's] interior life" (Fry 447). The exercise includes the repetition of passages in order to learn them by heart, and it involves the repetition of the text aloud so that the contemplative would eventually "live, move and have her being" in God. Eloisa's text is not the New Testament but Abelard's autobiography which occasions the beginning of the poem. Moreover, she does not repeat Psalm verses but Abelard's name as a way of appropriating him to herself. Her practice of the meditatio does not act as a stimulus to private prayer that would eventually engender a sense of union with God and peace. Rather, her inversion of the meditatio leads to "a sad variety of woe":

Soon as thy letters trembling I unclose,
That well-known name awakens all my woes.
Oh name for ever sad! for ever dear!
Still breath'd in sighs, still usher'd with a tear.

While the ill-effects of desolation touch most despairingly one's prayer life, there is another sense in which one's community life may suffer, too. Pope is careful to represent Eloisa's alienation from the other nuns of the Paraclete for whom she is responsible in her role as abbess. According to Eloisa, the other nuns live in "eternal sun-shine" while she roams restless amid "gloom"; they have "obedient slumbers" while her soul distills erotic dreams; they shed tears of joy and ecstasy while she weeps in frustration and longing for Abelard (Sena 452). Eloisa's role as abbess over her community of nuns is implicated here as well. According to the Rule of St. Benedict-the Rule that generally governed the life of the Order of the Paraclete-the abbess administers the monastery's affairs, even temporal affairs.

The Rule considers administration not as a separate task but an integral aspect of Eloisa's responsibility for the formation of her "daughters." For the Benedictines, there is no disincarnate spirituality; conversion embraces the whole of life and the abbess is meant to embody that conversion (Fry 370). This responsibility proves difficult for Eloisa. She suffers from deep distraction. As a result, material things are no longer sacramenta, symbols that reveal the beauty and goodness of God, but erotica, symbols that disfigure the beauty of goodness and divert things from their ordained purpose:

I waste the Matin lamp in sighs for thee,
Thy image steals between my God and me,
Thy voice I seem in ev'ry hymn to hear,
With ev'ry bead I drop too soft a tear.
When from the Censer clouds of fragrance roll,
And swelling organs lift the rising soul;
One thought of thee puts all the pomp to flight,
Priests, Tapers, Temples, swim before my sight:
In seas of flame my plunging soul is drown'd,
While Altars blaze, and Angels tremble round.

Eloisa's desire for Abelard contort these liturgical accouterments whose uses are meant to lead her to God. The Matin flame quivers not from prayers to God but from longing sighs for Abelard. She hears only his voice in hymns meant to praise God. The "clouds of fragrance" and "swelling organs" inaugurate a sexual fantasy in which the monastic reality before her-"Priests, Tapers, Temples"-turn extraordinarily luminous as her soul is drowned in flames of desire. In this particular moment, Eloisa relinquishes her role as Abbess for her role as Lover. Yet, buried within this passionate moment, there is a kernel of consolation for Eloisa and her community.

According to the Benedictine tradition, what defines the abbess is not her position as head of a community or institution but her relationship with others. The purpose of those relationships is educative because the monastic tradition understands the difficulty of coming to salvation unaided. The normal way of working out one's salvation is to learn from another human being who has made the journey and is able to guide another along the right path (Fry 355-56). Such an understanding of the monastic tradition leads us to be more tolerant of Eloisa so that we judge her less harshly than do those who abide by the dialectic of "nature and grace, virtue and passion."

Thomas Aquinas (1225-1274), whose contribution to the molding of the physiognomy of the religious state as we know it today was immense, claims in his Secunda secundae of the Summa theologiae, that a religious is striving for a goal-but she has not yet reached it: "He who enters the religious state is not obliged to have perfect charity, but to tend to it and work to attain it" (Summa, 2a, tae, q. 186, a. 1). Furthermore, the religious state, to which Eloisa aspires, is "a kind of discipline or exercise for attaining perfection" (q. 186, a. 2), an activity never finished this side of death. Chrysogonus Waddell, in his commentary on the Paraclete Statutes, elaborates on the nature of the spiritual life as unpredictable undulations between desolation and consolation:

But for the monk or nun who still lives within the monastic tradition of which Abelard and Eloisa were a part, this problem is a non-problem. No one this side of the beatific vision is ever perfectly "converted." There is always something of a gap between sincerely expressed and sincerely held ideals and one's inward conformity to and transformation by those ideals; and, to some extent, Eloisa's lament is the lament of even the most exemplary monk or nun. Here, of course, the qualifying phrase, "to some extent," is important; for according to Eloisa's self-perception, there is present in her case the element of deliberate voluntariness.

But the mere fact that this is so much a cause of anguish for her is proof positive that she is already well along the path of conversion, which, in the monastic tradition is an on-going process. There are degrees of humility, degrees of truth, degrees of love. The process of conversion is begun already with the very first step along the way of humility, truth, and love, but often enough remains something less than perfect up to the moment of one's final gasp. On which degree one happens to be standing at any given moment is less important than the fact that one has at least begun, be it ever so tentatively.

Eloisa's experiences of her overwhelming preoccupation with and passion for Abelard make her consummately human and, therefore, of greater benefit to her sisters in the community. She knows the nature of temptations, a knowledge which would not only allow her to be more understanding and less judgmental of others, but would, no doubt, inform her spiritual advice to those seeking guidance.'

That Eloisa recognizes her inability to distinguish Abelard

the Abbot from Abelard the Lover marks both her desolation and her bracing honesty about herself. In a spirit of secrecy Eloisa confesses: "Hide it, my heart, within that close disguise, / Where, mix'd with God's, his lov'd Idea lies". At the time of her religious profession, in which, standing before the altar and the Cross, she became the bride of Christ, Eloisa fastened her eyes not on the Cross before her but on Abelard: "Yet then, to those dread altars as I drew / Not on the Cross my eyes were fix'd, but you".

The irony in this scene, of course, is that Abelard is her Cross. For, as Elizabeth Walsh has suggested, Eloisa's love for him was not sanctioned by society and brought every kind of suffering upon her. This suffering, in turn, becomes her Cross and, like the Cross, becomes her way to God.' The date of the poem's composition underscores this theology of the cross. According to Geoffrey Tillotson's introduction to the poem in the Twickenham Edition, the poem seems to have been written during Holy Week of 1716. Christ's crucifixion intensifies this paradoxical moment. In addition, an understanding of St. Benedict's conception of the Abbot highlights the irony here and deepens Pope's representation of Eloisa's pain.

According to Timothy Fry's commentary on the Rule of St. Benedict, "the abbot is identified as another Christ-as the one who represents him in the monastery-by application to him of the very titles that define the role of Christ himself' (Fry 353): shepherd, physician, servant or steward of the household. The abbot is the mediator who bridges the gap between Christ and the monk, interpreting for him the Gospel teaching as it applies specifically to him, making the word of Christ alive and actual in the present moment. He is a channel through whom the word and will of Christ come to the monk.

Thus, Abelard represents the promise of Eloisa's redemption at the moment she sins, at the very moment she makes an idol of him. Furthermore, her "unbridled, immoderate love" for him causes her spiritual blindness and lures her to disrupt the hierarchy appropriate to the monastic context (Sena 450). Consequently, the idea of Abelard, the memory of him, and her profane desire for him constitute the

Cross she must bear in this world. Her salvation depends upon both the upright beam of the Cross represented by Abelard the Abbot, and the transverse beam represented by Abelard the Lover.

Moreover, her simultaneous action of replacing Abelard, the "vicar of Christ," with Abelard, the man of her "base" imagination, inverts the action of God in human history (Fairer 31). Roman Catholic theology avers that Christ became man to redeem a world riddled with just the kind of sin and suffering Eloisa manifests in her life. Symbolically in the poem, then, salvation is placed at the very centre of the Cross' perpendicular beams, the very crossroads where Abelard the Abbot intersects with Abelard the Lover.

Eloisa's desolation deeply compromises the intention of the rite of profession and makes her suffering more palpable:

Canst thou forget what tears that moment fell,
When, warm in youth, I bade the world farewell?
As with cold lips I kiss'd the sacred veil,
The shrines all trembled, and the lamps grew pale:
Heav'n scarce believ'd the conquest it survey'd,
And Saints with wonder heard the vows I made.

The taking of the veil and the making of vows symbolize the candidate's act of complete dispossession in favour of total possession by Christ In the Rule of St. Benedict, the novice writes out the vows and places the statement on the altar in the oratory. For Benedict, this petitio, the written document in which the novice states the terms of the promise, is both a formal donation of property and a donation of the candidate herself. However, Pope has Eloisa donate herself and her body to Abelard rather than to Christ and exclaim that her dispossession depends upon Abelard's love for her: "And if I lose thy love, I lose my all". Immediately following the description of her vows, she makes an effort to claim again what she has just surrendered in the rite of profession:

Come! with thy looks, thy words, relieve my woe;
Those still at least are left thee to bestow.
Still on that breast enamour'd let me lie,
Still drink delicious poison from thy eye,

Pant on thy lip, and to thy heart be prest;
Give all thou canst-and let me dream the rest. (119-24)

While she allows for Abelard's conversion, she cannot yet free herself from the "evil spirit" who binds her body to his, making her unable to "quit Abelard for God".

Eloisa cannot warm to the conferring of the veil: "As with cold lips I kiss'd the sacred veil". According to the Rule of St. Benedict, "the habit represents dispossession rather than holiness" (Fry 456). The stripping of the old clothes in favour of the habit symbolizes the renunciation of all possessions, including the body because the body is considered a material possession. On the day of profession the candidate is "well aware that from that day he will not have even his own body at his disposal" (Fry 270-71). Eloisa experiences the dispossession of her body in her death vision at the poem's conclusion, not during her profession ceremony. But that death vision has its roots, too, in the liturgy for the consecration of virgins which, traditionally for Benedictine nuns, is joined with the rite of religious profession and emphasizes the "completeness with which one belongs to God" as well as the desire to seek greater personal perfection through a more intense interior life (Kinish 123). Indeed, Eloisa's self-consciousness about her state reveals her intense interior life, albeit a life of desolation.

Eloisa recognizes the gap between her own turbulent inner life and the eschatological innocence made explicit in the liturgy for the consecration of virgins and its use of Revelation 14:1-5:

Next in my vision I saw Mount Zion, and standing on it a Lamb, who had with him a hundred and forty-four thousand people, all with his name and his Father's name written on their foreheads, I heard a sound coming out of the sky like the sound of the ocean or the roar of thunder; it seemed to be the sound of harpists playing their harps. There in front of the throne they were singing a new hymn in the presence of the four animals and the elders, a hymn that could only be learnt by the hundred and forty-four thousand who had been redeemed from the world. These are the ones who have kept their virginity and not been defiled with women; they follow the Lamb wherever he goes; they have been redeemed from amongst men to be the first-fruits for God and for the Lamb. They never allowed a lie to pass their lips and no fault can be found in them.

Unlike the perfect candidates who, upon profession, "have kept their virginity and not been defiled," and who have "never allowed a lie to pass their lips," Eloisa courageously acknowledges that her earthly frailties are redeemed in the next world-that her very sins are prerequisites to "eternal sleep". The world of song and hymn, of motion and activity evident in the reading from Revelation, stops in Eloisa's vision of stasis. "But all is calm in this eternal sleep; / Here grief forgets to groan, and love to weep, / Ev'n superstition loses every fear: / For God, not man, absolves our frailties here: The "hollow sound" of the voice beckoning Eloisa replaces the full-bodied music of the harps and the innocent, pure chorus singing a new hymn of praise for the Lamb. This voice beckons Eloisa to a place where no memory exists to haunt her spiritual life.

The "hollow" voice that calls Eloisa, "Come, sister, come", is reminiscent of those several verses in Revelation which report a voice heard from heaven (Rev. 1.11, 6.2-5, and 12.10, for example) and the hymn Veni Creator Spiritus, which dates from the twelfth century and which was sung during the rite of religious profession. From a strict Catholic family, Pope was likely to be familiar with the hymn that emphasizes the crucial word "come" throughout the poem, as well as the repeated images of the Holy Spirit:

Veni Creator Spiritus,
Mentes tuorum visita,
Imple superna gratia
Quae Tu creasti pectora.
Qui Paraclitus diceris,
Altissimi donum Dei,
Fons vivus, ignis, charitas,
Et spiritalis unctio.
(Come, Creator Spirit,

Visit the minds of your people,
Fill their hearts which you have created
With heavenly grace.
You are called the Paraclete,
The gift of God most high,
The living source, fire, love,
And spiritual balm].

Eloisa addresses her veni to Abelard as she takes the veil that is meant to protect her against the "surging heat of evil temptations" (Tavormina 393). Rather than begging the Holy Spirit to calm her senses, she submits herself to the memory of Abelard. But by the end of the poem Eloisa, in the final series of "comes," appears ready to plunge into the refining fire of the Paraclete:

I come, I come! prepare your roseate bow'rs,
Celestial palms, and ever-blooming flow'rs.
Thither, where sinners may have rest, I go,
Where flames refin'd in breasts seraphic glow.

Eloisa envisions not the communion of saints described in Revelation but communion with the dead, including, eventually, Abelard, where "one kind grave unite each hapless name". Thus the rite of religious profession, emblematic of Eloisa's marriage to Christ, is transformed into a marriage to Abelard. The symbolic dispossession called for in the ritual for profession and the consecration of virgins occurs for Eloisa at death when finally she is able to dispossess herself of her body.

Amid Eloisa's struggles with her motives at the time of her profession, Pope eventually brings her to a key moment in the poem when she meditates on death. Eloisa's meditation opens the door to grace because she realizes that things of this earth are passing, transitory: "O death all— eloquent! you only prove / What dust we doat on, when tis man we love". Marilyn Francus suggests that Eloisa's death vision is "morally inconclusive" because we cannot determine whether death is Eloisa's punishment or reward. One way out of the dilemma, writes Francus, "is to assert that the indeterminacy of the ending is purposeful, that Pope intends to leave the reader struggling, like Eloisa, for a resolution". In large measure I agree with Francus about Pope's emphasis on Eloisa's struggles. For example, in lines 277-80, Eloisa believes that grace is about to dawn upon her soul:

While prostrate here in humble grief I lie,
Kind, virtuous drops just gath'ring in my eye,
While praying, trembling, in the dust I roll,
And dawning grace is opening on my soul ....

Here, there are glimmers of grace, peace and a recognition that she will find some respite from her deep distractions. But the tidal wave of distraction rolls to shore again in lines 281-88 as she begs Abelard to "tear [her] from [her] God". However, Pope's use of St. Benedict's exhortation to "keep death constantly before our eyes" is not meant to have Eloisa live morbidly but to show her how to live fully in honesty and compassion, appreciating her participation in the dynamic movements between consolation and desolation (Freeman 96). In fact, she admits to these movements as she pleads halfway through the poem, "Assist me heav'n! but whence arose that pray'r? / Sprung it from piety, or from despair?" Eloisa's plea for help from heaven reveals a very positive self-consciousness about her spiritual state. She recognizes her need for grace and, later in the verse paragraph, asks questions central to opening her heart to God:

Ere such a soul regains its peaceful state,
How often must it love, how often hate!
How often, hope, despair, resent, regret,
Conceal, disdain-do all things but forget.
But let heav'n seize it, all at once 'tis fir'd,
Not touch'd, but rapt, not waken'd, but inspir'd.

By acknowledging how often the soul must sustain the journey through the incredible range of human emotions, Eloisa harbors the secret to consolation's arrival-necessary desolation.

IF we cannot resolve Eloisa's crisis along the dialectical lines of "nature"/"grace," "virtue"/"passion," then we are free to consider Pope's artistic act of redemption in the poem's startling conclusion. Pope creates a context for the spiritual movements of both desolation and consolation through his use of the heroic couplet, and he positions himself as redeemer of Eloisa and her cause at the poem's conclusion. Here, perhaps more than anywhere else in the poem, we see Pope's explicit poetic efforts "to put the image straight," which, in turn, demand a close reading of the poem because Pope so effectively mirrors the sometimes slow and painful spiritual process Eloisa experiences.

The moments of reminiscence, resignation and consolation, marked by balanced antitheses and parallelism, develop into outbursts of desolation. These eruptions within the heroic couplet signal Eloisa's inability to hold to God as her spiritual centre. Instead, she attempts to hold to Abelard for the fulfillment of her emotional life. For example, lines 177-206, a passage I discussed earlier, manifest this movement away from idolatry (177-94) in which Eloisa states her conflict sharply and within the "wrought iron" compression of balanced antitheses (Jones 112-13):

Ah wretch! believ'd the spouse of God in vain
Confess'd within the slave of love and man.
Assist me heav'n! but whence arose that pray'r?
Sprung it from piety, or from despair?
Ev'n here, where frozen chastity retires,
Love finds an altar for forbidden fires.
I ought to grieve, but cannot what I ought;
I mourn the lover, not lament the fault;
I view my crime, but kindle at the view,
Repent old pleasures, and sollicit new:
Now turn'd to heav'n, I weep my past offence,
Now turn to thee, and curse my innocence.
Of all affliction taught a lover yet,
'Tis sure the hardest science to forget!
How shall I lose the sin, yet keep the sense,
And love th' offender, yet detest th' offence?
How dear the object from the crime remove,
Or how distinguish penitence from love?

In this moment of discernment when Eloisa seems capable of dispensing with Abelard as idol, the iambic pentameter is very regular, broken only in those places where Pope wants to emphasize her willingness to repent her sin: "Assist me heav'n," "Sprung it," "Love finds," and "Repent old." Also, unlike other moments in the poem when the off-rhymes signal Eloisa's unsteady spiritual life, the rhyme scheme here sounds harmonious, as if all things incline to God, because Eloisa understands how her idolatry grips her.

But fear of ever being fulfilled by God breaks in upon the balanced antitheses Eloisa articulates in the previous passage. Earlier Eloisa describes the reality of temptation in paradoxes: "piety"/"despair"; "frozen chastity"/"forbidden fires"; "view the crime"/"kindle the view"; "repent old pleasures"/"sollicit new." Now, as she fears for herself, unable to reconcile her sin before God, the steady pace of possible consolation yields to the broken, repetitious and noisy voice of desolation:

Unequal task! a passion to resign,
For hearts so touch'd, so pierc'd, so lost as mine.
Ere such a soul regains its peaceful state,
How oft must it love, how oft hate!
How often, hope, despair, resent, regret,
Conceal, disdain-do all things but forget.
But let heav'n seize it, all at once 'tis fir'd,
Not touch'd, but rapt, not waken'd, but inspir'd!
Oh come! oh teach me nature to subdue,
Renounce my love, my life, my self-and you.
Fill my fond heart with God alone, for he
Alone can rival, can succeed to thee.

Eloisa's balanced view of her struggle manifested in her expression of antitheses and parallelisms cannot contain her confusion and fear. Longer periodic structures are overcome by repetitions of the main parts of the sentence: verbs, verb phrases, and nouns. Consider lines 196, 198-200, and 204. These repetitions often recur as if Eloisa desires to relive her past life (Jones 112).

But there is a further explanation, I think. Such repetitions are just that-re-petitions. That is, Eloisa is completely immersed in the critical dynamic essential to a lively spiritual life: of finding herself ready and able to give up her idols, of faltering through unchecked imagination and memory, and of petitioning again for God's assistance. She wavers on her spiritual journey, as is expected in the monastic tradition, and Pope accounts for both movements within the metrics of the poem. He redeems Eloisa through a poem that recreates the rhythm of her interior life.

Pope sustains this pattern of eruption within a controlling framework to the end of the poem. In lines 317-36 quoted above, imperative clauses govern the verse paragraph: "smooth my passage," "suck my last breath," "catches my flying soul." The verb imperatives are matched with nouns that are qualified by motion-not the stillness implied by the death vision but the violent death itself ("flames refin'd," "lips tremble," "eye-balls roll").

This last fit of passion subsides into longer rhythms that last until the poem's conclusion. As Jones notes, both the periodic structure and subordinate clauses return to the poem. Lines 337-42, for example, create both a less urgent tone and a sense that Eloisa gains some control over her emotions by projecting her own desires for peace onto Abelard. She recognizes the dual influence Abelard has over her, the effects of both desolation and consolation, and envisions for him a transcendent love of which she is now capable. The fuller periodic design eventually brings the poem, Eloisa, and Pope to their rest:

From the full quire when loud Hosanna's rise,
And swell the pomp of dreadful sacrifice,
Amid that scene, if some relenting eye
Glance on the stone where our cold reliques lie,
Devotion's self shall steal a thought from heav'n,
One human tear shall drop, and be forgiv'n.
And sure if fate some future Bard shall join
In sad similitude of griefs to mine,
Condemn'd whole years in absence to deplore,
And image charms he must behold no more, Such if there be, who loves so long, so well;
Let him our sad, our tender story tell;
The well-sung woes will Booth my pensive ghost;

He best can paint 'em, who shall feel 'em most.

Eloisa stakes her life, her salvation, on the poet who writes her story. This saving insight, however, descends on the poet and on Eloisa in opposite ways. Even though the poet succeeds, he does so by describing the apparent absence of grace in Eloisa. Eloisa, for her part, remains a "pensive ghost" caught eternally between her worldly love for Abelard and her spiritual love for God. Nonetheless, Eloisa anticipates her freedom and salvation through the work of the creator-poet and acknowledges that the past need not imprison her but compel her to move into the future, a future that can bring forth new possibilities where others who stand over the "pale marble" of Abelard's and Eloisa's tomb may recognize the dangers in possessive love: "Oh may we never love as these have lov'd!"

In this essay I have argued that critics' contributions to the debate about the dialectic of "grace and nature, virtue and passion" in Pope's Eloisa to Abelard tend to focus discussions on whether Eloisa succeeds in her life as a religious woman. Inevitably, this approach recasts interpretations of the poem to emphasize Eloisa's final redeemed or unredeemed status. Our attention is turned away from how Eloisa walks the spiritual path toward debates about whether she arrives at a destination appropriate to her station in life.

But another turn of the kaleidoscope brings into view Pope's startling emphasis on the monastic and Catholic dimensions of the poem and the possibility that Eloisa's "failure" to embrace God without compromise may be considered more successful than we might initially admit. If we focus on Eloisa's struggles and appreciate that the spiritual life exists in an alternation of gain and loss, pleasure and pain, hope and despair, then we see Eloisa's desolation for what it is: a necessary condition for consolation and for God's saving grace in her life.

Chapter 9

Alexander Pope and his Eighteenth-Century Women Readers

In the past ten or fifteen years, the study of eighteenth-century British literature and culture has been invigorated by a new attention to the relation between gender roles and cultural authority; both of the books under consideration make valuable contributions to this trend in criticism, albeit in different ways. The majority of the essays in the collection edited by Beth Fowkes Tobin clearly see themselves as pursuing the fruitful line of inquiry into the domestic sphere initiated by the literary critics Nancy Armstrong and Mary Poovey and the historians Catherine Hall and Lenore Davidoff; they are concerned with evaluating the rise of women's moral authority during the eighteenth century, and with the growing importance of private, affective relationships for men and women alike.

Methodologically, the essays in the Tobin volume take the inclusion of "History" in its title seriously; they by no means confine themselves to the analysis of literary texts. In contrast, Claudia Thomas's study of women writers' responses to Pope restricts its focus to female engagement with published literature. Like many of the essays in the Tobin collection, it is interested in disproving the notion that women in eighteenth-century Britain were the passive victims of patriarchal authority; however, it refutes this notion not through reference to the other forms of cultural authority women might exert, but through detailed analysis of the kinds of critical acuity women readers and writers brought to bear on the documents of male-dominated literary culture available to them.

According to Beth Fowkes Tobin's introduction, History, Gender and Eighteenth-Century Literature aims to contribute both to women's studies, and to the more general field of gender studies. Admirably, several of the essays do expand the rubric of gender studies to include the construction of masculinity during the period, including Tobin's own excellent study of Arthur Young's writings and the creation of the profession of estate manager, and Shawn Lisa Maurer's fascinating discussion of filial relations in early periodicals.

The volume also argues against a feminist essentialism; instead it seeks to "encourage feminists to turn to history and culture in their analyses of literary texts" and number of the essays inflect their discussions of gender roles with attention to pertinent social contexts. Susan Staves's article on "Fielding and the Comedy of Attempted Rape" continues her ground-breaking work on the imbrication of gender roles, legal concepts, and literary representation; both Maurer's piece and Beth Kowaleski-Wallace's article on "The Body, Class, and Art in Evelina and Frances Burney's Early Diaries" delineate the complex ways that middle-class economic identity, artistic and literary culture, and gender roles interacted during this period; Kathryn Kirkpatrick's investigation of metaphors of property in conduct book literature provides another interesting discussion of the relationship between class identities and constructions of femininity.

On the whole, these essays seem more adept at discussing the intricacies of English domestic culture than they do at extending those analyses to the context of English colonialism and imperialism. Often, when they do look at the relation between literature and the international arena, they rely on generalizations, rather than producing the kind of historically nuanced readings for which the introduction seems to call.

Diane Dugaw's article on Gay's sequel to the Beggar's Opera, Polly, for example, is useful for bringing this fascinating text to readers' attention, but relies heavily on an unexamined comparison between English woman and Caribbean slaves, claiming that the play is a "satire that exposes the European heroic ideal as an ethos of slavery: an enslaving gender ideology and an enslaving will to empire that mutually construct each other". Similarly, Ruth Perry's provocative comparison of four mid-eighteenth-century utopian novels ends with the proposal that "where women's claims to the life of the mind are honored and encouraged, it signals a belief in human potential - across gender and across the social dimensions of race, class and nation as well".

While it seems certain that the status of white women in eighteenth-century England was in some relation to the status of cultural others, it may be too all-encompassing to see sexual and racial oppression as two homogeneous, mutually exclusive, and thus analogous categories; such claims tend to ignore the heterogeneity of both dynamics, caused by the presence of gender difference in the colonies, for instance, or by ethnic differences among British women. Joseph Lew's article on "Mansfield Park and the Dynamics of Slavery" is an insightful analysis of the relation between the use of patriarchal power in the colonies and in the domestic space, but even he relies on the tempting, but imprecise, analogy between white English women and slaves to ground his argument.

Only Jill Campbell's article on Mary Wortley Montagu's descriptions of Turkey escapes from such generalizations, primarily because she discusses the interaction between two distinct sets of gender roles - English and Turkish - as well as examining the specificity of Lady Mary's responses to cultural differences.

Finally, it needs to be said of this collection that it has a quite specific idea of the dominant concerns of eighteenth-century England, particularly of the latter half of this period. These concerns include the reorganization of familial relationships, the structural importance of female propriety and moral authority to social organization, and the growth of evangelicalism as a source of feminine cultural power. While certainly not misplaced, a belief in the pre-eminence of these issues tends to produce an alternative canon of eighteenth-century texts, though I'm sure the contributors to this volume have nothing so prescriptive in mind. Yet the usual suspects are there: Sarah Scott, Fanny Burney, and two articles each on Hannah More and Jane Austen. Only two essays (on Gay and Montagu) treat subjects arguably not related to the construction of the middle classes. Thus, while the volume makes no claim to cover all the permutations of gender in eighteenth-century culture, it seems significant that its articles make no mention of writers of amatory fiction in the early eighteenth-century - Haywood, Behn, or Manley - the scandalous memoirists of mid-century - Charlotte Charke, among others - or the republican feminists of the later part of the century - Mary Wollstonecraft, for instance, or Mary Hays.

I mention this not as a criticism, but to point out its potential implications for literary periodization. If feminist literary historians see Mansfield Park (published 1814) as an eighteenth-century novel, but overlook novels such as The Memoirs of Emma Courtney (published 1796), which argue against the priority of home and family in women's lives, they may find they have renounced a male-dominated "Age of Johnson" only to find themselves constrained by the parameters of an "Age of Domesticity."

In contrast, Claudia Thomas's book covers one subject in considerable depth. This is an exhaustive, scrupulous investigation of the broad variety of women readers' responses to the work of Alexander Pope throughout the eighteenth century. She includes prose responses, as well as poetic ones, and writers who adopted Pope's formal qualities, along with writers who expanded on his thematic concerns. After compiling this evidence, Thomas powerfully and persuasively concludes that

Pope's eighteenth-century women readers suggest a model of fearless critical reading. Few of these women identified with Pope's constructions of femininity. Instead, women appropriated and revised Pope's images to suit their own contexts, whether more genteel, more devout, or more feminist. Current analysis implying that contemporary women were somehow victimized by Pope's gendered rhetoric should reconsider the critical acuity with which his female adience often read.

Although one might say that Thomas thus side-steps the potentially powerful impact of Pope's misogyny on his male readers, she nevertheless makes a crucial feminist statement in emphasizing female intelligence and critical agency.

Thomas provides a number of reasons why Pope would be a central figure in the intellectual milieu of eighteenth-century women, both during his lifetime and after his death. Analyzing Pope's early translations, Thomas concludes that such work "sought and addressed women readers", providing openings for them either to learn from his poetic technique, or to enter into dialogue with his opinions. Like Valerie Rumbold in Women's Place in Pope's World (1989), Thomas also points to Pope's own marginalization in English culture, by virtue of his class, religion and deformity, to explain why women readers who were his contemporaries might have found him a more accessible ally or opponent than other writers of the time.

As Pope assumed a position of cultural authority later in the century, Thomas argues, women's references to his work also served to legitimate their own writing. Denied the education that allowed male writers to signal authority through classical allusions, women turned to Pope to supply the place of the ancients.

Thomas's work rests on her exceptional scholarly labour in tracing the exact references to Pope's works in hundreds of relatively inaccessible texts by women writers. One unfortunate byproduct of this comprehensiveness is that, at times, it is difficult to follow the thread of the argument in the welter of citations Thomas supplies. This painstaking accumulation of detail, however, produces one of the major strengths of Thomas's book. She is able to show convincingly that women writers did not hold a unitary view of Pope or his work: indeed, they could not, since they were such a varied group themselves. Thus, Pope provided an attractive interlocuter for such aristocratic poets as Mary Wortley

Montagu and Anne Finch for different reasons than those for which he proved a valuable model for the working-class poet Mary Leapor, or the crippled shopkeeper, Mary Chandler.

This illuminating description of the way class and social context produced a variety of published female voices in eighteenth-century Britain makes Thomas's book an outstanding contribution to the project of historicization outlined by Tobin. Her attention to the public voices of women in the aristocracy and among the working classes also does the added work of showing that women's writing of the period was not completely circumscribed by domestic ideology.

THE DUNCIAD

The Dunciad is a landmark literary satire by Alexander Pope published in three different versions at different times. The first version (the "three book" *Dunciad*) was published in 1728. The second version, in which Pope confirmed his authorship of the work, appeared in the *Dunciad Variorum* in 1735. The *New Dunciad,* in four books and with a different hero, appeared in 1743. The poem celebrates the goddess Dulness and the progress of her chosen agents as they bring decay, imbecility, and tastelessness to the kingdom of Great Britain.

ORIGINS

Pope told Joseph Spence (in *Spence's Anecdotes*) that he had been working on a general satire of Dulness, with characters of contemporary scribblers, for some time and that it was the publication of *Shakespeare Restored* by Lewis Theobald that spurred him to complete the poem and publish it in 1728. Certainly Pope had written characters of the various "Dunces" prior to 1728. In his *Essay on Criticism,* Pope characterizes some witless critics. In his various *Moral Epistles,* Pope likewise draws characters of contemporary authors of poor taste. However, the general structure owes its origins to, on the one hand, the communal project of the Scribblerians and, on the other, the mock-heroic *MacFlecknoe* by John Dryden. The Scribblerian club comprised Jonathan Swift, John Gay, John Arbuthnot, Robert Harley, and Thomas Parnell most consistently, and the group met during the spring and summer of 1714. One group project was to write a satire of contemporary abuses in learning of all sorts, where the authors would combine to write the biography of the group's fictional founder, Martin Scriblerus. The resulting *The Memoirs of Martin Scriblerus* contained a number of parodies of the most lavish mistakes in scholarship.

For the mock-heroic structure of the *Dunciad* itself, however, the idea seems to have come most clearly from *MacFlecknoe. MacFlecknoe* is a poem celebrating the apotheosis of Thomas Shadwell, whom Dryden nominates as the dullest poet of the age. Shadwell is the spiritual son of Flecknoe, an obscure Irish poet of low fame, and he takes his place as the favourite of the goddess Dulness.

Pope takes this idea of the personified goddess of Dulness being at war with reason, darkness at war with light, and extends it to a full *Aeneid* parody. His poem celebrates a war, rather than a mere victory, and a process of ignorance, and Pope picks as his champion of all things insipid Lewis Theobald (1728 and '32) and Colley Cibber (1742).

THE THREE-BOOK *DUNCIAD A* AND THE DUNCIAD VARIORUM

Pope first published *The Dunciad* in 1728 in three books, with Lewis Theobald as its "hero." The poem was not signed, and he used only initials in the text to refer to the various Dunces in the kingdom of Dulness. However, "Keys" immediately came out to identify the figures mentioned in the text, and an Irish pirate edition was printed that filled in the names (sometimes inaccurately). Additionally, the men attacked by Pope also wrote angry denunciations of the poem, attacking Pope's poetry and person.

Pope endured attacks from, among others, George Duckett, Thomas Burnet, and Richard Blackmore. All of these, however, were less vicious than the attack launched by Edmund Curll, a notoriously unscrupulous publisher, who produced his own pirate copy of the Dunciad with astounding swiftness, and also published 'The Popiad' and a number of pamphlets attacking Pope. In 1729, Pope published an acknowledged edition of the poem, and the *Dunciad Variorum* appeared in 1732. The Variorum was substantially the same text as the 1729 edition, but it now had a lengthy prolegomenon. The prefatory material has Pope speaking in his own defence, although under a variety of other names; for example, "A Letter to the Publisher Occasioned by the Present Edition of the Dunciad" is signed by William Cleland (d. 1741), one of Pope's friends and father of John Cleland, but it was probably written by Pope himself.

In these prefatory materials, Pope points out that the Keys were often wrong about the allusions, and he explains his reluctance at spelling out the names. He says that he wishes to avoid elevating the targets of the satire by mentioning their names (which, of course, did happen, as a number of persons are only remembered for their appearances in the poem), but he similarly did not want innocents to be mistaken for the targets.

Pope also apologizes for using parody of the Classics (for his poem imitates both Homer and Virgil) by pointing out that the ancients also used parody to belittle unworthy poets. Pope's preface is followed by advertisements from the bookseller, a section called "Testimonies of Authors Concerning Our Poet and his Works" by "Martinus Scriblerus," and a further section named "Martinus Scriblerus, of the Poem."

Martinus Scriblerus was a corporate identity employed by Pope and the other members of the Scriblerians. Therefore, these two portions of the preface could have been written by any of its members, but they, like the other prefatory materials, were most likely written by Pope himself. The various Dunces had written responses to Pope after the first publication of *The Dunciad,* and they had not only written against Pope, but had explained why Pope had attacked other writers. In the "Testimonies" section, Martinus Scriblerus culls all the comments the Dunces made *about each other* in their replies and sets them side by side, so that each is condemned by another. He also culls their contradictory characterizations of

Pope, so that they seem to all damn and praise the same qualities over and over again.

The "Testimonies" also includes commendations from Pope's friends. The words of Edward Young, James Thomson and Jonathan Swift are brought together to praise Pope specifically for being temperate and timely in his charges. The conclusion asks the reader "to chuse whether thou wilt incline to the Testimonies of Authors avowed" (like Pope's friends) "or of Authors concealed" (like many of the Dunces)—in short, "of those who knew him, or of those who knew him not."

"TIBBALD" KING OF DUNCES

Alexander Pope had a proximal and long term cause for choosing Lewis Theobald as the King of Dunces for the first version of the *Dunciad*. The proximate cause was Theobald's publication of *Shakespeare Restored, or a Specimen of the many Errors as well Committed as Unamended by Mr Pope in his late edition of this poet; designed not only to correct the said Edition, but to restore the true Reading of Shakespeare in all the Editions ever published* in 1726.

Pope had published his own version of Shakespeare in 1725, and he had made a number of errors in it. He had "smoothed" some of Shakespeare's lines, had chosen readings that eliminated puns (which Pope regarded as low humour), and had, indeed, missed several good readings and preserved some bad ones. In the *Dunciad Variorum*, Pope complains that he had put out newspaper advertisements when he was working on Shakespeare, asking for anyone with suggestions to come forward, and that Theobald had hidden all of his material. Indeed, when Pope produced a second edition of his Shakespeare in 1728, he incorporated many of Theobald's textual readings.

Pope, however, had already a quarrel with Theobald. The first mention of Theobald in Pope's writings is the 1727, *Peri Bathos*, in *Miscellanies, Volume the Third* (which was actually the first volume), but Pope's attack there shows that Theobald was already a figure of fun. Regardless of the quarrels, though, Theobald was, in a sense, the nearly perfect King of Dunces.

The Dunciad's action concerns the gradual sublimation of all arts and letters into Dulness by the action of hireling authors. Theobald, as a man who had attempted the stage and failed, plagiarized a play, attempted translation and failed to such a degree that John Dennis referred to him as a "notorious Ideot," attempted subscription translation and failed to produce, and who had just turned his full attention to political attack writing, was an epitome, for Pope, of all that was wrong with British letters.

Additionally, Pope's goddess of Dulness begins the poem already controlling state poetry, odes, and political writing, so Theobald as King of Dunces is the man who can lead her to control the stage as well. Theobald's writings for John Rich, in particular, are singled out within the *Dunciad* as abominations for their mixing of tragedy and comedy and their "low" pantomime and opera; they are not the first to bring the Smithfield muses to the ears of kings, but they ferried them over in bulk.

The central premise of the poem is the same as that of *MacFlecknoe*: the crowning of a new King of Dulness. However, Pope's poem is far more wide-ranging and specific than Dryden's had been. His satire is political and cultural in very specific ways. Rather than merely lambasting "vice" and "corruption," Pope attacks very particular degradations of political discourse and particular degradations of the arts.

The political attack is on the Whigs, and specifically on the Hanoverian Whigs. The poem opens, in fact, with the goddess Dulness noting that "Still Dunce the second rules like Dunce the first," which is an exceptionally daring reference to George II, who had come to the throne earlier in the year. Furthermore, although the King of Dunces, Theobald, writes for the radical Tory *Mist's Journal*, Pope consistently hammers at radical Protestant authors and controversialists.

Daniel Defoe is mentioned almost as frequently as anyone in the poem, and the booksellers picked out for abuse both specialized in partisan Whig publications. The cultural attack is broader than the political one, and it may underlie the whole. Pope attacks, over and over again, those who write for pay.

While Samuel Johnson would say, half a century later, that no man but a blockhead ever wrote but for money, Pope's attack is not on those who get paid, but those who will write on cue for the highest bid. Pope himself was one of the earliest poets to make his living solely by writing, and so it is not the *professional* author, but the *mercenary* author that Pope derides.

He attacks hired pens, the authors who perform poetry or religious writing for the greatest pay alone, who do not believe in what they are doing. As he puts it in book II, "He (a patron) chinks his purse, and takes his seat of state... And (among the poets) instant, fancy feels th' imputed sense" (II 189-91). He objects not to professional writers, but to hackney writers. His dunce booksellers will trick and counterfeit their way to wealth, and his dunce poets will wheedle and flatter anyone for enough money to keep the bills paid.

The plot of the poem is simple. Dulness, the goddess, appears at a Lord Mayor's Day in 1724 and notes that her king, Elkannah Settle, has died. She chooses Lewis Theobald as his successor. In honour of his coronation, she holds heroic games. He is then transported to the Temple of Dulness, where he has visions of the future. The poem has a consistent setting and time, as well. Book I covers the night after the Lord Mayor's Day, Book II the morning to dusk, and Book III the darkest night. Furthermore, the poem begins at the end of the Lord Mayor's procession, goes in Book II to the Strand, then to Fleet Street (where booksellers were), down by Bridewell Prison to the Fleet ditch, then to Ludgate at the end of Book II; in Book III, Dulness goes through Ludgate to the City of London to her temple.

THE ARGUMENTS OF THE THREE BOOKS

The poem begins with an epic invocation, "Books and the Man I sing, the first who brings/ The Smithfield Muses to the Ear of Kings" (Smithfield being the site of Bartholomew Fair entertainments, and the man in question was Elkanah Settle, who had written for Bartholomew Fair after the Glorious Revolution; Pope makes him the one who brought pantomime, farce, and monster shows to the royal theaters).

The goddess Dulness notes that her power is so great that, "Time himself stands still at her command,/ Realms shift their place, and Ocean turns to land," and thus claims credit for the routine violation of the Unities of Aristotle in poetry. On Lord Mayor's Day of 1724, when Sir George Thorold was Lord Mayor, Dulness announces the death of the current King of Dunces, Elkanah Settle. Settle had been the City Poet, and his job had been to commemorate Lord Mayor's Day pageants. Thanks to his hard work in stultifying the senses of the nation, Dulness claims control of all official verse, and all current poets are her subjects ("While pensive Poets painful vigils keep,/ Sleepless themselves to give their readers sleep" I. 91-92).

She mentions Thomas Heywood, Daniel Defoe (for writing political journalism), Ambrose Philips, Nahum Tate, and Sir Richard Blackmore as her darlings. However, her triumph is not complete, and she aspires to control dramatic poetry as well as political, religious, and hack poetry. She therefore decides that Theobald will be the new King.

The action shifts to the library of Lewis Theobald, which is "A Gothic Vatican! of Greece and Rome/ Well-purg'd, and worthy Withers, Quarles, and Blome" (a Vatican Library for Northern European authors, and especially notable for vainglorious and contentious writing and criticism). Theobald is despairing of succeeding in writing dull poetry and plays, and he is debating whether to return to being a lawyer (for that had been Theobald's first trade) or to become a political hack. He decides to give up poetry and become an entirely hired pen for Nathaniel Mist and his *Mist's Journal*. He therefore collects all the books of bad poetry in his library along with his own works and makes a virgin sacrifice of them (virgin because no one has ever read them) by setting fire to the pile.

The goddess Dulness appears to him in a fog and drops a sheet of *Thule* (a poem by Ambrose Philips that was supposed to be an epic, but which only appeared as a single sheet) on the fire, extinguishing it with the poem's perpetually wet ink. Dulness tells Theobald that he is the new King of Dunces and points him to the stage. She shows him,

"How, with less reading than makes felons 'scape,
Less human genius than God gives an ape,
Small thanks to France and none to Rome or Greece,
A past, vamp'd, future, old, reviv'd, new piece,
'Twixt Plautus, Fletcher, Congreve, and Corneille,
Can make a Cibber, Johnson, or Ozell." (I. 235-40)

The book ends with a hail of praise, calling Theobald now the new King Log (from Aesop's fable).

A BOOK II

Book II centers on the highly scatological "heroic games." Theobald sits on throne of Dulness, which is a velvetine tub ("tub" being the common term for the pulpit of Dissenters), and Dulness declares the opening of heroic games to celebrate his coronation. Therefore, all her sons come before her on the Strand in London, leaving half the kingdom depopulated, for she summons both dull writers, their booksellers, *and* all who are stupid enough to patronize dull writers.

The first game is for booksellers. (Booksellers at the time purchased manuscripts from authors, and the proceeds from book sales went entirely to the bookseller, with the author getting no more than the advance price.) Dulness therefore decides upon a race for the booksellers. She creates a phantom Poet,

"No meagre, muse-rid mope, adust and thin,
In a dun night-gown of his own loose skin," (II. 33-4)

but, instead, a fat, well dressed poet (and therefore a wealthy, noble one who would command sales by his title). The phantom poet is named More, a reference to James Moore Smythe, who had plagiarized both Arbuthnot (*Historico-physical Account of the South-Sea Bubble*) and Pope (*Memoirs of a Parish Clark*), and whose only original play had been the failed *The Rival Modes*. The booksellers immediately set out running to be the first to grab Moore, with Bernard Lintot setting forth with a roar (Lintot had been James Moore Smythe's publisher), only to be challenged by Edmund Curll:

"As when a dab-chick waddles thro' the copse,
On feet and wings, and flies, and wades, and hops;

So lab'ring on, with shoulders, hands, and head,
Wide as a windmill all his figure spread . . .
Full in the middle way there stood a lake,
Which Curl's Corinna chanc'd that morn to make,
(Such was her wont, at early down to drop
Her evening cates before his neighbour's shop,)
Here fortun'd Curl to slide; loud shout the band,
And Bernard! Bernard! rings thro' all the Strand." (II 59-70)

The race seemingly having been decided by progress through bed-pan slops, Curll prays to Jove, who consults the goddess Cloacina. He hears the prayer, passes a pile of feces down, and catapults Curll to the victory. As Curll grabs the phantom Moore, the poems it seemed to have fly back to their real authors, and even the clothes go to the unpaid tailors who had made them (James Moore Smythe had run through an inherited fortune and bankrupted himself by 1727). Dulness urges Curll to repeat the joke, to pretend to the public that his dull poets were really great poets, to print things by false names. (Curll had published numerous works by "Joseph Gay" to trick the public into thinking they were by John Gay.)

For his victory, she awards Curll a tapestry showing the fates of famous Dunces. On it, he sees Daniel Defoe with his ears chopped off, John Tutchin being whipped publicly through western England, two political journalists clubbed to death (on the same day), and himself being wrapped in a blanket and whipped by the schoolboys of Westminster (for having printed an unauthorized edition of the sermons of the school's master, thereby robbing the school's own printer).

The next contest Dulness proposes is for the phantom poetess, Eliza (Eliza Haywood). She is compared to their Hera. Where Hera was "cow-eyed" in *Iliad*, and "of the herders," Haywood inverts these to become a

". . . Juno of majestic size,
With cow-like-udders, and with ox-like eyes" (II 155-6).

The booksellers will urinate to see whose urinary stream is the highest. Curll and Chetham compete. Chetham's efforts are insufficient to produce an arc, and he splashes his own face. Curll, on the other hand, produces a stream over his own head, burning (with an implied case of venereal disease) all the while. For this, Chetham is awarded a kettle, while Curll gets the phantom lady's works and company.

The next contest is for authors, and it is the game of "tickling": getting money from patrons by flattery. A very wealthy nobleman, attended by jockeys, huntsmen, a large sedan chair with six porters, takes his seat. One poet attempts to flatter his pride. A painter attempts to paint a glowing portrait. An opera author attempts to please his ears. John Oldmixon simply asks for the money (Oldmixon had attacked Pope in *The Catholic Poet,* but Pope claims that his real crime was plagiarism in his *Critical History of England,* which slandered the Stuarts and got him an office from the Whig ministry), only to have the lord clench his money tighter. Finally, a young man with no artistic ability sends his sister to the lord and wins the prize.

Another contest, primarily for critics, comes next. In this, Dulness offers up the prize of a "catcall" and a drum that can drown out the braying of asses to the one who can make the most senseless noise and impress the king of monkeys. They are invited to improve mustard-bowl thunder (as the sound effect of thunder on the stage had been made using a mustard bowl and a shot previously, and John Dennis had invented a new method) and the sound of the bell (used in tragedies to enhance the pitiful action). Pope describes the resulting game thus:

"Twas chatt'ring, grinning, mouthing, jabb'ring all,
And Noise, and Norton, Brangling, and Breval,
Dennis and Dissonance; and captious Art,
And Snip-snap short, and Interruption smart.
'Hold (cry'd the Queen) A Catcall each shall win,
Equal your merits! equal is your din!" (II. 229-234)

The critics are then invited to all bray at the same time. In this, Richard Blackmore wins easily:

"All hail him victor in both gifts of Song,
Who sings so loudly, and who sings so long." (II. 255-6)

(Blackmore had written six epic poems, a "Prince" and "King" Arthur, in twenty books, an *Eliza* in ten books, an *Alfred* in twelve books, etc. and had earned the nickname "Everlasting Blackmore." Additionally, Pope disliked his overuse of the verb "bray" for love and battle and so had chosen to have Blackmore's "bray" the most insistent.)

The assembled horde go down by Bridewell (the women's prison) between 11:00 AM and 12:00 PM, when the women prisoners are being whipped, and go "To where Fleet-ditch with disemboguing streams/ Rolls the large tribute of dead dogs to Thames" (II 267-8). The Fleet Ditch was the sewer outlet for the city at the time, where all of the gutters of the city washed into the river. It was silted, muddy, and mixed with river and city waters.

In the ditch, the political hacks are ordered to strip off their clothes and engage in a diving contest. Dulness says, "Who flings most filth, and wide pollutes around/ The stream, be his the Weekly Journals, bound" (II 267-8), while a load of lead will go to the deepest diver and a load of coal to the others who participate. "The Weekly Journals" was a collective noun, referring to *London Journal, Mist's Journal, British Journal, Daily Journal, inter al.* In this contest, John Dennis climbs up as high as a post and dives in, disappearing forever. Next, "Smedly" (Jonathan Smedley, a religious opportunist who criticized Jonathan Swift for gain) dives in and vanishes. Others attempt the task, but none succeed like Leonard Welsted (who had satirized Pope, Gay, and Arbuthnot's play *Three Hours after Marriage* in 1717), for he goes in swinging his arms like a windmill (to splash all with mud): "No crab more active in the dirty dance,/ Downward to climb, and backward to advance" (II 296-7). He wins the *Journals,* but Smedly reappears, saying that he had gone all the way down to Hades, where he had seen that a branch of Styx flows into the Thames, so that all who drink city water grow dull and forgetful from Lethe.

Smedly becomes Dulness's high priest, and the company move to Ludgate. There, the young critics are asked to weigh the difference between Richard Blackmore and John "Orator" Henley. The one who can will be the chief judge of Dulness. Three sophomores from Cambridge University and three lawyers from Temple Bar attempt the task, but they all fall asleep.

The entire company slowly falls asleep, with the last being Susanna Centlivre (who had attacked Pope's translation of Homer before its publication) and "Norton Defoe" (another false identity created by a political author who claimed to be the "true son" of Daniel Defoe). Finally, Folly herself is killed by the dullness of the works being read aloud. The result is, appropriately, that there is no judge for Dulness, for Dulness requires an absence of judgment.

A BOOK III

Book three is set in the Temple of Dulness in the City. Theobald sleeps with his head on the goddess's lap, with royal blue fogs surrounding him. In his dream, he goes to Hades and visits the shade of Elkannah Settle. There he sees millions of souls waiting for new bodies as their souls transmigrate. Bavius dips each soul in Lethe to make it dull before sending it to a new body. (In classical mythology, the souls of the dead were put into Lethe to forget their lives before passing on to their final reward, but these are dipped in Lethe before being born.)

Elkannah Settle hails Theobald as the great promised one, the messiah of Dulness, for Bavius had dipped him over and over again, from lifetime to lifetime, before he was perfected in stupidity and ready to be born as Theobald. Theobald had formerly been a Boeotian, several Dutchmen, several monks, all before being himself: "All nonsense thus, of old or modern date, / Shall in thee centre, from thee circulate" (III 51-2).

Settle gives Theobald full knowledge of Dulness. This is his baptism: the time when he can claim his divine role and begin his mission (in a parody of Jesus being blessed by the Holy Spirit). Settle shows Theobald the past triumphs of Dulness in its battles with reason and science. He surveys the *translatio stultitia*: the Great Wall of China and the emperor burning all learned books, Egypt and Omar I burning the books in the Ptlomaean library. Then he turns to follow the light of the sun/learning to Europe and says,

"How little, mark! that portion of the ball,
Where, faint at best, the beams of Science fall.
Soon as they dawn, from Hyperborean skies,
Embody'd dark, what clouds of Vandals rise!" (III 75-8)

Goths, Alans, Huns, Ostrogoths, Visigoths, and Islam are all seen as destroyers of learning. Christianity in the medieval period is also an enemy of learning and reason in Settle's view:

"See Christians, Jews, one heavy sabbath keep;
And all the Western World believe and sleep." (III 91-2)

Pope lambasts the medieval popes for destroying statuary and books that depicted Classical gods and goddesses and for vandalizing others, for making statues of Pan into Moses.

Settle then surveys the future. He says that Grub Street will be Dulness's Mount Parnassus, where the goddess will "Behold a hundred sons, and each a dunce" (III 130). He names two sons of contemporary dunces who were already showing signs of stupidity: Theophilus Cibber (III 134) and the son of Bishop Burnet.

Settle turns to examine the present state of "duncery", and this section of the third book is the longest. He first looks to literary critics, who are happiest when their authors complain the most. Scholars are described as:

"A Lumberhouse of Books in every head,
For ever reading, never to be read." (III 189-90)

William Hogarth made this engraving entitled "A Just View of the English Stage" in 1727. It shows the managers of the Drury Lane theater (including Colley Cibber (centre)) concocting an absurd farce with every possible stage effect, simply to get the better of John Rich. The toilet paper in the privy is labelled "Hamlet" and "Way of Ye World."

From critics, he turns to the contrastive of triumphant dunces and lost merit. Orator Henley gets special attention here (lines 195 ff.). Henley had set himself up as a professional lecturer. On Sundays, he would discuss theology, and on Wednesdays any other subject, and those who went to hear him would pay a shilling each ("Oh great Restorer of the good old Stage,/ Preacher at once, and Zany of thy Age!" 201-202), while learned bishops and skilled preachers spoke to empty congregations. Next come the theatres: a *Dr. Faustus* was the toast of the 1726-1727 season, with both Lincoln's Inn Fields and Drury Lane competing for more and more lavish stage effects to get the audiences in:

"Gods, imps, and monsters, music, rage, and mirth,
A fire, a jig, a battle, and a ball,
Till one wide Conflagration swallows all." (III 233-6)

Even though Pope was on good terms with some of the men involved (e.g. Henry Carey, who provided music for the Drury Lane version), the two companies are fighting to see who can make the least sense. This competition of vulgarity is led by two theaters, and each has its champion of decadence. At Lincoln's Inn Fields is the "Angel of Dulness," John Rich:

"Immortal Rich! how calm he sits at ease
Mid snows of paper, and fierce hail of pease;
And proud his mistress' orders to perform,
Rides in the whirlwind, and directs the storm." (III 257-260)

Rich's ability to ride in a stage whirlwind (in parody of God in the Book of Job) is matched by Colley Cibber and Barton Booth, patentees of the Drury Lane theater, who mount the stage in purple dragons and have an aerial battle. Dulness is the winner in these contests, for she benefits. Settle urges Theobald to refine these entertainments, to hammer them home and get them all the way to court, so that Dulness can be the true empress of the land. He prophesizes that Theobald will live in an age that will see Laurence Eusden the Poet Laureate and Colley Cibber the "Lord Chancellor of plays".

Settle then reveals some current triumphs of dullness over good sense. He mentions William Benson as the proper judge of architecture,

"While Wren with sorrow to the grave descends,
Gay dies un-pension'd with a hundred Friends.
Hibernian Politicks, O Swift, thy doom,
And Pope's translating three whole years with Broome." (III 325-328)

William Benson was a fool who had taken the place of Sir Christopher Wren and told the House of Lords that the house was unsound and falling down. It was not.

John Gay never obtained a pension and yet was often remarked as one of the most jovial, intelligent, and compassionate wits of the age. Jonathan Swift had been "exiled" to Ireland, where he had become involved in Irish politics. Pope himself had spent three years translating Homer. Settle sees in these things great prospects for the coming age of darkness. The poem ends with a vision of the apocalypse of nonsense:

"Lo! the great Anarch's ancient reign restor'd,
Light dies before her uncreating word." (III 339-40)
Settle invokes the second coming of stupidity, urging,
"Thy hand great Dulness! lets the curtain fall,
And universal Darkness covers all." (III 355-6)

At the very conclusion, Theobald cannot take any more joy, and he wakes. The vision goes back through the ivory gate of Morpheus.

THEMES OF THE THE DUNCIAD A

The Three Book *Dunciad* has an extensive inversion of Virgil's *Aeneid,* but it also structures itself heavily around a Christological theme. To some degree, this imagery of unholy consecration had been present in Dryden's *MacFlecknoe,* but Pope's King of Dunces is much more menacing than Thomas Shadwell could ever have been in Dryden's poem. It is not a case of an unworthy man getting praised that spurs the poem, but rather a force of degradation and decadence that motivates it.

Pope is not targeting one man, but rather a social decline that he feels is all but irrevocable. Nevertheless, the poem is still a satire and not a lamentation. The top of society (the kings) may be dulled by spectacle and freak shows, but Dulness is only one force. She is at war with the men of wit, and she can be opposed. In the Four Book *Dunciad* (or *Dunciad B*), any hope of redemption or reversal is gone, and the poem is even more nihilistic.

THE FOUR BOOK *DUNCIAD B* OF 1743

In 1741, Pope wrote a fourth book of the *Dunciad* and had

it published the next year as a stand-alone text. He also began revising the whole poem to create a new, integrated, and darker version of the text. The four-book *Dunciad* appeared in 1743 as a new work. Most of the critical and pseudo-critical apparatus was repeated from the *Dunciad Variorum* of 1738, but there was a new "Advertisement to the Reader" by Bishop Warburton and one new substantial piece: a schematic of anti-heroes, written by Pope in his own voice, entitled *Hyper-Critics of Ricardus Aristarchus.*

The most obvious change from the three book to the four book *Dunciad* was the change of hero from Lewis Theobald to Colley Cibber.

COLLEY CIBBER: KING OF DUNCES

Colley Cibber's *Apology for the Life of Colley Cibber, Comedian* appeared in 1740. In "A Letter from Mr. Cibber, to Mr. Pope", published in 1762, Cibber tells an anecdote of going with Pope and friends to a brothel. Since Pope was only about 4' tall, with a hunch back, due to a childhood tubercular infection of the spine, Cibber regarded taking Pope to a prostitute as a joke, and he congratulates himself on saving English poetry by pulling Pope off of an unsafe woman.

Whether this betrayal of trust and scandalous anecdote is true or not, Pope's explanation of the change of hero is more than sufficient without recourse to such biographical details. First, Cibber, and his son, Theophilus, had been satirized in the three book *Dunciad* (see above). Secondly, the *Apology* was inarguably a work of personal vanity that the age in general found offensive. Moreover, Pope, in the guise of Ricardus Aristarchus, explains in detail why Colley Cibber is the perfect hero for a mock heroic parody.

Aristarchus's "hyper-criticism" establishes a science for the mock heroic and follows up some of the ideas set forth by Pope in *Peri Bathos* in the *Miscellanies, Volume the Third* (1727). In this piece, the rules of heroic poetry could be inverted for the proper mock-heroic. The epic hero, Pope says, has wisdom, courage, and love. Therefore, the mock-hero should have "*Vanity, Impudence, and Debauchery.*" As a wise man knows without being told, Pope says, so the vain man listens to no opinion but his own, and Pope quotes Cibber as saying, "Let all the world impute to me what Folly or weakness they please; but till *Wisdom* can give me something that will make me more heartily happy, I am content to be Gazed at."

Courage becomes a hero, Pope says, and nothing is more perversely brave that summoning all one's courage just to the face, and he quotes Cibber's claim in the *Apology* that his face was almost the best known in England. Chivalric love is the mark of a hero, and Pope says that this is something easy for the young to have. A mock-hero could keep his lust going when old, could claim, as Cibber does, "a man has his Whore" at the age of 80. When the three qualities of wisdom, courage, and love are combined in an epic hero, the result is, according to Pope, magnanimity that induces admiration in the reader.

On the other hand, when vanity, impudence, and debauchery are combined in the "lesser epic" hero (Pope uses the term "lesser epic" to refer to the satirical epic that would function like a satire play in the Classical theater), the result is "Buffoonry" that induces laughter and disgust. Finally, Pope says that Cibber's offenses are compounded by the outlandishness of his claims. Although he was "a person never a hero even on the Stage," he sets himself out as an admirable and *imitable* person who expects applause for his vices.

THE ARGUMENT OF THE FOUR BOOK DUNCIAD

Most of the argument of the *Dunciad B* is the same as that of *Dunciad A*: It begins with the same Lord Mayor's Day, goes to Dulness contemplating her realm, moves to *Cibber* (called "Bays," in honour of his being Poet Laureate and thereby having the laurel wreath and butt of sherry) in despair, announces Cibber's choice as new King of Dunces, etc. Other than a change of hero, however, Pope made numerous adaptations and expansions of key passages. Not only are the topical references altered to fit Cibber's career, but Pope consistently changes the nature of the satire subtly by increasing the overarching metaphor of Cibber as "Anti-Christ of Wit," rather than Classical hero of Dulness. Most of the adaptations increase the parody of the Bible at the expense of the parody of Virgil.

B BOOK I

The invocation changes from "the one who brings" the Smithfield muses to the ears of kings to "The Mighty Mother, and her Son who brings," thus immediately making Cibber the fatherless son of a goddess, and the poem addresses "how the Goddess bade Britannia sleep,/ And pour'd her Spirit o'er the land and deep" (I 7-8). From the invocation, the poem moves to an expanded description of the Cave of Poverty and Poetry, near Bedlam.

Cibber is the co-master of the cave, as "o'er the gates [of Bedlam], by his fam'd father's hand/ Great Cibber's brazen, brainless brothers stand" (I 31-2) (referring to statues constructed by Caius Cibber, Colley Cibber's father), and the cave is now the source of "Journals, Medleys, Merc'ries, Magazines" (I 42). These changes introduce the Biblical and apocalyptical themes that Book IV, in particular, will explore, as Dulness's spirit parodies the Holy Spirit dwelling upon the face of the waters in the Book of Genesis.

When Dulness chooses her new king, she settles on Bays, who is seen in his study surveying his own works: "Nonsense precipitate, like running Lead,/ That slip'd thro' Cracks and Zig-zags of the Head" (I 123-4) and "Next, o'er his Books his eyes began to roll,/ In pleasing memory of all he stole" (*B* I 127-8). The base of Cibber's pile of sacrificed books is several commonplace books, which are the basis of all his own productions.

Although Cibber confesses "Some Daemon stole my pen... And once betray'd me into common sense," he prays to Dulness for inspiration, insisting that "Else all my Prose and Verse were much the same;/ This, prose on stilts; that, poetry fall'n lame" (I 187-90). The accidental common sense was *The Careless Husband.* When Cibber casts about for new professions, he, unlike Theobald in 1732, decides, "Hold-to the Minister I more incline;/ To serve his cause, O Queen! is serving thine" (I 213-4). The "minister" is Robert Walpole, an extremely unpopular Whig leader, and the "queen" is both Dulness and Queen Caroline of Hanover, who was a Tory enemy for her reconciliation of George II with Walpole.

When the new king is about to burn his books in despair, Pope heightens the religious imagery, for Cibber says to his books, "Unstain'd, untouch'd, and yet in maiden sheets;/ While all your smutty sisters walk the streets" (I. 229-30), and it is better that they be burned than that they be wrapped in "Oranges, to pelt your Sire" (I. 236). Again, Dulness extinguishes the pyre with a sheet of the ever-wet *Thule.*

Cibber goes to Dulness's palace, and Pope says that he feels at home there, and "So Spirits ending their terrestrial race,/ Ascend, and recognize their Native Place" (I 267-8). The Christian Heaven-home of Puritan songs is altered for Cibber to the originating sleep of Dulness.

While in the *Dunciad A* the palace had been empty, it is here crowded with ghosts (the same dunces mentioned in 1727, but all having died in the interim). Dulness calls forth her servants to herald the new king, and the book ends with Dulness's prayer, which takes an apocalyptic tone in the new version:

"O! when shall rise a Monarch all our own,
And I, a Nursing-mother, rock the throne,
'Twixt Prince and People close the Curtain draw,
And suckle Armies, and dry-nurse the land:
'Till Senates nod to Lullabies divine,
And all be sleep, as at an Ode of thine." (Dunciad B I 311-18)

B BOOK II

Most of Book II of the *Dunciad B* is the same as *Dunciad A.* The Dunce Games are largely the same, with a few changes in personnel. Cibber watches all, with "A brain of feathers, and a heart of lead" (II 44). The contest of booksellers is generally as it was in 1727, with Curll slipping on bedpan slops. However, when Curll prays to Cloacina, Pope provides more motivation for her hearing his prayer:

"Oft had the Goddess heard her servant's call,
From her black grottos near the Temple wall,

List'ning delighted to the jest unclean
Of link-boys vile, and watermen obscene." (B II 97-100)

Further, Cloacina aids Curll win the race herself, and not by intercession with Jove, and Pope here explains *how* she propels him to victory: she makes the ordure nourishment to Curll, and he "Imbibes new life, and scours and stinks along" (*B* II 106). Again, the phantom poet, More, vanishes. The game for Eliza Heywood's person and poetry is the same as the previous version, except that the promised gift for the victor is a chamber pot. Curll here competes with Osborne, a bookseller who had claimed to sell Pope's subscription edition of *Iliad* at half price, when he had merely pirated it, cut the size of the book to octavo, and printed on low quality paper. Curll win's Eliza, and Osborne is crowned with the pot.

The "tickling" contest is the same, except that Thomas Bentley, nephew of Richard Bentley the classicist, replaces Richard Blackmore. This Bentley had written a fawning ode on the son of Robert Harley (a former friend of Pope's with whom he seems estranged). In the noise battle, Dulness tells her poets,

"With Shakespear's nature, or with Johnson's art,
Let others aim: 'Tis yours to shake the soul
With Thunder rumbling from the mustard bowl." (B II 224-6)

In the braying contest that follows, there is a noise that seems to come "from the deep Divine;/ There Webster! peal'd thy voice, and Whitfield! thine" (*B* II 257-8). Webster was a radical Protestant religious writer who had demanded the scourging of the church, and Whitfield was George Whitfield, the notable collaborator with John Wesley, whom Pope describes as "a Field-preacher thought the only means of advancing Christianity was by the old death of fire and faggot" who agreed with Webster only "to abuse all the sobre Clergy" (note to line 258). Richard Blackmore appears again as the single singer with the loudest "bray."

The progress by Bridewell to Fleet-ditch and the muck-diving games are the same, but, again, with some changes of dunces. Oldmixon, who had appeared in 1727 as one of the ticklers, is here the elderly diver who replaces John Dennis.

Smedley and Concanen are the same, but Pope adds a new section on party political papers:

> *"Next plung'd a feeble, but a desp'rate pack,*
> *With each a sickly brother at his back:*
> *Sons of a Day! just buoyant on the flood,*
> *Then number'd with the puppies in the mud.*
> *Ask ye their names? I could as soon disclose*
> *The names of these blind puppies as of those." (B 305-310)*

These "sons of a day" are the daily newspapers that only had lifespans of a single issue. They were frequently printed with two different papers on the same sheet of paper (front and back), and Pope quotes the investigation into Robert Harley, 1st Earl of Oxford (conducted by Walpole's administration) as showing that the Tory ministry of Pope's friends had spent over fifty thousand pounds to support political papers.

The dead gazettes are mourned only by "Mother Osborne" (James Pitt, who had run the *London Journal* under the name of "Father Osborne"; he had been called "Mother Osborne" for his dull, pedantic style).

The champion of splattering in *Dunciad B* is William Arnal, a party author of the *British Journal* who had gotten ten thousand pounds as a political hack. In keeping with the insertion of Webster and Whitfield, earlier, Pope takes a new turn and has the winner of the depth dive be the Archbishop of Canterbury, John Potter (1674 - 1747), and he is surrounded by an army of minor authors, "Prompt to guard or stab, to saint or damn./ Heav'n's Swiss, who fight for any God, or Man" (*B* II 357-8). These trimming religious authors are people like Benjamin Hoadley (who had been an aid to Smedley) and John "Orator" Henley.

Potter describes the vision of Hades and the Styx pouring into the Thames, but it is not merely Lethe that pours in. Lethe and the effluvia of dreams go into the Thames, so the effect is that it "Intoxicates the pert, and lulls the grave" (*B* II 344). The Archbishop of Canterbury becomes the Archbishop of Dulness.

The book concludes with the contest of reading Blackmore and Henley.

B BOOK III

Book III is, like Book II, largely the same text as the *Dunciad Variorum*. In light of the new fourth book and the subtle changes of Book I, however, some passages take on more menace. The opening, where Cibber rests with his head in Dulness's lap, is here a clear parody of the Madonna with child.

The vision granted Cibber is less Christological, as Cibber is not given a mission in the same way with an infusion of the Unholy Spirit, as Book IV provides a new ending, but the general vision of Hades is the same. Cibber visits the shade of Elkannah Settle and is shown the *translatio studii* and its inverse, the *translatio stultitia,* as learning moves ever westward across the world, with the sun, and darkness springs up right behind it.

In the survey of the formless poets waiting to be born (in print), Cibber sees the same faces as Theobald had, but with a few excisions and additions. The implied homosexual couple of critics from the *Dunciad A* are cut, but a mass of nameless poets contend, "who foremost shall be dam'd to Fame" (*B* III 158) (both cursed with fame and damned by the goddess Fama for being an idiot), and altogether,

"Down, down they larum, with impetuous whirl,
The Pindars, and the Miltons of a Curl." (B III 163-4)

As in the previous version, these struggling hack writers and political character assassins are contrasted to the glorious dunces who win all the money and fame of the kingdom, while worthy ministers and divines go ignored. Thus, Settle features Orator Henley as a paragon,

". . . his breeches rent below;
Imbrown'd with native bronze, lo! Henley stands,
Tuning his voice, and balancing his hands." (B III 197-200)

As in the three book *Dunciad,* Settle shows the happy triumph of Dulness on the stage, but the lines are compressed and take on a new parodic context:

"All sudden Gorgons hiss, and Dragons glare,
And ten-horn'd fiends and Giants rush to war.
Hell rises, Heav'n descends, and dance on Earth;
Gods, imps, and monsters, music, rage, and mirth,

A fire, a jigg, a battle, and a ball,
'Till one wide conflagration swallows all.
Thence a new world to Nature's laws unknown,
Breaks out refulgent, with a heav'n its own." (B III 235-42)

The theater is providing a mockery of the Apocalypse and the second coming, an inverted, man-made spectacle of the divine. For these accomplishments, Settle blesses Cibber and mourns his own failure in Dulness's service. For Cibber,

"Happier thy fortunes! like a rolling stone,
Thy giddy dulness still shall lumber on,
Safe in its heaviness, shall never stray,
But lick up ev'ry blockhead in the way." (B III 293-6).

Settle then takes a glance at the loss of learning incipient in the age. In architecture, the fool triumphant is Ripley, who was making a new Admiralty building, while "Jones' and Boyle's" fail. Settle wishes for the day to come soon when Eton and Westminster are in permanent holiday. As with the earlier version of the poem, the book ends with Cibber excitedly waking from his dream.

BOOK IV

Book IV was entirely new to the *Dunciad B* and had been published first as a stand-alone concluding poem. Pope himself referred to the four-book version "the *Greater Dunciad,*" in keeping with the *Greater Iliad.* It is also "greater" in that its subject is larger.

Book IV can function as a separate piece or as the conclusion of the *Dunciad*: in many ways its structure and tone is substantially different from the first three books, and it is much more allegorical.

It opens with a second, nihilistic invocation:

"Yet, yet a moment, one dim Ray of Light
Indulge, dread Chaos, and eternal Night!" (B IV 1-2)
"Suspend a while your Force inertly strong,
Then take at once the Poet, and the Song." (ibid. 7-8)

The fourth book promises to show the obliteration of sense from England. The Dog-star shines, the lunatic prophets speak, and the daughter of Chaos and Nox (Dulness) rises to "dull and venal a new World to mold" (*B* IV 15) and begin a Saturnian age of lead.

Dulness takes her throne, and Pope describes the allegorical tableau of her throne room. Science is chained beneath her foot-stool. Logic is gagged and bound. Wit has been exiled from her kingdom entirely. Rhetoric is stripped on the ground and tied by sophism. Morality is dressed in a gown that is bound by two cords, of furs (the ermines of judges) and lawn (the fabric of bishops sleeves), and at a nod from Dulness, her "page" (a notorious hanging judge named Page who had had over one hundred people executed) pulls both cords tight and strangles her. The Muses are bound in tenfold chains and guarded by Flattery and Envy.

Only mathematics is free, because it is too insane to be bound. Nor, Pope says, could Chesterfield refrain from weeping upon seeing the sight (for Chesterfield had opposed the Licensing Act of 1737, which is the chaining of the Muses). Colley Cibber, however, slumbers, his head in Dulness's lap. (In a note, Pope says that it is proper for Cibber to sleep through the whole of Book IV, as he had had no part in the actions of book II, slept through book III, and therefore ought to go on sleeping.)

Into the audience chamber, a "Harlot form" "with mincing step, small voice, and languid eye" comes in (*B* IV 45-6). This is opera, who wears patchwork clothing (for operas being made up of the patchwork of extant plays and being itself a mixed form of singing and acting). Opera then speaks to Dulness of the Muses:

"Chromatic tortures soon shall drive them hence,
Break all their nerves, and fritter all their sense:
One Trill shall harmonize joy, grief, and rage,
Wake the dull Church, and lull the ranting Stage;
To the same notes thy sons shall hum, or snore,
And all thy yawning daughters cry, encore." (B IV 55-60)

However, Opera warns Dulness that Handel is a threat to her. His operas make too much sense, have too strong a plot, and are too masculine in their performance. Accordingly, Dulness banishes Handel to Ireland.

An illustration of Othello striking Desdemona from Thomas Hanmer's ornate 1743 edition of William Shakespeare. The text was based on Pope's edition.

Fame blows her "posterior trumpet," and all the dunces of the land come to Dulness's throne. There are three classes of dunce. First, there are the naturally dull. These are drawn to her as bees are to a queen bee, and they "adhere" to her person. The second are the people who do not wish to be dunces but are, "Whate'er of mungril no one class admits,/ A wit with dunces, and a dunce with wits" (*B* IV 89-90). These dunces orbit Dulness. They struggle to break free, and they get some distance from her, but they are too weak to flee. The third class are "false to Phoebus, bow to Baal;/ Or impious, preach his Word without a call" (*B* IV 93-4).

They are men and women who do dull things by supporting dunces, either by giving money to hacks or by suppressing the cause of worthy writers. These people come to Dulness as a comet does: although they are only occasionally near her, they habitually do her bidding. Of this last group, Pope classes Sir Thomas Hanmer, a "decent knight," who absurdly thinks himself a great Shakespeare editor and uses his own money to publish an exceptionally lavish and ornate edition (with a text that was based on Pope's own edition).

He is outshone in darkness by one Benson, who is even more absurd, in that he begins putting up monuments of John Milton, striking coins and medals of Milton, and translating Milton's Latin poetry and who had then passed from excessive Milton fanaticism to fanaticism for Arthur Johnston, a Scottish physician and Latin poet. Unable to be the most fantastically vain man, Hamner prepares to withdraw his edition, but "Apollo's May'r and Aldermen" (*B* IV 116) take the page from him. (This was a reference to Oxford University Press, with which Pope had a quarrel based on their denying Bishop Warburton a doctorate in 1741). Dulness tells her followers to imitate Benson and tack their own names to statues and editions of famous authors, to treat standard authors as trophies (the busts made of them like hunting trophies), and thus "So by each Bard an Alderman shall sit" (*B* IV 131).

All of the dunces press forward, vying to be the first to speak, but a ghost comes forward who awes them all and makes all to shake in fear. Doctor Busby, headmaster of Westminster School appears, "Dripping with Infant's blood, and Mother's tears" (*B* IV 142) from the birch cane that he used to whip boys, and every man in the hall begins to tremble. Busby tells Dulness that he is her true champion, for he turns geniuses to fools, "Whate'er the talents, or howe'er design'd,/ We hang one jingling padlock on the mind" (161-2). Dulness agrees and wishes for a pedant king like James I again, who will "stick the Doctor's Chair into the Throne" (177), for only a pedant king would insist on what her priests (and only hers) proclaim: "The RIGHT DIVINE of Kings to govern wrong" (188), for Cambridge and Oxford still uphold the doctrine.

As soon as she mentions them, the professors of Cambridge and Oxford (except for Christ Church college) rush to her, "Each fierce Logician, still expelling Locke". (John Locke had been censured by Oxford University in 1703, and his *Essay on Human Understanding* had been banned.) These professors give way to their greatest figure, Richard Bentley, who appears with his Quaker hat on and refuses to bow to Dulness.

Bentley tells Dulness that he and critics like him are her true champions, for he had "made Horace dull, and humbled Milton's strains" and, no matter what her enemies do, critics will always serve Dulness, for "Turn what they will to Verse, their toil is vain,/ Critics like me shall make it Prose again". Picking fine arguments on letters and single textual variants and correcting authors, he will make all wits useless, and clerics, he says, are the purely dull, though the works of Isaac Barrow and Francis Atterbury might argue otherwise. He says that it is "For thee explain a thing till all men doubt it,/ And write about it, Goddess, and about it". They cement over all wit, throwing stone back onto the figures that authors had chiselled out of marble. As he makes his boast, he sees "A whore, a pupil, and a French governor" come forward, and the devout Bentley skulks away.

The French governor attempts to speak to Dulness but cannot be heard over the French horn sound that emerges, so the pupil tells his story. The "governor" is an English nobleman who went to school and college without learning anything, then went abroad on the Grand Tour, where "Europe he saw, and Europe saw him too".

He went to Paris and Rome and "he saunter'd Europe round,/ And gather'd ev'ry Vice on Christian ground" (*B* IV 311-312). At the end of his travels, he is "perfectly well bred,/ With nothing but a Solo in his head", and he has returned to England with a despoiled nun following him. She is pregnant with his child (or the student's) and destined for the life of a prostitute (a kept woman), and the lord is going to run for Parliament so that he can avoid arrest. Dulness welcomes the three — the devious student, the brainless lord, and the spoiled nun — and spreads her own cloak about the girl, which "frees from sense of Shame."

After the vacuous traveller, an idle lord appears, yawning with the pain of sitting on an easy chair. He does nothing at all. Immediately after him, Annius speaks. He is the natural predator for idling nobles, for he is a forger of antiquities (named for Annio di Viterbo) who teaches the nobles to value their false Roman coins above their houses and their forged Virgil manuscripts above their own clothing. He serves Dulness by teaching her servants to vaunt their stupidity with their wealth.

Chapter 10

Project Gutenberg

Project Gutenberg, abbreviated as PG, is a volunteer effort to digitize, archive and distribute cultural works. Founded in 1971 by Michael S. Hart, it is the oldest digital library. Most of the items in its collection are the full texts of public domain books. The project tries to make these as free as possible, in long-lasting, open formats that can be used on almost any computer.

As of December 2007[update], Project Gutenberg claimed over 25,000 items in its collection. Project Gutenberg is affiliated with many projects that are independent organizations which share the same ideals, and have been given permission to use the *Project Gutenberg* trademark.

Wherever possible, the releases are available in plain text, but other formats are included, such as HTML. Most releases are in the English language, but many non-English works are also available. There are multiple affiliated projects that are providing additional content, including regional and language-specific works. Project Gutenberg is also closely affiliated with Distributed Proofreaders, an internet-based community for proofreading scanned texts.

Project Gutenberg has been criticized for lack of scholarly rigor in its e-texts: for example, there is usually inadequate information about the edition used and often omission of original prefaces. However, John Mark Ockerbloom of the University of Pennsylvania noted that PG is responsive about addressing errors once they are identified, and the texts now include specific source edition citations. In many cases the editions also are not the most current scholarly editions, for these later editions are not usually in the public domain. While the works in Project Gutenberg represent a valuable sample of publications that span several centuries, there are some issues of concern for linguistic analysis. Some content may have been modified by the transcriber because of editorial changes or corrections (such as to correct for obvious proofsetter or printing errors). The spelling may also have been modified to conform with current practices. This can mean that the works may be problematic when searching for older grammatical usage. Finally, the collected works can be weighted heavily towards certain authors (such as Charles Dickens), while others are barely represented.

In March 2004, a new initiative was begun by Michael Hart and John S. Guagliardo to provide low-cost intellectual properties. The initial name for this project was *Project Gutenberg* 2 (PG II), which created controversy among PG volunteers because of the re-use of the project's trademarked name for a commercial venture.

THE PROLOGUE TO THE SATIRES CRITICISM

Alexander Pope, English poet, was born in Lombard Street, London, on the 21st of May 1688. His father, Alexander Pope, a Roman Catholic, was a linen-draper who afterwards retired from business with a small fortune, and fixed his residence about 1700 at Binfield in Windsor Forest. Pope's education was desultory. His father's religion would have excluded him from the public schools, even had there been no other impediment to his being sent there. Before he was twelve he had obtained a smattering of Latin and Greek from various masters, from a priest in Hampshire, from a schoolmaster at Twyford near Winchester, from Thomas Deane, who kept a school in Marylebone and afterwards at Hyde Park Corner, and finally from another priest at home.

Between his twelfth and his seventeenth years excessive application to study undermined his health, and he developed the personal deformity which was in so many ways to distort his view of life. He thought himself dying, but through a friend, Thomas (afterwards the Abbe) Southcote, he obtained the advice of the famous physician John Radcliffe, who prescribed diet and exercise. Under this treatment the boy recovered his strength and spirits. "He thought himself the better," Spence says, "in some respects for not having had a regular education. He (as he observed in particular) read originally for the sense, whereas we are taught for so many years to read only for words."

He afterwards learnt French and Italian, probably in a similar way. He read translations of the Greek, Latin, French and Italian poets, and by the age of twelve, when he was finally settled at home and left to himself, he was not only a confirmed reader, but an eager aspirant to the highest honours in poetry. There is a story, which chronological considerations make extremely improbable, that in London he had crept into Will's coffee-house to look at Dryden, and a further tale that the old poet had given him a shilling for a translation of the story of Pyramus and Thisbe; he had lampooned his schoolmaster; he had made a play out of John Ogilby's *Iliad* for his schoolfellows; and before he was fifteen he had written an epic, his hero being Alcander, a prince of Rhodes, or, as he states elsewhere, Deucalion.

There were, among the Roman Catholic families near Binfield, men capable of giving a direction to his eager ambition, men of literary tastes, and connexions with the literary world. These held together as members of persecuted communities always do, and were kept in touch with one another by the family priests. Pope was thus brought under the notice of Sir William Trumbull, a retired diplomatist living at Easthampstead, within a few miles of Binfield.

Thomas Dancastle, lord of the manor of Binfield, took an active interest in his writings, and at Whiteknights, near Reading, lived another Roman Catholic, Anthony Englefield, "a great lover of poets and poetry." Through him Pope made the acquaintance of Wycherley and of Henry Cromwell, who was a distant cousin of the Protector, a gay man about town, and something of a pedant. Wycherley introduced him to William Walsh, then of great renown as a critic. Before the poet was seventeen he was admitted in this way to the society of

London "wits" and men of fashion, and was cordially encouraged as a prodigy.

Wycherley's correspondence with Pope was skilfully manipulated by the younger man to represent Wycherley as submitting, at first humbly and then with an ill-grace, to Pope's criticisms. The publication (Elwin and Courthope, vol. v.) of the originals of Wycherley's letters from MSS. at Longleat showed how seriously the relations between the two friends, which ceased in 1710, had been misrepresented in the version of the correspondence which Pope chose to submit to the public.

Walsh's contribution to his development was the advice to study "correctness." "About fifteen," he says, "I got acquainted with Mr. Walsh. He used to encourage me much, and used to tell me that there was one way left of excelling; for, though we had several great poets, we never had any one great poet that was correct, and he desired me to make that my study and aim" (Spence, p. 280). Trumbull turned Pope's attention to the French critics, out of the study of whom grew the *Essay on Criticism*; he suggested the subject of *Windsor Forest*, and he started the idea of translating Homer.

It says something for Pope's docility at this stage that he recognized so soon that a long course of preparation was needed for such a magnum opus, and began steadily and patiently to discipline himself. The epic was put aside and afterwards burnt; versification was industriously practised in short "essays"; and an elaborate study was made of accepted critics and models. He learnt most, as he acknowledged, from Dryden, but the harmony of his verse also owed something to an earlier writer, George Sandys, the translator of Ovid. At the beginning of the 18th century Dryden's success had given great vogue to translations and modernizations.

The air was full of theories as to the best way of doing such things. What Dryden had touched, Pope did not presume to meddle with — Dryden was his hero and master; but there was much more of the same kind to be done. Dryden had rewritten three of the *Canterbury Tales*; Pope tried his hand at the *Merchant's Tale*, and the *Prologue to the Wife of Bath's Tale*, and produced also an imitation of the *House of Fame*. Dryden had translated Virgil; Pope experimented on the *Thebais* of Statius, Ovid's *Heroides* and *Metamorphoses*, and the *Odyssey*. He knew little Latin and less Greek, but there were older versions in English which helped him to the sense; and, when the correspondents to whom he submitted his versions pointed out mistranslations, he could answer that he had always agreed with them, but that he had deferred to the older translators against his own judgment.

It was one of Pope's little vanities to try to give the impression that his metrical skill was more precocious even than it was, and we cannot accept his published versions of Statius and Chaucer (published in "miscellanies" at intervals between 1709 and 1714) as incontrovertible evidence of his proficiency at the age of sixteen or seventeen, the date, according to his own assertion, of their composition. But it is indisputable that at the age of seventeen his skill in verse astonished a veteran critic like Walsh, and some of his pastorals were in the hands of Sir George Granville (afterwards Lord Lansdowne) before 1706. His metrical letter to Cromwell, which Elwin dates in 1707, when Pope was nineteen, is a brilliant feat of versification, and has turns of wit in it as easy and spirited as any to be found in his mature satires. Pope was twenty-one when he sent the "Ode on Solitude" to Cromwell, and said it was written before he was twelve years old.

Precocious Pope was, but he was also industrious; and he spent some eight or nine years in arduous and enthusiastic discipline, reading, studying, experimenting, taking the advice of some and laughing in his sleeve at the advice of others, "poetry his only business," he said, "and idleness his only pleasure," before anything of his appeared in print. In these preliminary studies he seems to have guided himself by the maxim formulated in a letter to Walsh (dated July 2, 1706) that "it seems not so much the perfection of sense to say things that had never been said before, as to express those best that have been said oftenest."

His first publication was his "Pastorals." Jacob Tonson,

the bookseller, had seen these pastorals in the hands of Walsh and Congreve, and sent a polite note (April 20, 5706) to Pope asking that he might have them for one of his miscellanies. They appeared accordingly in May 1709 at the end of the sixth volume of Tonson's *Poetical Miscellanies*, containing contributions from Ambrose Philips, Sheffield, Garth and Rowe, with "January and May," Pope's version of Chaucer's "Merchant's Tale." Pope's next publication was the *Essay on Criticism* (1711), written two years earlier, and printed without the author's name. "In every work regard the writer's end" (1.255) is one of its sensible precepts, and one that is often neglected by critics of the essay, who comment upon it as if Pope's end had been to produce an original and profound treatise on first principles.

His aim was simply to condense, methodize, and give as perfect and novel expression as he could to floating opinions about the poet's aims and methods, and the critic's duties, to "what oft was thought, but ne'er so well expressed " (1.298). "The town" was interested in *belles lettres*, and given to conversing on the subject; Pope's essay was simply a brilliant contribution to the fashionable conversation. The youthful author said that he did not expect the sale to be quick because "not one gentleman in sixty, even of liberal education, could understand it."

The sales were slow until Pope caused copies to be sent to Lord Lansdowne and others, but its success was none the less brilliant for the delay. The town was fairly dazzled by the young poet's learning, judgment, and felicity of expression. Many of the admirers of the poem doubtless would have thought less of it if they had not believed all the maxims to be original. "I admired," said Lady Mary Wortley Montagu, "Mr Pope's *Essay on Criticism* at first very much, because I had not then read any of the ancient critics, and did not know that it was all stolen." Pope gained credit for much that might have been found, where he found it, in the *Institutes* of Quintilian, in the numerous critical writings of Rene Rapin, and in Rene le Bossu's treatise on epic poetry.

Addison has been made responsible for the exaggerated

value once set on the essay, but Addison's paper (*Spectator*, No. 253) was not unmixed praise. He deprecated the attacks made by Pope on contemporary literary reputations, although he did full justice to the poet's metrical skill.

Addison and Pope became acquainted with one another, and Pope's sacred eclogue, "Messiah," was printed as No. 378 of the *Spectator*. In the *Essay on Criticism* Pope provoked one bitter personal enemy in John Dennis, the critic, by a description of him as Appius, who "stares, tremendous, with a threat'ning eye." Dennis retorted in *Reflections.. upon a late Rhapsody* .. (1712), abusing Pope among other things for his personal deformity. Pope never forgot this brutal attack, which he described in a note inserted after Dennis's death, as late as 1743, as written "in a manner perfectly lunatic." *The Rape of the Lock* in its first form appeared in 1712 in Lintot's *Miscellanies*; the "machinery" of sylphs and gnomes was an afterthought, and the poem was republished as we now have it early in 1714.

William, 4th Baron Petre, had surreptitiously cut off a lock of Miss Arabella Fermor's hair, and the liberty had been resented; Pope heard the story from his friend John Caryll, who suggested that the breach between the families might be healed by making the incident the subject of a mock-heroic poem like Boileau's *Lutrin*. Pope caught at the hint; the mock-heroic treatment of the pretty frivolities of fashionable life just suited his freakish sprightliness of wit, and his studies of the grand epic at the time put him in excellent vein. *The Rape of the Lock* is admitted to be a masterpiece of airiness, ingenuity, and exquisite finish. But the poem struck Taine as a piece of harsh, scornful, indelicate buffoonery, a mere succession of oddities and contrasts, of expressive figures unexpected and grinning, an example of English insensibility to French sweetness and refinement.

Sir Leslie Stephen objected on somewhat different grounds to the poet's tone towards women. His laughter at Pope's raillery was checked by the fact that women are spoken of in the poem as if they were all like Belinda. The poem shows the hand of the satirist who was later to assert that "every woman is at heart a rake," in the epistle addressed to Martha Blount.

Windsor Forest, modelled on Sir John Denham's *Cooper's Hill,* had been begun, according to Pope's account, when he was sixteen or seventeen. It was published in March 1713 with a flattering dedication to the secretary for war, George Granville, Lord Lansdowne, and an opportune allusion to the peace of Utrecht.

This was a nearer approach to taking a political side than Pope had yet made. His principle had been to keep clear of politics, and not to attach himself to any of the sets into which literary men were divided by party. Although inclined to the Jacobites by his religion, he never took any part in the plots for the restoration of the Stuarts, and he was on friendly terms with the Whig coterie, being a frequent guest at the coffee-house kept by Daniel Button, where Addison held his "little senate."

He had contributed his poem, "The Messiah" to the *Spectator*; he had written an article or two in the *Guardian,* and he wrote a prologue for Addison's *Cato*. Nevertheless he induced Lintot the bookseller to obtain from John Dennis a criticism of *Cato*. On the publication of Dennis's remarks, the violence of which had, as Pope hoped, made their author ridiculous, Pope produced an anonymous pamphlet, *The Narrative of Dr Robert Norris concerning the Frenzy of Mr John Dennis* (1713), which, though nominally in defence of Addison, had for its main purpose the gratification of Pope's own hostility to Dennis. Addison disavowed any connivance in this coarse attack in a letter written on his behalf by Steele to Lintot, saying that if he noticed Dennis's attack at all it would be in such a way as to allow him no just cause of complaint.

Coolness between Addison and Pope naturally followed this episode. When the *Rape of the Lock* was published, Addison, who is said to have praised the poem highly to Pope in private, dismissed it in the *Spectator* with two sentences of patronizing faint praise to the young poet, and, coupling it with Tickell's "Ode on the Prospect of Peace," devoted the rest of the article to an elaborate puff of "the pastorals of Mr Philips." When Pope showed a leaning to the Tories in *Windsor Forest,* the members of Addison's coterie made insidious war on him.

Within a few weeks of the publication of the poem, and when it was the talk of the town, there began to appear in the *Guardian* (Nos. 22, 23, 28, 30, 32) a series of articles on "Pastorals." Not a word was said about *Windsor Forest*, but everybody knew to what the general principles referred. Modern pastoral poets were ridiculed for introducing Greek moral deities, Greek flowers and fruits, Greek names of shepherds, Greek sports and customs and religious rites. They ought to make use of English rural mythology — hobthrushes, fairies, goblins and witches; they should give English names to their shepherds; they should mention flowers indigenous to English climate and soil; and they should introduce English proverbial sayings, dress, and customs.

All excellent principles, and all neglected by Pope in *Windsor Forest*. The poem was fairly open to criticism in these points; there are many beautiful passages in it, showing close though somewhat professional observation of nature, but the mixture of heathen deities and conventional archaic fancies with modern realities is incongruous, and the comparison of Queen Anne to Diana was ludicrous. But the sting of the articles did not lie in the truth of the oblique criticisms. The pastorals of Ambrose Philips, published four years before, were again trotted out. Here was a true pastoral poet, the eldest born of Spenser, the worthy successor of Theocritus and Virgil!

Pope took an amusing revenge, which turned the laugh against his assailants. He sent Steele an anonymous paper in continuation of the articles in the *Guardian* on pastoral poetry, reviewing the poems of Mr Pope by the light of the principles laid down. Ostensibly Pope was censured for breaking the rules, and Philips praised for conforming to them, quotations being given from both. The quotations were sufficient to dispose of the pretensions of poor Philips, and Pope did not choose his own worst passages, accusing himself of actually deviating sometimes into poetry.

Although the *Guardian*'s principles were also brought into ridicule by burlesque exemplifications of them after the manner of Gay's *Shepherd's Week*, Steele, misled by the opening sentences, was at first unwilling to print what appeared to be a direct attack on Pope, and is said to have asked Pope's consent to the publication, which was graciously granted.

The estrangement from Addison was completed in connexion with Pope's translation of Homer. This enterprise was definitely undertaken in 1713. The work was to be published by subscription, as Dryden's *Virgil* had been. Men of all parties subscribed, their unanimity being a striking proof of the position Pope had attained at the age of twenty-five. It was as if he had received a national commission as by general consent the first poet of his time.

But the unanimity was broken by a discordant note. A member of the Addison clique, Tickell, attempted to run a rival version. Pope suspected Addison's instigation; Tickell had at least Addison's encouragement. Pope's famous character of Addison as "Atticus" in the *Epistle to Dr Arbuthnot* (ii. 193-215) was, however, inspired by resentment at insults that existed chiefly in his own imagination, though Addison was certainly not among his warmest admirers. Pope afterwards claimed to have been magnanimous, but he spoiled his case by the petty inventions of his account of the quarrel.

The translation of Homer was Pope's chief employment for twelve years. The new pieces in the miscellanies published in 1717, his "Elegy on an Unfortunate Lady," and his "Eloisa to Abelard," were probably written some years before their publication. His "Eloisa to Abelard " was based on an English translation by John Hughes of a French version of the Letters, which differed very considerably from the original Latin. *The Iliad* was delivered to the subscribers in instalments in 1715, 1717, 1718 and 1720. Pope's own defective scholarship made help necessary.

William Broome and John Jortin supplied the bulk of the notes, and Thomas Parnell the preface. For the translation of the *Odyssey* he took Elijah Fenton and Broome as coadjutors, who between them translated twelve out of the twenty-four books. It was completed in 1725. The profitableness of the work was Pope's chief temptation to undertake it. His receipts for his earlier poems had totalled about £150, but he cleared more than £8000 by the two translations, after deducting all payments to coadjutors — a much larger sum than had ever been received by an English author before.

The translation of Homer had established Pope's reputation with his contemporaries, and has endangered it ever since it was challenged. Opinions have varied on the purely literary merits of the poem, but with regard to it as a translation few have differed from Bentley's criticism, "A fine poem, Mr Pope, but you must not call it Homer." His collaboration with Broome and Fenton involved him in a series of recriminations. Broome was weak enough to sign a note at the end of the work understating the extent of Fenton's assistance as well as his own, and ascribing the merit of their translation, reduced to less than half its real proportions, to a regular revision and correction — mostly imaginary — at Pope's hands.

These falsehoods were deemed necessary by Pope to protect himself against possible protests from the subscribers. In 1722 he edited the poems of Thomas Parnell, and in 1725 made a considerable sum by an unsatisfactory edition of Shakespeare, in which he had the assistance of Fenton and Gay.

Pope, with his economical habits, was rendered independent by the pecuniary success of his Homer, and enabled to live near London. The estate at Binfield was sold, and he removed with his parents to Mawson's Buildings, Chiswick, in 1716, and in 1719 to Twickenham, to the house with which his name is associated. Here he practised elaborate landscape gardening on a small scale, and built his famous grotto, which was really a tunnel under the road connecting the garden with the lawn on the Thames. He was constantly visited at Twickenham by his intimates, Dr John Arbuthnot, John Gay, Bolingbroke (after his return in 1723), and Swift (during his brief visits to England in 1726 and 1727), and by many other friends of the Tory party. With Atterbury, bishop of Rochester, he was on terms of affectionate intimacy, but he blundered in his evidence when he was called as a witness on his behalf in 1723.

In 1717 his father died, and he appears to have turned to the Blounts for sympathy in what was to him a very serious bereavement. He had early made the acquaintance of Martha and Teresa Blount, both of them intimately connected with his domestic history. Their home was at Mapledurham, near Reading, but Pope probably first met them at the house of his neighbour, Mr Englefield of Whiteknights, who was their grandfather.

He begun to correspond with Martha Blount in 1712, and after 1717 the letters are much more serious in tone. He quarrelled with Teresa, who had apparently injured or prevented his suit to her sister; and although, after her father's death in 1718, he paid her an annuity, he seems to have regarded her as one of his most dangerous enemies. His friendship with Martha lasted all his life. So long as his mother lived he was unwearying in his attendance on her, but after her death in 1733 his association with Martha Blount was more constant. In defiance of the scandal-mongers, they paid visits together at the houses of common friends, and at Twickenham she spent part of each day with him. His earlier attachment to Lady Mary Wortley Montagu was apparently a more or less literary passion, which perished under Lady Mary's ridicule.

The year 1725 may be taken as the beginning of the third period of Pope's career, when he made his fame as a moralist and a satirist. It may be doubted whether Pope had the staying power necessary for the composition of a great imaginative work, whether his crazy constitution would have held together through the strain. He toyed with the idea of writing a grand epic. He told Spence that he had it all in his head, and gave him a vague (and it must be admitted not very promising) sketch of the subject and plan of it. But he never put any of it on paper. He shrank as with instinctive repulsion from the stress and strain of complicated designs.

Even his prolonged task of translating weighed heavily on his spirits, and this was a much less formidable effort than creating an epic. He turned rather to designs that could be accomplished in detail, works of which the parts could be separately laboured at and put together with patient care, into which happy thoughts could be fitted that had been struck out at odd moments and in ordinary levels of feeling.

Edward Young's satire, *The Universal Passion,* had just appeared, and been received with more enthusiasm than any thing published since Pope's own early successes. This alone would have been powerful inducement to Pope's emulous temper. Swift was finishing *Gulliver's Travels,* and came over to England in 1726. The survivors of the Scriblerus Club — Swift, Pope, Arbuthnot, and Gay — resumed their old amusement of parodying and otherwise ridiculing bad writers, especially bad writers in the Whig interest. Two volumes of their *Miscellanies in Prose and Verse* were published in 1727. A third volume appeared in 1728, and a fourth was added in 1732. According to Pope's own history of the *Dunciad, an Heroic Poem in Three Books,* which first appeared on the 28th of May 1728, the idea of it grew out of this.

Among the *Miscellanies* was a "Treatise of the Bathos or the Art of Sinking in Poetry," in which poets were classified, with illustrations, according to their eminence in the various arts of debasing instead of elevating their subject. No names were mentioned, but the specimens of bathos were assigned to various letters of the alphabet, which, the authors boldly asserted, were taken at random. But no sooner was the treatise published than the scribblers proceeded to take the letters to themselves, and in revenge to fill the newspapers with the most abusive falsehoods and scurrilities they could devise. This gave Pope the opportunity he had hoped for, and provided him with an excuse for the personalities of the *Dunciad,* which had been in his mind as early as 1720.

Among the most prominent objects of his satire were Lewis Theobald, Colley Cibber, John Dennis, Richard Bentley, Aaron Hill and Bernard Lintot, who, in spite of his former relations with Pope, was now classed with the piratical Edmund Curll.

The book was published with the greatest precautions. It was anonymous, and professed to be a reprint of a Dublin edition. When the success of the poem was assured, it was republished in 1729, and a copy was presented to the king by Sir Robert Walpole. Names took the place of initials, and a defence of the satire, written by Pope himself, but signed by his friend William Cleland, was printed as "A letter to the Publisher." Various indexes, notes and particulars of the attacks on Pope made by the different authors satirized were added. To avoid any danger of prosecution, the copyright was assigned to Lord Oxford, Lord Bathurst and Lord Burlington, whose position rendered them practically unassailable.

We may admit that personal spite influenced Pope at least as much as disinterested zeal for the honour of literature, but in the dispute as to the comparative strength of these motives, a third is apt to be overlooked that was probably stronger than either. This was an unscrupulous elfish love of fun, and delight in the creations of a humorous imagination. Certainly to represent the *Dunciad* as the outcome of mere personal spite is to give an exaggerated idea of the malignity of Pope's disposition, and an utterly wrong impression of the character of his satire. He was not, except in rare cases, a morose, savage, indignant satirist, but airy and graceful in his malice, revengeful perhaps and excessively sensitive, but restored to good humour as he thought over his wrongs by the ludicrous conceptions with which he invested his adversaries.

The most unprovoked assault was on Richard Bentley, whom he satirized in the reconstruction and enlargement of the Dunciad made in the last years of his life at the instigation, it is said, of William Warburton. In the earlier editions the place of hero had been occupied by Lewis Theobald, who had ventured to criticize Pope's Shakespeare. In the edition which appeared in Pope's *Works* (1742), he was dethroned in favour of Colley Cibber, who had just written his *Letter from Mr Cibber to Mr Pope* inquiring into the motives that might induce him in his satyrical writings to be so frequently fond of Mr Cibber's name (1742). Warburton's name is attached to many new notes, and one of the preliminary dissertations by Ricardus Aristarchus on the hero of the poem seems to be by him.

The four epistles of the *Essay on Man* (1733) were also intimately connected with passing controversies. They belong to the same intellectual movement with Butler's *Analogy* — the effort of the 18th century to put religion on a rational basis. But Pope was not a thinker like Butler. The subject was suggested to him by Henry St John, Lord Bolingbroke, who had returned from exile in 1723, and was a fellow-member of the Scriblerus Club. Bolingbroke is said — and the statement is supported by the contents of his posthumous works — to have furnished most of the arguments. Pope's contribution to the controversy consisted in brilliant epigram and illustration.

In this didactic work, as in his *Essay on Criticism,* he put together on a sufficiently simple plan a series of happy sayings, separately elaborated, picking up the thoughts as he found them in miscellaneous reading and conversation, and trying only to fit them with perfect expression. His readers were too dazzled by the verse to be severely critical of the sense. Pope himself had not comprehended the drift of the arguments he had adopted from Bolingbroke, and was alarmed when he found that his poem was generally interpreted as an apology for the free-thinkers. Warburton is said to have qualified its doctrines as "rank atheism," and asserted that it was put together from the "worst passages of the worst authors." The essay was soon translated into the chief European languages, and in 1737 its orthodoxy was assailed by a Swiss professor, Jean Pierre de Crousaz, in *an Examen de l'essay de M. Pope sur l'homme.*

Warburton now saw fit to revise his opinion of Pope's abilities and principles — for what reason does not appear. In any case he now became as enthusiastic in his praise of Pope's orthodoxy and his genius as he had before been scornful, and proceeded to employ his unrivalled powers of sophistry in a defence of the orthodoxy of the conflicting and inconsequent positions adopted in the *Essay on Man*. Pope was wise enough to accept with all gratitude an ally who was so useful a friend and so dangerous an enemy, and from that time onward Warburton was the authorized commentator of his works.

The *Essay on Man* was to have formed part of a series of philosophic poems on a systematic plan. The other pieces were to treat of human reason, of the use of learning, wit, education and riches, of civil and ecclesiastical polity, of the character of women, &c. Of the ten epistles of the *Moral Essays,* the first four, written between 1731 and 1735, are connected with this scheme, which was never executed. There was much bitter, and sometimes unjust, satire in the *Moral Essays* and the *Imitations of Horace.*

In these epistles and satires, which appeared at intervals, he was often the mouthpiece of his political friends, who were all of them in opposition to Walpole, then at the height of his power, and Pope chose the object of his attacks from among the minister's adherents. Epistle III, "Of the Use of Riches," addressed to Allen Bathurst, Lord Bathurst, in 1732, is a direct attack on Walpole's methods of corruption, and on his financial policy in general; and the two dialogues (1738) known as the "Epilogue to the Satires," professedly a defence of satire, form an eloquent attack on the court. Pope was attached to the Prince of Wales's party, and he did not forget to insinuate, what was indeed the truth, that the queen had refused the prince her pardon on her deathbed. The "Epistle to Dr Arbuthnot" contains a description of his personal attitude towards the scribblers and is made to serve as a "prologue to the satires."

The gross and unpardonable insults bestowed on Lord Hervey and on Lady Mary Wortley Montagu in the first satire "to Mr Fortescue" provoked angry retaliation from both. The description of Timon's ostentatious villa in Epistle IV, addressed to the Earl of Burlington, was generally taken as a picture of Canons, the seat of John Brydges, duke of Chandos, one of Pope's patrons, and caused a great outcry, though in this case Pope seems to have been innocent of express allusion. Epistle II, addressed to Martha Blount, contained the picture of Atossa, which was taken to be a portrait of Sarah Jennings, Duchess of Marlborough. One of the worst imputations on Pope's character was that he left this passage to be published when he had in effect received a bribe of £1000 from the duchess of Marlborough for its suppression through the agency of Nathanael Hooke (d. 1763). As the passage eventually stood, it might be applied to Katherine, duchess of Buckingham, a natural daughter of James II. Pope may have altered it with the intention of diverting the satire from the original object.

He was scrupulously honest in money matters, and always independent in matters of patronage; but there is some evidence for this discreditable story beyond the gossip of Horace Walpole (*Works*, ed. P. Cunningham, i. cxliv.), though not sufficient to justify the acceptance it received by some of Pope's biographers. To appreciate fully the point of his allusions requires an intimate acquaintance with the political and social gossip of the time. But apart from their value as a brilliant strongly-coloured picture of the time Pope's satires have a permanent value as literature. It is justly remarked by Mark Pattison that "these Imitations are among the most original of his writings." The vigour and terseness of the diction is still unsurpassed in English verse.

Pope had gained complete mastery over his medium, the heroic couplet, before he used it to express his hatred of the political and social evils which he satirized. The elaborate periphrases and superfluous ornaments of his earlier manner, as exemplified in the *Pastorals* and the *Homer*, disappeared; he turned to the uses of verse in the ordinary language of conversation, differing from everyday speech only in its exceptional brilliance and point. It is in these satires that his best work must be sought, and by them that his position among English poets must be fixed. It was the *Homer* chiefly that Wordsworth and Coleridge had in their eye when they began the polemic against the "poetic diction" of the 18th century, and struck at Pope as the arch-corrupter.

They were historically unjust to Pope, who did not originate this diction, but only furnished the most finished examples of it. At the beginning of the 19th century Pope still had an ardent admirer in Byron, whose first satires are written in Pope's couplet. The much abused pseudo-poetic diction in substance consisted in an ambition to "rise above the vulgar style," to dress nature to advantage — a natural ambition when the arbiters of literature were people of fashion. If one compares Pope's "Messiah" or "Eloisa to Abelard," or an impassioned passage from the *Iliad,* with the originals that he paraphrased, one gets a more vivid idea of the consistence of pseudo-poetic diction than could be furnished by pages of analysis. But Pope merely made masterly use of the established diction of his time, which he eventually forsook for a far more direct and vigorous style. A passage from the *Guardian*, in which Philips was commended as against him, runs: "It is a nice piece of art to raise a proverb above the vulgar style and still keep it easy and unaffected. Thus the old wish, 'God rest his soul,' is very finely turned: —

Then gentle Sidney liv'd, the shepherd's friend,
Eternal blessings on his shade attend!

Pope would have despised so easy a metamorphosis as this at any period in his career, and the work of his coadjutors in the *Odyssey* may be distinguished by this comparative cheapness of material. Broome's description of the clothes-washing by Nausicaa and her maidens in the sixth book may be compared with the original as a luminous specimen. Pope's wit had won for him the friendship of many distinguished men, and his small fortune enabled him to meet them on a footing of independence. He paid long visits at many great houses, especially at Stanton Harcourt, the home of his friend Lord Chancellor Harcourt; at Oakley, the seat of Lord Bathurst; and at Prior Park, Bath, where his host was Ralph Allen. With the last-named he had a temporary disagreement owing to some slight shown to Martha Blount, but he was reconciled to him before his death.

He died on the 30th of May 1744, and he was buried in the parish church of Twickenham. He left the income from his property to Martha Blount till her death, after which it was to go to his half-sister Magdalen Rackett and her children. His unpublished MSS. were left at the discretion of Lord Bolingbroke, and his copyrights to Warburton.

If we are to judge Pope, whether as a man or as a poet, with human fairness, and not merely by comparison with standards of abstract perfection, there are two features of his times that must be kept steadily in view — the character of political strife in those days and the political relations of men of letters. As long as the succession to the Crown was doubtful, and political failure might mean loss of property, banishment or death, politicians, playing for higher stakes, played more fiercely and unscrupulously than in modern days, and there was no controlling force of public opinion to keep them within the bounds of common honesty. Hence the age of Queen Anne is preeminently an age of intrigue.

The government was almost as unsettled as in the early days of personal monarchy, and there was this difference — that it was policy rather than force upon which men depended for keeping their position. Secondly, men of letters were admitted to the inner circles of intrigue as they had never been before and as they have never been since. A generation later Walpole defied them, and paid the rougher instruments that he considered sufficient for his purpose in solid coin of the realm; but Queen Anne's statesmen, whether from difference of tastes or difference of policy, paid their principal literary champions with social privileges and honourable public appointments.

Hence men of letters were directly infected by the low political morality of the unsettled time. And the character of their poetry also suffered. The most prominent defects of the age — the lack of high and sustained imagination, the genteel liking for "nature to advantage dressed," the incessant striving after wit — were fostered, if not generated, by the social atmosphere.

Pope's own ruling passion was the love of fame, and he had no scruples where this was concerned. His vanity and his childish love of intrigue are seen at their worst in his petty manoeuvres to secure the publication of his letters during his lifetime. These intricate proceedings were unravelled with great patience and ingenuity by Charles Wentworth Dilke, when the false picture of his relations with his contemporaries, which Pope had imposed on the public, had been practically accepted for a century. Elizabeth Thomas, the mistress of Henry Cromwell, had sold Pope's early letters to Henry Cromwell to the bookseller Curll for ten guineas. These were published in Curll's *Miscellanea* in 1726 (dated 1727), and had considerable success.

This surreptitious publication seems to have suggested to Pope the desirability of publishing his own correspondence, which he immediately began to collect from various friends on the plea of preventing a similar clandestine transaction. The publication by Wycherley's executors of a posthumous volume of the dramatist's prose and verse furnished Pope with an excuse for the appearance of his own correspondence with Wycherley, which was accompanied by a series of unnecessary deceptions. After manipulating his correspondence so as to place his own character in the best light, he deposited a copy in the library of Edward, second earl of Oxford, and then he had it printed.

The sheets were offered to Curll by a person calling himself P. T., who professed a desire to injure Pope, but was no other than Pope himself. The copy was delivered to Curll in 1735 after long negotiations by an agent who called himself R. Smythe, with a few originals to vouch for their authenticity. P. T. had drawn up an advertisement stating that the book was to contain answers from various peers. Curll was summoned before the House of Lords for breach of privilege, but was acquitted, as the letters from peers were not in fact forthcoming. Difficulties then arose between Curll and P. T., and Pope induced a bookseller named Cooper to publish a *Narrative of the Method by which Mr Pope's Private Letters were procured by Edmund Curll, Bookseller* (1735).

These preliminaries cleared the way for a show of indignation against piratical publishers and a "genuine" edition of the *Letters of Mr Alexander Pope* (1737, fol. and 4to). Unhappily for Pope's reputation, his friend Caryll, who died before the publication, had taken a copy of Pope's letters before returning them. This letter-book came to light in the middle of the 19th century, and showed the freedom which Pope permitted himself in editing. The correspondence with Lord Oxford, preserved at Longleat, afforded further evidence of his tortuous dealings. The methods he employed to secure his correspondence with Swift were even more discreditable. The proceedings can only be explained as the measures of a desperate man whose maladies seem to have engendered a passion for trickery. They are related in detail by Elwin in the introduction to vol. i. of Pope's *Works*.

A man who is said to have "played the politician about cabbages and turnips," and who "hardly drank tea without a stratagem," was not likely to be straightforward in a matter in which his ruling passion was concerned. Against Pope's petulance and "general love of secrecy and cunning" have to be set, in any fair judgment of his character, his exemplary conduct as a son, the affection with which he was regarded in his own circle of intimates, and many well-authenticated instances of genuine and continued kindliness to persons in distress.

Chapter 11

The War of the Spanish Succession Criticism

Pope is not only the foremost literary figure of his age, but the representative man of a system or style of writing which for a hundred years before and after him pervaded English poetry. The writers in this style are sometimes spoken of as the "school of Pope." But the title is a misnomer. A school coexists along with other schools from which it is distinguished by some special characteristics; all the contemporaneous schools taken together bearing the common and more general stamp of their age. During the period now under review, which extends, speaking roughly, from the Restoration to the French Revolution, the whole of English literary effort, but especially poetical effort, has one aim and is governed by one principle.

This is the desire to attain perfection of form; a sense of the beauty of literary composition as such. It was the rise within the vernacular language of that idea, which impregnating the Latin language as written and spoken in the fifteenth century had produced the revived, neo-latin literature of the Renaissance. Pope himself (Sat and Ep. 5), in describing this "manner," spoke of it as French, and attributed it to the imitation of French fashions introduced into England at the Restoration.

We conquer'd France, but felt our captive's charms;
Her arts victorious triumph'd o'er our arms;
Britain to soft refinements less a foe,
Wit grew polite, and numbers learn'd to flow.

De Quincey (Works, vol. 9) expatiates upon the

deficiencies of this explanation of a revolution in literary taste. Certainly the court of Louis XIV exercised a great influence in all matters of taste. But this influence of fashion ceased when the ascendency of France was broken by the war of the Spanish succession, while the direction which had been impressed upon English poetry continued to dominate it till towards the close of the eighteenth century.

A better denomination for the period of our literature which extends from the Restoration to the French Revolution is "the classical period." And this is not to be taken to mean that English writers now imitated the Greek and Latin writers, or consciously formed themselves upon classical models, as the Latinists of the Renaissance imitated Cicero and Virgil. English writers had begun to perceive that there was such an art as the art of writing; that it was not enough to put down words upon paper anyhow, provided they conveyed your meaning.

They found that sounds were capable of modulation, and that pleasure could be given by the arrangement of words, as well as instruction conveyed by their import. The public ear was touched by this new harmony, and began imperatively to demand its satisfaction and from that moment the rude volubility of the older time seemed to it as the gabble of savages. A poem was no longer to be a story told with picturesque imagery, but was to be a composition in symmetry and keeping.

A thought or a feeling was not to be blurted out in the first words that came, but was to be matured by reflection and reduced to its simplest expression. Condensation, terseness, neatness, finish — all qualities hitherto unheard of in English — had to be studied. It was found to be possible to please by your manner as well as by your matter. And having been shown to be possible, it became necessary. No writer who neglected the graces of style could gain acceptance by the public.

This fastidiousness of the public ear required on the part of writers greatly increased labour. It was no longer possible to take a sheet of paper, and write out your thoughts as fast as the pen would move. "The mob of gentlemen who wrote with ease" were distanced in the race.

It was evident that, under the new standard thus set up, the prize would be to him who should be willing to take most trouble about his style. Pope was willing. As a boy he took as his life's lesson the advice given him by "knowing Walsh," who used to tell him "there was one way left of excelling; for though we had several great poets, we never had any one great poet that was correct; and desired me to make that my study and aim." De Quincey, misconstruing Walsh's meaning, has been at the pains so show that Pope's verses abound in grammatical incorrectnesses. "The language," he says, "does not realise the idea; it simply suggests or hints it." That conveyance by suggestion, instead of a perfect and plenary deliverance, is just what Pope aimed at, and what Walsh inculcated, though he may not have chosen the very best word for what he meant.

Pope at once took the lead in the race of writers because he took more pains than they. He laboured day and night so form himself for his purpose, that viz. of becoming a writer of finished verse. To improve his mind, to enlarge his view of the world, to store up knowledge — these were things unknown to him. Any ideas, any thoughts, such as custom, chance, society or sect may suggest, are good enough, but each idea must be turned over till it has been reduced to its neatest and most epigrammatic expression.

If this definition of the literary aim which dominated all writing during the hundred years which followed 1660 be just, it follows from it that the period would be more favourable to prose than to poetry. What in fact came to pass was that a compromise was effected between poetry and prose, and the leading writers adopted as the most telling form of utterance prosaic verse, metre without poetry. It is by courtesy that the versifiers of this century from Dryden to Churchill are styled poets, seeing that the literature they have bequeathed us wants just that element of inspired feeling, which is present in the feeblest of the Elizabethans.

But if these versifiers are not poets in the noblest sense of the term, it does not follow that what they produced is destitute of value. In the romantic reaction at the beginning of this century, the worthlessness of eighteenth-century poetry was part of the revolutionary creed. Sheer lawlessness was then admired, while labour was disdained as the badge of an unimaginative and artificial school. The sounder judgment of a riper period of criticism can now do justice to the writers of our classical period.

What they had not got we know well enough. They wanted inspiration, lofty sentiment, the heroic soul, chivalrous devotion, the inner eye of faith — above all, love and sympathy. They could not mean greatly. But such meaning as they had they laboured to express in the neatest, most terse and pointed form which our language is capable of. If not poets they were literary artists. They showed that a couplet can do the work of a page, and a single line produce effects which in the infancy of writing would require sentences.

Of these masters of literary craft Pope is the most consummate. In two directions, in that of condensing and pointing his meaning, and in that of drawing the utmost harmony of sound out of the couplet, Pope carried versification far beyond the point at which it was when he took it up. Historical parallels are proverbially misleading. Yet the analogy between what Virgil did for the Latin hexameter as he received it from Lucretius, and Pope's maturing the ten-syllable couplet which he found as Dryden left it, is sufficiently close to be of use in aiding us to realise Pope's merit. Because, after Pope, his trick of versification became common property, and "every warbler had his tune by heart," we are apt to overlook the merit of the first invention.

But epigrammatic force and musical flow are not the sole elements of Pope's reputation. The matter which he worked up into his verse has a permanent value, and is indeed one of the most precious heirlooms which the eighteenth century has bequeathed us. And here we must distinguish between Pope when he attempts general themes, and Pope when he draws that which he knew, viz. the social life of his own day. When in the Pastorals he writes of natural beauty, in the Essay on

Criticism he lays down the rules of writing, in the Essay on Man he versifies Leibnitzian optimism, he does not rise above the herd of eighteenth-century writers, except in so far as his skill of language is more accomplished than theirs. The Rape of the Lock and The Dunciad have a little more interest, because they treat of contemporary manners. But even in these poems, because the incidents are trivial and the personages contemptible, Pope is not more than pretty in The Rape of the Lock, and forcible, where force is ludicrously misplaced, in The Dunciad.

It is where he comes to describe the one thing which he knew, and about which he felt sympathy and antipathy, viz. the court and town of his time, in the Moral Essays, and the Satires and Epistles, that Pope found the proper material on which to lay out his elaborate workmanship. And even in these capital works we must distinguish between Pope's general theorems and his particular portraits. Where he moralises, or deduces general principles, he is superficial, second-hand, and onesided as the veriest scribbler. For example: in the splendid lines on the Duke of Wharton (Mor. Ess. 1.174) we must separate the childish theory of "the ruling passion" from the telling accumulation of epigram on epigram which follows under that spurious rubric.

Or again, we might instance his Epistle to Augustus (Ep. 5) sparkling with lines of wit and pregnant sense, and yet offering as our literary history the grotesque theory, that the French style, which came in with the Restoration, was a consequence of the conquest of France in the fifteenth century.

In short, Pope, wherever he recedes from what was immediately close to him, the manners, passions, prejudices, sentiments, of his own day, has only such merit — little enough — which wit divorced from truth can have. He is at his best only where the delicacies and subtle felicities of his diction are employed to embody some transient phase of contemporary feeling. Pope has small knowledge of books. Though he was, as Sir W. Hamilton says, "a curious reader," he read for style, not for facts. Of history, of science, of nature, of anything except "the town" he knows nothing. He just shares the ordinary prejudices of the ordinary "wit" of his day. He was a Tory-Catholic, like any other Tory-Catholic of George II's day.

His sentiments reflect the social medium in which he lived. The complex web of society, with its indefinable shades, its minute personal affinities and repulsions, is the world in which Pope lived and moved, and which he has drawn in a few vivid lines, with the keenness and intensity of which there is nothing in our literature that can compare. Clarendon's portraits in his gallery of characters are more complete and discriminating, and infinitely more candid.

But they do not flash the personage, or the situation, upon the imagination, and fix it in the memory, as one of Pope's incisive lines does. Like all the greatest poets, Pope is individual and local. He can paint with his full power only what he sees. When he attempts abstract truth, general themes, past history, his want of knowledge makes itself felt in feeble and distorted views.

The first production of Pope to appear in print was his Pastorals, published 1709, when the author was twenty-one, but written some years earlier. As the work of a youth of seventeen they are a marvellous feat of melodious versification. In any other respect they are only worthy of mention as already exemplifying the false taste which Pope never got rid of when he attempted any other theme than manners.

Of this false taste his Messiah is an elaborate specimen. This poem is an adaptation of Virgil's fourth Eclogue, Pollio, to Christ, grafting upon the lines of the Latin poet the images supplied by the prophecies of Isaiah. The ingenuity with which the double imitation is carried through is only surpassed by the mastery shown over the melody of the couplet, and the exhibition of a complete poetical vocabulary. These brilliant qualities carried by storm the admiration of Pope's contemporaries, and continued to command the homage of the eighteenth century down to Johnson.

Language experience, enforced by the precept and example of Wordsworth, makes our age too keenly feel that the pathos and sublimity of the Hebrew prophet are destroyed by the artificial embroidery with which Pope has overlaid them. Pope's Messiah reads to us like a sickly paraphrase, in which all the majesty of the original is dissipated. "Righteousness" becomes "dewy nectar"; "sheep" are the "fleecy care"; the call to Jerusalem to "arise and shine" is turned into an invocation to "exalt her tow'ry head."

The "fir-tree and box-tree" of Isaiah are "the spiry fir and shapely box." In his translation of the prediction "the sucking child shall play on the hole of the asp, and the weaned child shall put his hand on the cockatrice den," Pope makes the cockatrice a "crested basilisk," and the asp "a speckled snake"; they have both scales of a "green lustre," and a "forky tongue," and with this last the "smiling infant shall innocently play." "The leopard," says Isaiah, "shall lie down with the kid, and the young lion and the fatling together, and a little child shall lead them"; Pope could not leave this exquisite picture undecorated, and with him "boys in flowery bands the tiger lead."

The alternative is an example of the justice of De Quincey's observation that "the Arcadia of Pope's age was the spurious Arcadia of the opera theatre." (Elwin.)

The Essay on Criticism appeared in 1711. This is a didactic poem of which the remote prototype is Horace's Ars poetica, and the immediate, Boileau's Art poetique. It differs from these models in its subject, which is the Art of Criticism. To Dr. Johnson this production appeared "to display such extent of comprehension, such nicety of distinction, such acquaintance with mankind, and such knowledge both of ancient and modern learning, as are not often attained by the matured age and the longest experience."

This verdict of Johnson may be cited to show the great advance which criticism has made in England in the course of a century. We should now say that the precepts of Pope's Essay are conventional truisms, the ordinary rules of composition which may be found in all school manuals, and which we taught to boys as part of their prosody. "The Essay," says De Quincey, "is a mere versification, like a metrical multiplication table, of commonplaces the most mouldy with which criticism has baited its rattraps." It required very little reading of the French textbooks to find the maxims which Pope has here strung together. But he has dressed them so neatly, and turned them out with such sparkle and point, that these truisms have acquired a weight not their own, and they circulate as proverbs among us in virtue of their pithy form rather than their truth.

They exemplify his own line "What oft was thought, but ne'er so well expressed." Pope told Spence that he had "gone through all the best critics," specifying Quintilian, Rapin and Le Bossu. But whatever trouble he took in collecting what to say, his main effort is expended upon how to say it. The Essay on Criticism abounds in those striking couplets which have lodged in all our memories, and given their last and abiding shape to dicta which have been extant in substance since literature began. A good example of this art is supplied by the couplet which has just been quoted from;

True wit is nature to advantage dressed;
What oft was thought, but ne'er to well expressed.

which is Pope's compressed form of the following prose of Boileau; "Qu'est-ce qu'une pensee neuve, brillante, extraordinaire? Ce n'est point comme se le persuadent les ignorants, une pensee que personne n'a jamais eue, ni du avoir. C'est au contraire une pensee qui a du venir a tout Ie monde, et que quelqu'un s'avise Ie premier d'exprimer. Un bon mot n'est bon mot qu'en ce qu'il dit une chose que chacun pensoit, et qu'il la dit d'une maniere vive, fine, et nouvelle."

But though the Essay abounds with sparkle and point and memorable lines, it is very far from being composed throughout of nothing but such. Besides the general fault, which pervades all Pope's longer efforts, of want of coherent texture and consecutiveness of argument, the Essay on Criticism offers too many weak lines, obscure expressions, and monotonous rhymes. Negligences of versification, such as no piece of Pope's composition is entirely free from, abound in the Essay. One instance of this slovenliness is the want of variety in his endings. There are twelve couplets rhyming to "wit," and ten rhyming to "sense."

Unhappy wit, like most mistaken things,
Atones not for that envy which it brings.

"Mistaken things" here means "things wrongly taken by others," which is not the natural sense of the words; and "atones" stands for "compensates." "But sense survived when merry jests were passed." It requires explanation that "were passed" here means "had passed away."

Critics...
Form short ideas, and offend in arts
As most in manners, from a love to parts.

In this one couplet are three expressions, "short ideas," "offend in arts," and "love to parts," the meaning of which has to be guessed, or gathered from the context; it is not apparent on the face of the words used. In some styles of poetry enigmatical expression is not a fault; in an Aeschylean chorus it is of the essence of the charm that the revelations should be shrouded in clouds. But Pope's verse, like French prose, is constructed on the principle of being immediately intelligible; the moment it is not so, its "raison d'etre" is gone.

The Rape of the Lock is a mock-heroic poem, the style of which was suggested to Pope by Boileau's Lutrin. Pope followed his model in entitling his work "An heroicomical poem," the epithet employed by Boileau its the 1709 edition of his Lutrin. It was founded upon an incident which had caused great commotion in the circle of Catholic families in which Pope, though not himself a member of it, had friends. Lord Petre, in a moment of youthful frolic, had cut off a lock of hair from Miss Arabella Fermor's head, a liberty which was keenly resented, and had caused a violent quarrel between the families.

Mr. Caryll, a Sussex squire, nephew to the Mr. John Caryll who had been Secretary to Mary, James II's Queen, suggested to Pope to write a poem, which by treating the incident playfully, might induce the offended family to take a more lenient view of what they regarded as an outrage. This was the motive of the first draft of the poem, as it was printed in Tonson's Miscellany, 1712, in two cantos, and no more than 330 lines. This first sketch was written off in a fortnight, but its author, pleased with the success of his work, elaborated it afterwards, and enlarged it especially by the introduction of what he calls the "machinery," or the agency of supernatural beings of the fairy species, whom he calls "sylphs." It is universally admitted that the later additions, and this invention especially, are great improvements, thus forming an exception to the rule that a poet should never recast, or supplement, a piece which he has turned out well in the first instance.

The heroine of the poem, Belinda, is Miss Fermor; the Baron is Lord Petre; Thalestris is Mrs. Morley; Sir Plume is Mrs. Morley's brother, Sir George Brown of Keddingon. Pope obtained permission to dedicate the poem to Miss Fermor; but notwithstanding that he takes care to tell her that "Belinda resembles her in nothing but in beauty," the lady was more offended than flattered by the representation given of her. Sir George Brown was indignant at being made to talk nothing but nonsense. In bringing about its professed aim, the reconciliation of the two families, the poem was entirely unsuccessful.

But with the public it was otherwise. On its first publication Addison pronounced it a delicious little thing; "merum sal." Criticism the most hostile to Pope, of which there has been abundance in the modern reaction against his influence, has agreed to spare the Rape. Macaulay pronounces it his best poem. De Quincey, who never spares Pope when he is weak, goes beyond Macaulay, and declares it "the most exquisite monument of playful fancy that universal literature offers." The Rape of the Lock, writes Hazlitt, "is the most exquisite specimen of filigree work ever invented.

It is made of gauze and silver spangles. The most glittering appearance is given to everything; to paste, pomatum, billets-doux, and patches. Airs, languid airs breathe around the atmosphere is perfumed with affectation. A toilet is described with the solemnity of an altar raised to the goddess of vanity, and the history of a silver bodkin is given with all the pomp of heraldry. No pains are spared, no profusion of ornament, no splendour of poetic diction to set off the meanest things....

It is the triumph of insignificance, the apotheosis of foppery and folly. It is the perfection of the mock-heroic." And Professor Conington thinks "there can be little to say about a poem so exquisite in its peculiar style of art as to make the task of searching for faults almost hopeless, that of commending beauties simply impertinent."

Such warmth of encomium as this is at least testimony to the admiration which the skill of the poet can still excite in the reader. But it is criticism which touches the workmanship rather than the work. Pope's execution is so clever as always to charm us even when his subject is most devoid of interest. The secret of the peculiar fascination of The Rape of the Lock lies, I believe, not merely in the art and management, but in the fact that here, for the first time, Pope is writing of that which he knew, of the life he saw and the people he lived with.

For Windsor Forest, though he lived in it, he had no eyes; but a drawing-room, a fop, and a belle, these were the objects which had struck his young fancy when he emerged from the linen-draper's villa, and he had studied them. About these things he can be real and truthful; when he writes of Abelard and Heloise he is making believe, he is an actor trying to think himself into his part. Only in his Satires and Epistles and in the characters of his Moral Essays will he again succeed in hitting upon congenial matter on which to lay out his extraordinary power of versification.

Nor is the reflection of social life and manners which the Rape offers confined to superficial forms only. The most intimate sentiments of the time find their representation here. As an instance we may point to the mean estimation of women. Contempt veiled under the show of deference, a mockery of chivalry, its form without its spirit, — this is the attitude assumed towards women by the poet in this piece. "The world of fashion is displayed in its most gorgeous and attractive hues, and everywhere the emptiness is visible beneath the outward splendour. The beauty of Belinda, the details of her toilet, her troops of admirers, are all set forth with unrivalled grace and fascination, and all bear the impress of vanity and vexation. Nothing can exceed the art with which the satire is blended with the pomp, mocking without disturbing the unsubstantial gewgaw. The double vein is kept up with sustained skill in the picture of the outward charms and the inward frivolity of women.

With varying vanities from every part
They shift the moving toyshop of their heart;

this is the tone throughout. Their hearts are toyshops. They reverse the relative importance of things; the little with them is great, and the great little. (Elwin.) This feeling towards women is not the poet's idiosyncrasy; here he is but the representative of his age. The degradation of woman in England does not date from the Restoration. It was complete before the Commonwealth, and is aptly symbolised in the behaviour of James I, who compelled all ladies to kneel on being presented to him. But the combination of the forms of chivalrous devotion with the reality of cynical contempt, was the peculiar tone of manners which came in with the court of Charles II, and gradually spread downwards through the lower social strata. The poem in our literature which gives the most finished representation of this sentiment is The Rape of the Lock.

It was to the translation of Homer, undertaken as a commercial speculation, that Pope owed, more than to anything else he produced, the great reputation he attained in his lifetime. The verdict of later times has reversed the decision of an age little versed in Greek, and whose artificial manners were alien from the primeval simplicity and savagery of Homer. Pope translated from the Latin version, from the French of Dacier, from the English of Chapman. But it was less his ignorance of Greek, than his theory of poetical expression, which led him astray.

His solicitude is entirely spent upon the words he is using, and not upon the thing he is describing. He introduced ornaments which are not only foreign, but false and out of keeping. He reproduced neither the naivete or the dignity of the original. Pope's moonlight scene provoked Wordsworth's remark that "the eye of the poet had never been steadily fixed upon its object," and that "it shows to what a low state knowledge of the most obvious and important phenomena had sunk." Yet no selection from Pope would be complete which did not offer a specimen of the Homer. We give the moonlight scene from the 8th Book, partly for the sake of comparison with Chapman's rendering of the same lines, (see above, vol. i.p. 519), and also because it is a striking example of both the faults and excellences of the translation. We have in these few lines more than average infidelity to the original; we have unhomeric embroidery, such as "refulgent lamp of night"; but we have at the same time twenty-four lines (eleven in the Greek) of finished versification, the rapid, facile, and melodious flow of which, concentrating all the felicities of Pope's higher style, has never been surpassed in English poetry.

The translation of Homer occupied Pope during the ten best years of his life. The Odyssey was finished in 1725, and Pope turned to very different work, the composition of The Dunciad. The Dunciad is a personal satire, or lampoon, directed against the small authors of the day, who are bespattered with much mud and little wit, without any pretence of disguise, and under their own names. The Dunciad has been the parent of a numerous progeny, The Scribleriad, The Baviad, The Pursuits of Literature, English Bards and Scotch Reviewers, all of which have had much vogue in their day, and lost their savour when the generation they libelled has passed away.

It must not be concealed that critics of reputation have spoken with approbation of this amalgam of dirt, ribaldry, and petty spite. De Quincey has allowed himself to say that The Dunciad is Pope's "greatest work." Thackeray, who had no toleration for similar offences when Swift was the offender, thought that the conclusion of The Dunciad "shows the author to be the equal of all poets of all times"; and Conington considers the poem as "unquestionably a very great satire." It certainly shows Pope's peculiar skill as an artist in its perfection. He has now (1727) attained a complete mastery over the couplet, and can compel it to do the work he requires of it. To the literary historian the value of The Dunciad is great, as a chapter of contemporary life, a record of small celebrities, otherwise lost to fame. But of its absolute merit as a poem, a just taste must agree with Taine (Litt. Angl. t. 4), that "seldom has so much talent been expended to produce so much ennui."

The motive of the satire is not the desire of the moral reformer to improve mankind, but the rancour and malevolence of literary jealousy. And against whom is this petty irritation felt? Against feeble journalists, brutal pamphleteers, starving rhymesters, a crew of hackney authors, bohemians of ink and paper below literature. To sting and wound these unfortunates gave Pope pleasure as he sate, meditating stabs, in his elegant villa, the resort of the rich and the noble! By attacking these, he lowers himself to their level. The first poet of the age — of the century — chooses to hand himself down to posterity as bandying scurrilities with the meanest scribblers hired defamers, the banditti of the printing-office, ready at the shortest notice to deliver half a crown's worth of slander.

To be even with these miserable outcasts Pope condescended to employ one of the worst of them, Savage, as a spy and informer to bring him gossip from their haunts. When every other taunt fails him Pope can gibbet the poverty of these unsuccessful authors as a crime, and turn them into ridicule for wanting a dinner. The superfluous vehemence with which he rails against these insignificant enemies betrays the hollowness of the pretence that the satire was aimed not at individuals, but at the spirit of dullness or stupid conservatism. Of Pope's ignorance of everything, except society and the art of versifying, The Dunciad offers one signal instance.

The first scholar in Europe, one possessing a genius for criticism to which philologians of all countries still pay admiring homage, was an Englishman, and a contemporary of Pope. Pope looked on Richard Bentley but knew him not. The lines (included in our selection) in which the great critic is quizzed, are a typical specimen of the fatal flaw in Pope's writings, viz. that the workmanship is not supported by the matter; a palpable falsehood, is enshrined in immortal lines.

The composition of The Dunciad had revealed to Pope

where his true strength lay, in blending personalities with moral reflection. During the next decade, 1730-40, he confined himself to the one style of composition upon which his reputation as an English poet must rest, and in which he has never had a rival. The pieces which appear in his collected works under the various titles of Moral Essays, Essay on Man, Epistle to Dr. Arbuthnot, Imitations of Horace, Epilogue to the Satires, were brought out singly at various time during these ten years.

The most celebrated of these poems are the four epistles addressed to Lord Bolingbroke, and known by the collective title of the Essay on Man. It is a didactic or argumentative poem, not on Man, as the title bears, but a theodicee or vindication of the ways of Providence.

The view attempted to be presented is that of Leibnitzian optimism; the end of the universe is the general good of the whole; it was impossible to realise this without admitting partial evil. Man is not the end of creation, but only one in a graduated scale of beings; it is his pride which leads him to complain when he finds that everything has not been ordered for his benefit.

The reasoning of the Essay on Man is feeble, the philosophy either trite or inconsistent, or obscure. But the less the intrinsic value of the argument, the more is our admiration excited by the literary skill and brilliant execution displayed in the management. The particular illustrations, the episodes and side-lights, always sparkle with wit, and are sometimes wants with feeling, when the main thesis is jejune and frigid. "Whilst Pope frequently wastes his skill in gilding refuse, he is really most sensitive to the noblest sentiments of his contemporaries, and when he has good materials to work upon, his verse glows with unusual fervour." (Leslie Stephen.) Ruskin points to the couplet

Never elated, while one man's oppressed;
Never dejected whilst another's blessed

as "the most complete, concise, and lofty expression of moral temper existing in English words." "If the Essay on Man were shivered into fragments, it would not lose its value for it is precisely its details which constitute its moral as well as literary beauties." (A. W. Ward.)

The Moral Essays, from which our next specimen is taken, consist of five epistles composed at different times, and placed in the works under a common title. Of these the same may be said as of the Essay on Man, that the ethical doctrine is not worthy of the exquisite workmanship. Our extract is from the first epistle, and includes the celebrated character of Philip Lord Wharton, a piece of portraiture which rank, with those of Addison, the Duchess of Marlborough, Lord Hervey, and the death-bed of Villiers Duke of Buckingham. They are masterpieces of English versification, medals cut with such sharp outlines and such vigour of hand that they have lost none of their freshness by lapse of time. "When the poet engraves one of these figures, his compendious imagery, the surprises of his juxtaposition, the sustained and multiplied antitheses, the terse texture of each line, the incessant shocks from the play of his eloquence directed and concentrated continually upon one point, from these things the memory receives an impression which it never loses." (Taine.)

Pope's peculiar powers found their most perfect development in the pieces, which in the collected works are entitled Satires and Epistles of Horace Imitated. Casually suggested by Bolingbroke in the course of conversation, and calling themselves an imitation, these "satires and epistles" are the most original of Pope's writings, and the most natural and spontaneous outcome of his genius.

These pieces, nine in number, including a Prologue, and two Epistles, form a total of some 2000 lines, and were the product of the four years 1735-8, and therefore of Pope's meridian period between his fortieth and fiftieth year. The ferocity of Pope's invective and the malice of his antipathies are here subdued, and though the coarser horse-laugh of the old time breaks out every now and then, yet on the whole the finer play of sarcasm and witty innuendo has taken the place of hard names and slander.

The Epistle to Dr. Arbuthnot, or Prologue to the Satires may be singled out as Pope's most characteristic piece. We give it entire in our selections. It contains the two famous portraits, that of Lord Hervey (Sporus) and that of Addison (Atticus). The libel, for such it is, on Lard Hervey cannot be excused even by the rancour of political party.

This accomplished nobleman was Vice-Chamberlain in the court of George II, a position easy enough to a mere fribble, but which was sure to mark out a man of parts and wit such as Lord Hervey, as the object of hatred to the tory and jacobite opposition. Even as art, Pope must be considered in this sketch to have failed from overcharging his canvas with odious and disgusting images. Yet "it is impossible not to admire, however we may condemn, the act by which acknowledged wit, beauty and gentle manners, the Queen's favour, and even a valetudinary diet are travestied into the most odious defects and offences." (Croker.)

The satire on Addison, in a more refined style, but not less unjust in fact, had been written twenty years before, during Addison's lifetime. Pope regarded the piece with the affection with which an author regards the product of much time and labour; and he had meditated each stab in this finished lampoon for years. Having printed it separately in 1727, he now finally adapted it into this Prologue to the Satires, only suppressing the real name, but not concealing it under the thin disguise of "Atticus." The art of these malignant lines is much greater than that of those on Lord Hervey. Pope here not only avoids any images which were in themselves offensive, but allows his victim many virtues and accomplishments.

Chapter 12

Epistle to Bathurst and the Meaning of Finance

A large amount of recent scholarly and critical writing on the various relationships between economics and literature in the late seventeenth and early eighteenth centuries has been based on the notion that financial innovations in the late seventeenth century precipitated anxiety about the form and nature of linguistic exchanges such as the writing and reading of poetry.

The general thesis of such work is that the shift from fixed value in land to unstable and fluctuating value in paper money, stocks, and government bonds had an effect on, even a corollary in, language: linguistic signs could no longer be presumed to have a fixed referent because, just as the referents of signs in financial transactions may rise or fall in value at any time, the referent of a linguistic sign may vary and alter.

Such a thesis is often combined with a recognition of the rise of the literary market place, in order to demonstrate the newly closer connection between economic and literary transactions: words themselves are now the objects of trade and even speculation. I want to suggest that Alexander Pope is aware of the instability of value, not in new financial practices alone, but also in the idea of value itself, and that this extends to his awareness of linguistic value. Instability, however, is not meaninglessness, and Pope is concerned to show how instability of value becomes meaningful. In short, I believe the increasingly large literature surrounding eighteenth-century poetry and economics is founded on a false premise about the nature of language, literary language in particular, in relation to economy, and that it is precisely the way in which this premise is exposed as false in the Epistle to Bathurst that makes it such a good poem.

Early on in the Epistle Pope presents his readers with a crucial and memorable turn in his argument. He has been arguing that "What Nature wants, commodious Gold bestows," suggesting all the while that the benefits of gold are meager in comparison to the corruption it brings. Eventually, gold "bribes a Senate, and the Land's betray'd" (line 34).

Pope then seems to indulge in a form of nostalgia for older types of exchange, predating the valuation of everything in terms of gold, as this would make corruption physically more difficult.

Oh! that such bulky Bribes as all might see, Still, as of old, incumber'd Villainy! In vain may Heroes fight, and Patriots rave; If secret Gold saps on from knave to knave. Could France or Rome divert our brave designs, With all their brandies or with all their wines? What could they more than Knights and Squires confound, Or water all the Quorum ten miles round? (lines 35-42)

A list of examples furthers the condemnation of gold, until a peak is reached. Blest paper-credit! last and best supply! That lends Corruption lighter wings to fly! Gold imp'd by thee, can compass hardest things, Can pocket States, can fetch or carry Kings; A single leaf shall waft an Army o'er, Or ship off Senates to a distant Shore; A leaf, like Sibyl's, scatter to and fro Our fates and fortunes, as the winds shall blow: Pregnant with thousands flits the Scrap unseen, And silent sells a King or buys a Queen. (lines 69-78)

The ease that paper money and credit bring to transactions is lamentable, as it makes the corruption and alienation of civic duty that is possible in any economic medium less open to detection. Paper credit is variable, scattered like the leaves of classical prophecy, and probably to be trusted only as far. It is associated with the feminine and the grotesque: the scrap of paper is not just pregnant, but pregnant with thousands, its fecundity monstrous. Wind and flight are prominent:

corruption flies; armies are wafted; leaves, fates, and fortunes blow; and scraps flit.

Paper credit, particularly on a public scale, introduces a state of uncertainty and incomprehension into the world, where established forms of government can be altered or changed at once and the people of a nation are never certain of their allegiances, as they are no longer obliged to a person or an institution, but to a credit slip.

This passage illustrates thoroughly the thesis that Pope was staunchly opposed to the financial innovations that took place under William III, against whom and his Hanoverian followers much of the invective of the passage could be directed.

It illustrates also Pope's distrust of paper credit, its association with feminine and dangerously variable characters and modes of understanding one's place in the world. It also suggests, in the preceding argument, that there was a time when things were better, when values and allegiances, fates and fortunes were somehow fixed. It might be added that Pope's tightly controlled couplets attempt to fix what has been rendered unstable by financial and political events, to give words a recognizable place and meaning despite apparent flux.

Such a reading of the passages I have just quoted undeniably illustrates aspects of Pope's political commitments and his attitudes toward women and market economics. I would like to suggest, however, that this position of extreme uncertainty and nostalgia is belied by the tone and indeed the logic of the rest of the poem, and that Pope's position is more sophisticated and skeptical than this line of reading proposes. Paul J. Alpers recognizes that Pope's nostalgia is qualified: "Surely Pope does not say that tangible oxen are better for man than intangible paper."

The old form of bribe is no more acceptable or less harmful than the new: the bribe in kind could certainly inebriate a nation, and drunken "Knights and Squires" are no more capable of civic virtue than are rich knights and squires, probably even less. Pope suggests that any bribe is an abuse of value, and that there are no incorruptible or invariable values. I will begin by giving an account of the grounds for the imputation of simple nostalgia from which I am trying to clear Pope.

Earl R. Wasserman, in his exemplary commentary on the poem, states that "the subject of his [Pope's] satire is not the limited one of the tastelessness and social indelicacy of conspicuous consumption, but the whole corruptness of the new moneyed society he sees mushrooming about him and invading his values."

Chapter 13

Pope's Portrayal of Belinda and Her Society in The Rape of the Lock

In 'The Rape of the Lock' Alexander Pope (1688-1744) employs a mock-epic style to satirise the 'beau-monde' (fashionable world, society of the elite) of eighteenth century England. The richness of the poem, however, reveals more than a straightforward satirical attack. Alongside the criticism we can detect Pope's fascination with, and perhaps admiration for, Belinda and the society in which she moves.

Pope himself was not part of the 'beau-monde'. He knew the families on which the poem is based but his own parents, though probably comfortably off, were not so rich or of the class one would have to be in to move in Belinda's circle. He associated with learned men and poets, and there can have been little common ground between the company he kept at Will's Coffee House and those who frequented Hampton Court.

The incident at the centre of the poem is the Baron's theft of a lock of hair and the ensuing estrangement of two families. The opening lines of the poem introduce the reader to the satirical stance he is taking towards the society portrayed in the poem.

What dire Offence from am'rous Causes springs,
What mighty Contests rise from trivial Things, [I.1-2]

Pope suggests that they are taking a trivial incident too seriously, displaying an exaggerated sense of their own importance. Throughout the poem Pope continues to make this point through his use of the mock-epic style, which itself takes a trivial incident too seriously, and uses dispro-portionately grand language to describe an unworthy subject.

Belinda is belittled early in the poem by the revelation of Ariel [l.27-114], who tells her that part of her will survive after her death.

Think not, when Woman's transient Breath is fled,
That all her Vanities at once are dead:
Succeeding Vanities she still regards,
And tho' she plays no more, o'erloks the Cards.
Her Joy in gilded Chariots, when alive,
And Love of Ombre, after Death survive.
For when the Fair in all their Pride expire,
To their first Elements their Souls retire: [l.51-9]

We might expect this part, the deepest and most essential part of her being, the 'first Elements', to be her soul, but in Belinda's case it is her 'Vanities', her 'Joy in gilded Chariots' and her 'Love of *Ombre*', suggesting that her soul consists of nothing more that vanity and a love of pleasure.

Belinda's vanity is seem to take the form of religious devotion in the passage describing her morning toilette.

And now, unveil'd, the Toilet stands display'd,
Each Silver Vase in mystic Order laid.
First, rob'd in White, the Nymph intent adores
With Head uncover'd, the Cosmetic Pow'rs.
A heav'nly Image in the Glass appears,
To that she bends, to that her Eyes she rears; [l.121-6]

The ironic transposition of 'cosmic powers' in '*Cosmetic* Pow'rs' indicates the excessive value she attributes to her make-up, and bowing to her own image shows her devotion to her religion of narcissism. The passage is a mock version of the arming of the epic hero, her weaponry of cosmetics being ridiculed by the implicit comparison with the swords and shields of the epic hero. The passage includes a mock catalogue.

Here Files of Pins extend their shining Rows,
Puffs, Powders, Patches, Bibles, Billet-doux. [l.137-8]

This catalogue, echoing the catalogue of troops and weaponry found in epics, is one of the many indications of the jumbled values to be found in Belinda's society. The Bible is seen as a trinket for the adornment of her dressing table, along with the puffs and powders. The main force of this passage is satire, but alongside the satire Pope reveals a hint of fascination with the charm and delicacy of Belinda and her cosmetic devotion.

From each she nicely culls with curious Toil,
And decks the Goddess with the glitt'ring Spoil,
This Casket India's glowing Gems unlocks,
And all Arabia breathes from yonder Box. [l.131-4]

The rich imaginative vision in a passage such as this shows more than a desire to deprecate; it suggests that he too is at least partly fascinated by glitter. Pope appreciates the cosmetics in terms of the wider context of their origins and purpose, which Belinda could not do, and his tone reveals an attitude of amused, detached, fascination rather than straightforward disapproval.

In the second Canto Pope turns his mocking attention to the Baron. Pope's ridicule of the Baron is more severe, and the hint of admiration detected in his treatment of Belinda is absent.

In *The Aeneid* when Aeneas builds an altar Virgil is reminding us of his piety; his humility before divine powers. The Baron's worship is presented in terms of ridiculous excess. His altar is made from the profane escapist literature of romance, and his trophies, 'three Garters, half a Pair of Gloves' [ll.39] are ridiculous in comparison with the booty collected by conquering armies.

There is a parallel between the passages describing Belinda's toilette and the Baron's worship, each revealing the idealised image he/she holds of him/her self - Belinda as a goddess and the Baron as a hero - and it is through the absurdity of these ideals taken to extremes that Pope deflates them. Pope mocks the Baron not only as a poor parody of an epic hero but also for adopting an affected stance as a traditional courtly lover.

With tender Billet-doux he lights the Pyre,
And breathes three am'rous Sighs to raise the Fire,
Then prostrate falls, and begs with ardent Eyes
Soon to obtain, and long possess the Prize: [ll.41-4]

Pope is showing us a profane world in which a man worships the woman, and the woman worships herself. The ridicule achieved by the comparison between the struggle between Belinda and the Baron and an epic battle reaches its peak in the battles of Cantos 3 and 5.

In Canto 3 the glory and excitement of epic warfare is evoked, but the warriors are mere cards in a game of ombre. In Canto 5 the belle and the Baron tussle with the weapons of a snuff box and a bodkin, and Pope evokes scenes of farce and slapstick.

A Charge of Snuff the wily Virgin threw;
The Gnomes direct, to ev'ry Atome just,
The pungent Grains of titillating Dust.
Sudden, with starting Tears each Eye o'erflows,
And the high Dome re-echoes to his Nose.
Now meet thy Fate incens'd Belinda cry'd,
And drew a deadly Bodkin from her Side. [V.82-8]

In this dramatic scene we see supposedly civilised and sophisticated people behaving like squabbling children, and the violent emotions which can lurk under the dignified surface of the 'beau-monde' are revealed.

One of the effects of the whole poem is to show that the glitter and refinement of this world can be a veneer to cover the basest human motives.

Pope also shows us, in a mock version of the heroic underworld, the human casualties of the 'beau-monde'.

There Affectation with a sickly Mien
Shows in her Cheek the Roses of Eighteen,
Practis'd to Lisp, and hang the Head aside,
Faints into Airs, and languishes with Pride; [IV.31-4]

This is harsh criticism, but since we see these people in a context of suffering the response Pope demands seems to include as much pity as laughter. Although condemning the 'beau-monde' for its triviality and lack of proper moral values,

Pope is sensitive to the plight of the human beings caught up in its 'rat-race'.

Behind the ridicule which Pope achieves through his satire, we detect a depth of understanding in his attitude towards Belinda's predicament. Belinda's honour is very important for her future, even if in a broader context her idea of 'honour' is seen to mean little more than 'reputation'. Belinda has to steer a difficult path on which she has to attract prospective husbands yet not get a reputation as a coquette. The words of Thalestris represent a very real danger if she should veer too far on one direction.

Methinks already I your Tears survey,
Already hear the horrid things they say,
Already see you a degraded Toast,
And all your Honour in a Whisper lost! [IV.107-10]

The words of Clarissa show the danger of the other extreme:

Since painted, or not painted, all shall fade,
And she who scorns a Man, must die a Maid; [V.27-8]

This understanding and sympathy renders the poem more likely to be accepted by Mrs Arabella Fermor, to whom it is addressed, and more likely to achieve its intended aim of reconciling the Fermor and Petre families.

Behind the comparisons between the epic world and the 'beau-monde' Pope also looks at the contrast between the ideals and the reality of the 'beau-monde' itself. The opening lines of the second paragraph introduce this theme:

Say what strange Motive, Goddess! cou'd compel
A well-bred Lord t'assault a gentle Belle?
Oh say what stranger Cause, yet unexplor'd,
Cou'd make a gentle Belle reject a Lord? [I.7-10]

The 'motives' and 'causes' are as basic as human motives and causes anywhere. Sexual passion, for example, would hardly be openly admitted in polite society, yet it always lurks just below the surface. One example of this is in the title of the poem, for the act of cutting off a lock of hair can be seen, even if only as a joke, as sublimated rape. Sexuality is also implicit in this couplet:

On her white Breast a sparkling Cross she wore,
Which Jews might kiss, and Infidels adore. [ll.7-8]

Here we have an obvious double meaning which not only exposes the trivialising of a Christian symbol but also reveals the underlying purpose of Belinda's meticulous attention to her appearance. The Sylphs, the guardian spirits of 'beau-monde' belles, are well aware of the possible outcome of sophisticated pleasantries with lords:

To Fifty chosen Sylphs, of special Note,
We trust th'important Charge, the Petticoat:
Oft have we known that sev'nfold Fence to fail,
Tho' stiff with Hoops, and arm'd with Ribs of Whale. [ll.117-20]

If we look for an explicit moral message in the poem we must look to Clarissa's speech [V.7-34], which Pope included specifically for that purpose. This is the most sobre passage in the poem and it embodies Pope's message to the 'beau-monde', and in particular to the Fermor and Petre families. It is a plea for maturity and good sense, for virtue and care of the soul; all the things which the satire has shown to be lacking.

By asking them to see their lives in a wider context he hopes to persuade them to adopt a more rational sense of proportion. By laughing at the mock-epic style they will have to admit that they are laughing at themselves, and Pope hopes this will inculcate a spirit of good humour and reconciliation.

Although not himself of the 'beau-monde' Pope was part of the same era. The finesse and delicacy of 'beau-monde' manners is matched by Pope's style, and the good humour, wit, and charm which characterises Pope's manner must represent an expression of the same ideals pursued by the Baron and other courtly men of the age.

An affinity between them is revealed by Pope's empathy, fine judgements, and carefully aimed criticisms, and Pope must have been at least a little fascinated by the 'beau-monde' to apply his talents to this poem which, in an ironic way, celebrates Belinda and her world and, as Pope himself suggests in the final couplet of the poem, has preserved them for posterity.

This Lock, the Muse shall consecrate to Fame,
And mid'st the Stars inscribe Belinda's Name! [V.149-50]

COMPARISON OF SWIFT'S "THE LADY'S DRESSING ROOM" AND POPE'S "RAPE OF THE LOCK"

In these poems, Swift and Pope satirize female vanity, but in tone, language, and form, the works diverge greatly. Pope wrote "Rape of the Lock" expressly at the request of his friend, John Caryll, in an effort to make peace between real-life lovers. The incident of the lock of hair was factual; Pope's intention was to dilute with humour the ill feelings aroused by the affair. He was, in fact, putting a minor incident into perspective, and to this end, chose a mock-heroic form, composing the poem as a "take-off" epic poetry, particularly the work of Milton.

He is inviting the individuals involved to laugh at themselves, to see how emotion had inflated their response to what was really an event of no consequence. For the reader, the incident becomes a statement about human folly, a lesson on female vanity, and a satire of the rituals of courtship. Perhaps Pope also intended to comment on the meaningless lives of the upper classes. The poem was published in 1712 and again in 1714; probably the satire is more biting in the later version than in the one presented to Miss Fermor. Pope could hardly have hope to soothe the lady's wounded pride by pointing out her vanity and empty-headedness.

The circumstances which provoked Swift to write "The Lady's Dressing Room" are to me unknown. The poem doesn't even appear in *The Norton Anthology of English Literature* , the Bible of my undergraduate years, nor is it mentioned in the biographical sketch of Swift which that book contains. Swift was somewhat of a misanthrope, and did not accept the view that human nature is essentially good:

To the 'philanthropic' flattery that sentimentalism and Deistic rationalism were paying to human nature, Swift opposed a more ancient and plausible view: that human nature is deeply and permanently flawed, and that we can do nothing with or for the human race until we recognize its moral and intellectual limitations.

In his poetry, Swift revealed human imperfection, and cosmetic vanity was one evil he chose to attack. In this particular poem, he really rubs our nose in it.

Is the vulgarity of his humour more shocking to us than it would have been to his contemporaries? Or is it so striking to us because it is missing from almost all of the other poetry we read in college courses? "Bathroom humour" isn't exactly absent from 20th century popular culture, after all.

The reader can't pretend to being ignorant that such humour exists and is enjoyed by a certain audience. Swift's style is deliberately "unpoetic" in diction and crude in humour, perhaps because he wished to force his readers to confront what he saw as the truth about our humanity: "he hated 'that animal called man' in general, and offered a new definition of the species as not animal rationale, but as merely animal rationis capax (an animal capable of reason)" (Norton 1978).

Nevertheless, the effect of Swift's bawdiness is to make him seem crude — and angry. His style reflects on him as a man, so that the intensity of his social criticism is somewhat undermined. The reader wants to say that of course Celia shits, but so does Strephon — and so does Swift. What of it? Pope seems to be more in control of tone in "Rape" than Swift is in "The Lady's Dressing Room." His style does not deflect his satiric arrows from their true target.

In keeping with his choice of mock-heroic form, Pope employs a "high-toned" poetic diction and the stately iambic pentameter of dignified epics like "Paradise Lost." And of course, Pope's mastery of the heroic couplet, and the balanced, measured rhythms of his lines, lend an even greater air of solemnity. To achieve this effect, he inverts the syntax of ordinary speech, as in these lines: "Her lively looks a spritely mind disclose" (ii, 9), ""Favors to none, to all she smiles extends" (II, 11), and "Bright as the sun, her eyes the gazers strike" (ii, 13). The effect of this inversion is to add rhetoric weight to the end of the line; the sentence feels particularly "complete."

At the same time, the reader is always aware that the poem is a joke. Pope comes right out and says so. For example, one epic tradition is to open with a statement of purpose and an invocation to the Muse. Pope states his purpose as being to sing of the "dire offense" that springs from "amorous causes" and the "mighty contests" that rise from "trivial things" (1-2) — hardly the lofty and weighty subjects of epic poetry — and names his Muse "Caryll" for his friend John Caryll, the relative of the young lord who stole the lock of hair from Arabella Fermor — not the proper sort of Muse for epic poetry. By way of mythological spirits hovering over earthly concerns, Pope gives us sylphs that are really the spirits of young women like Belinda.

Milton's Adam had the angel Raphael looking out for him; Belinda has Ariel, one of the "light militia of the lower sky". He jokingly raises Belinda to the exalted stature proper to epic heroines by addressing her as "Fairest of mortals, thou distinguished care/ Of thousands bright inhabitants of air" and exorts her: "thy own importance know"; but because Belinda is really only a "gentle belle", a pampered and privileged young woman, capable of mere "infant thought", the effect is humorous.

The stakes in this mock-heroic epic are Belinda's maidenhood, and the convention of the epic warning comes by way of Ariel's reading of bad omens: "Late as I ranged the crystal wilds of air,/ In the clear mirror of thy ruling star/ I saw, alas! some dread event impend/ . . . Beware of all, but most beware of Man!". Belinda's performance of her toilette, assisted by Betty, her "inferior priestess", is described as the arming of the epic hero: "Now awful Beauty put on all its arms", and the images evoked in Pope's description of the various creams and perfumes on Belinda's vanity invests them with a value and exoticism they don't deserve: "Unnumbered treasures," "glittering spoil," "India's glowing gems," "all Arabia breathes from yonder box," "The tortoise here and elephant unite". By means of hyperbole, Pope manages to reveal the true worthlessness of these substances.

Coombes advocates the use of concrete, Saxonate words over abstract, Latinate ones in poetry, and offers numerous examples from 18th century poetry of how the effect of abstraction is to show a lack of emotional engagement and possibly even a physical distance between the poet and his subject. Yet Coombes defends Miltonian "poetic diction," such as Pope employs in "Rape," as sometimes being the most proper and natural style for a particular poet to use. Certainly such a style is well-suited to "The Rape of the Lock," exactly because it does strike the reader as "too much," as "too high" for the subject matter.

"Not with more glories, in the ethereal plain,/ The sun first rises o'er the purpled main,/ Than, issuing forth, the rival of his beams/ Launched on the bosom of the silver Thames" (ii, 1-4). The use of such "high falutin'" rhetoric to describe a young lady on her way to Hampton Court to play cards is witty and hilarious. Further, it allows the reader a sense of satisfaction to be "in" on the joke. Besides, Pope balances such abstract, Miltonian description with concrete images as well. He explains, for instance, that such female vanities as a "love of ombre" survive after death, certainly a specific, concrete image, and shows us "lapdogs giv[ing] themselves the rousing shake".

Particularly effective is when Pope combines the abstract with the concrete in a single couplet, as in such lines as "Think what an equipage thou hast in air,/ And view with scorn two pages and a chair", or when he combines Miltonian style with upper class English slang, as in "If to her share some female errors fall,/ Look on her face, and you'll forget 'em all" (ii, 17-18).

Iambic pentameter and poetic diction would not serve Swift's purposes in "The Lady's Dressing Room." He has no intention of redeeming Celia with even a mock-heroic tone. (Interestingly, it can be argued that ultimately, the tone of Swift's poem is "darker" than that of Pope"s, despite the fact that by reason of the meter, it should be the other way around.) Swift's poem is written in iambic tetrameter, an even number of metric feet per line; this lends a greater sense of "completion" or of "balance" to each line (according to Barbara Drake, in *Writing Poetry,* the text my students are reading in English 266).

The reader stops at the end of every line, rather than moving on in the way we read heroic couplets, or pausing at a caesura in the middle of a line, as we do when reading Pope Thus the end rhyme of successive lines in Swift's poem is stressed, and the comic tone of the poem is heightened. Some lines deviate from the iambic and end in a feminine rhyme: "The goddess from her chamber issues,/ Arrayed in lace, brocades and tissues", for example, and "But oh! it turned poor Strephon's bowels,/ When he beheld and smelled the towels" (43-44). Feminine rhyme isn't necessarily associated with comic effect, although triple rhyme is (Holman and Harmon 408). Nevertheless, in Swift's poem, the rhyme scheme certainly underscores the humour. It also lends itself to the bawdy humour Swift favors here.

Unlike Pope's imagery, which tends to be more abstract, Swift's is concrete to the point of being graphic. Most of "the Lady's Dressing Room" is a description of Celia's vanity, and Swift's imagery is quite concrete, and certainly as inventive as Pope's. Just as Pope uses hyperbole to invest Belinda's creams and perfumes with qualities of the rare and the exotic, so Swift uses hyperbole — but to give the contents of Celia's "gallypots" a quality of horror.

"Some filled with washes, some with paste,/ Some with pomatum, paints and slops,/ And ointments good for scabby chops". The sheer awfulness of this description may be unparalleled in literature, with the possible exception of the weird sisters' cauldron in Macbeth. Not only do Celia's cosmetics demonstrate her vanity, her artifice and hypocrisy, but they suggest her underlying ugliness, both physical and spiritual. Celia, Swift tells us, not only has "scabby chops" but hairs growing low on her forehead, suggesting a simian appearance, bristles on her chin, and worms in her nose. Celia uses puppy water as a wash and has unfeelingly used her pet dog Tripsy's hide to make a pair of gloves.

Like Pope, Swift nevertheless elevates his character to the stature of a goddess, although the rest of the poem effectively strips her of this undeserved title. And in the last stanza, another goddess, Vengeance, punishes Strephon for his "peeping" (119-120). Also like Pope, Swift employs the epic convention of the extended simile. In lines 83-90, he compares Strephon, lifting the lid of Celia's chamber pot , to the mythological character of Epimetheus opening Pandora's box and releasing all human evils. The effect is highly humorous, and had he stopped here, Swift would have been all right. But he couldn't resist carrying this scene beyond the limits of good taste. In lines 99-112 , he draws another extended simile, comparing the process by which cooking meat is "poisoned" by the smoke of the oil it exudes on the cooking fire, to the way Celia's "parts" are tainted by the "excremental smell" of her . . . excrement (What would Kenner say about this as an image? I wonder.).

Although it succeeds as a simile, what kind of a mind would expend the time required to concoct such a conceit? I give Swift credit as a poet for his inventiveness, and grudgingly confess I find his views a change (though not exactly a "refreshing" one) from the tired (and insincere) conceits of Petrarchan love sonnets, but surely his talents deserved better expression than this. The first simile demonstrates his wit and poetic genius; the second reveals how low he can stoop as a man.

In Swift's defence, it must be noted that, although Celia, specifically, and female vanity in general are the principal subjects of the poem and the objects of Swift's ridicule, Strephon isn't exactly a hero, nor does the poet expect us to see him as such. Sneaking around behind both Celia's and the maid's back, snooping and sniffing in places he has no right to be, Strephon reveals himself to be something of a dog, certainly no better than any woman who attempts to seem more fastidious than she really is. Who exactly Strephon is, is unclear. He may be a servant, or perhaps a male suitor who, enamored of Celia, wants to go through her things (perhaps to find a souvenir?)

His attitude is clear enough: spiteful and "disgusted", until he leaves her room "repeating in his amorous fits,/ Oh! Celia, Celia, Celia shits!". Is he exclaiming inanely over this proof of his love's humanity? Or is he planning to "tell all" to anyone who will listen? The character of Strephon adds a farcical element to the poem. Throughout the poem, we are reminded of his presence, his need that will not be denied to poke his nose where it doesn't belong. The description of Celia's "dirty smock," complete with "besmeared armpits", her "filthy basin" "fouled with the scouring of her hands" and "the scrapings of her teeth and gums", and her "snotty" handkerchief and smelly stockings are somehow more awful for the presence of Strephon, and the comedy is heightened by his bungling and his responses, as when he is frightened by his own reflection in the magnifying glass.

Fully one-third of the poem, lines 69-114, is devoted to describing Celia's chamber pot (more a cabinet than a mere "pot"). It isn't just the fact that Celia has spent five hours dressing that rankles the poet, or the fact that creams and tints applied to the face present an artificial kind of beauty that may yet conceal a spiritual ugliness; but that her efforts have been expended on trying to deny the facts of her flesh: sweat, earwax, spit, oil, body odor, shit. These are the essence of our humanity, Swift seems to insist. And the chamber pot, or cabinet, can be seen as a metaphor for Celia herself, having been fashioned to look like a piece of fine furniture: "With rings and hinges counterfeit/ To make it seem in this disguise/ A cabinet to vulgar eyes".

Celia — and by extension all women — becomes the brunt of Swift's satire in the last stanza, when Strephon comes to associate all women with any "unsavory odors". Celia becomes "Everywoman," but Strephon is not "Everyman," when Swift speaks in first person at the end of the poem (deus ex machina?) to put matters in perspective. "If Strephon would but stop his nose. . . / He soon would learn to think like me,/ And bless his ravished sight to see/ Such order from confusion sprung,/ Such gaudy tulips raised from dung". In their natural state, women are "dung," in their unnatural state, they are "gaudy" tulips. Strephon is punished, and appropriately so, but his bad conduct is merely glossed over. Swift is superior to them both, or so he would have us believe. His satire comes off finally as a reflection of his own obsession with the animal aspects of other people's human nature. In "The Rape of the Lock" Pope focuses on a particular woman and thus succeeds in creating a convincing portrait that the reader accepts and applies to a general population of young women. Belinda may be superficial and rather empty-headed, possessed of "a sprightly mind . . ./ Quick as her eyes, and as unfixed as those", but she is charming and innocent, too. She is the product of her culture, her social class and the times. When Pope says, "Yet graceful ease, and sweetness void of pride,/ Might hide her faults, if belles had faults to hide" (II, 15-16) the reader knows he's being generous; we've already seen her faults.

By contrast, Swift focuses on a particular woman and then makes generalizations which he forces on us. As a result, our minds resist. His attack on Celia seems too mean-spirited to be entirely deserved and his criticism is unrelieved. He gives Celia no redeeming virtues, and so his satire is darker than Pope's is in "The Rape of the Lock." Swift's techniques seem to me to be less effective than Pope's because they reflect poorly on the poet himself, so much so that "The Lady's Dressing Room" seems to undercut Coombe's argument for concrete language and the emotional engagement of the poet.

Chapter 14

Alexander Pope's "Essay on Criticism"

Pope's "Essay on Criticism" is a didactic poem in heroic couplets, begun, perhaps, as early as 1705, and published, anonymously, in 1711. The poetic essay was a relatively new genre, and the "Essay" itself was Pope's most ambitious work to that time. It was in part an attempt on Pope's part to identify and refine his own positions as poet and critic, and his response to an ongoing critical debate which centered on the question of whether poetry should be "natural" or written according to predetermined "artificial" rules inherited from the classical past.

The poem commences with a discussion of the rules of taste which ought to govern poetry, and which enable a critic to make sound critical judgements. In it Pope comments, too, upon the authority which ought properly to be accorded to the classical authors who dealt with the subject; and concludes (in an apparent attempt to reconcile the opinions of the advocates and opponents of rules) that the rules of the ancients are in fact identical with the rules of Nature: poetry and painting, that is, like religion and morality, actually reflect natural law.

The "Essay on Criticism," then, is deliberately ambiguous: Pope seems, on the one hand, to admit that rules are necessary for the production of and criticism of poetry, but he also notes the existence of mysterious, apparently irrational qualities — "Nameless Graces," identified by terms such as "Happiness" and "Lucky Licence" — with which Nature is endowed, and which permit the true poetic genius, possessed of adequate "taste," to appear to transcend those same rules. The critic, of course, if he is to appreciate that genius, must possess similar gifts.

True Art, in other words, imitates Nature, and Nature tolerates and indeed encourages felicitous irregularities which are in reality (because Nature and the physical universe are creations of God) aspects of the divine order of things which is eternally beyond human comprehension. Only God, the infinite intellect, the purely rational being, can appreciate the harmony of the universe, but the intelligent and educated critic can appreciate poetic harmonies which echo those in nature.

Because his intellect and his reason are limited, however, and because his opinions are inevitably subjective, he finds it helpful or necessary to employ rules which are interpretations of the ancient principles of nature to guide him — though he should never be totally dependent upon them. We should note, in passing, that in "The Essay on Criticism" Pope is frequently concerned with "wit" — the word occurs once, on average, in every sixteen lines of the poem. What does he mean by it?

Pope then proceeds to discuss the laws by which a critic should be guided — insisting, as any good poet would, that critics exist to serve poets, not to attack them. He then provides, by way of example, instances of critics who had erred in one fashion or another. What, in Pope's opinion (here as elsewhere in his work) is the deadliest critical sin — a sin which is itself a reflection of a greater sin? All of his erring critics, each in their own way, betray the same fatal flaw.

The final section of the poem discusses the moral qualities and virtues inherent in the ideal critic, who is also the ideal man — and who, Pope laments, no longer exists in the degenerate world of the early eighteenth century.

This eminent English poet was born in London, May 21, 1688. His parents were Roman Catholics, and to this faith the poet adhered, thus debarring himself from public office and employment. His father, a linen merchant, having saved a moderate competency, withdrew from business, and settled on a small estate he had purchased in Windsor Forest.

He died at Chiswick, in 1717. His son shortly afterwards took a long lease of a house and five acres of land at Twickenham, on the banks of the Thames, whither he retired with his widowed mother, to whom he was tenderly attached and where he resided till death, cultivating his little domain with exquisite taste and skill, and embellishing it with a grotto, temple, wilderness, and other adjuncts poetical and picturesque. In this famous villa Pope was visited by the most celebrated wits, statesmen and beauties of the day, himself being the most popular and successful poet of his age.

His early years were spent at Binfield, within the range of the Royal Forest. He received some education at little Catholic schools, but was his own instructor after his twelfth year. He never was a profound or accurate scholar, but he read Latin poets with ease and delight, and acquired some Greek, French, and Italian. He was a poet almost from infancy, he "lisped in numbers," and when a mere youth surpassed all his contemporaries in metrical harmony and correctness. His pastorals and some translations appeared in 1709, but were written three or four years earlier. These were followed by the Essay on Criticism, 1711; Rape of the Lock (when completed, the most graceful, airy, and imaginative of his works), 1712-1714; Windsor Forest, 1713; Temple of Fame, 1715. In a collection of his works printed in 1717 he included the Epistle of Eloisa and Elegy on an Unfortunate Lady, two poems inimitable for pathetic beauty and finished melodious versification.

From 1715 till 1726 Pope was chiefly engaged on his translations of the Iliad and Odyssey, which, though wanting in time Homeric simplicity, naturalness, and grandeur, are splendid poems. In 1728-29 he published his greatest satire—the Dunciad, an attack on all poetasters and pretended wits, and on all other persons against whom the sensitive poet had conceived any enmity. In 1737 he gave to the world a volume of his Literary Correspondence, containing some pleasant gossip and observations, with choice passages of description but it appears that the correspondence was manufactured for publication not composed of actual letters addressed to the parties whose names are given, and the collection was introduced to the public by means of an elaborate stratagem on the part of the scheming poet.

Between the years 1731 and 1739 he issued a series of poetical essays moral and philosophical, with satires and imitations of Horace, all admirable for sense, wit, spirit and brilliancy of these delightful productions, the most celebrated is the Essay on Man to which Bolingbroke is believed to have contributed the spurious philosophy and false sentiment, but its merit consists in detached passages, descriptions, and pictures. A fourth book to the Dunciad, containing many beautiful and striking lines and a general revision of his works, closed the poet's literary cares and toils. He died on the 30th of May, 1744, and was buried in the church at Twickenham. Pope was of very diminutive stature and deformed from his birth. His physical infirmity, susceptible temperament, and incessant study rendered his life one long disease.

He was, as his friend Lord Chesterfield said, "the most irritable of all the genus irritabile vatum, offended with trifles and never forgetting or forgiving them." His literary stratagems, disguises, assertions, denials, and (we must add) misrepresentations would fill volumes. Yet when no disturbing jealousy vanity, or rivalry intervened was generous and affectionate, and he had a manly, independent spirit. As a poet he was deficient in originality and creative power, and thus was inferior to his prototype, Dryden, but as a literary artist, and brilliant declaimer satirist and moralizer in verse he is still unrivaled. He is the English Horace, and will as surely descend with honors to the latest posterity.

[The title, An Essay on Criticism hardly indicates all that is included in the poem. It would have been impossible to give a full and exact idea of the art of poetical criticism without entering into the consideration of the art of poetry. Accordingly Pope has interwoven the precepts of both throughout the poem which might more properly have been styled an essay on the Art of Criticism and of Poetry.]

The Stagirite—Aristotle, born at the Greek town of Stageira on the Strymonic Gulf (Gulf of Contessa, in Turkey)

384 B.C., whose treatises on Rhetoric and the Art of Poetry were the earliest development of a Philosophy of Criticism and still continue to be studied.

The poet contradicts himself with regard to the principle he is here laying down in lines 271-272 where he laughs at Dennis for Concluding all were desperate sots and fools. Who durst depart from Aristotle's rules.] Secure from flames.—The poet probably alludes to such fires as those in which the Alexandrine and Palatine Libraries were destroyed. From envy's fiercer rage.—Probably he alludes to the writings of such men as Maevius and Zoilus, a sophist and grammarian of Amphipolis, who distinguished himself by his criticism on Isocrates, Plato, and Homer, receiving the nickname of _Homeromastic (chastiser of Homer).

Destructive war—Probably an allusion to the irruption of the barbarians into the south of Europe. And all-involving age; that is, time. This is usually explained as an allusion to 'the long reign of ignorance and superstition in the cloisters,' but it is surely far-fetched, and more than the language will bear.]

Dennis, the son of a saddler in London, born 1657, was a mediocre writer, and rather better critic of the time, with whom Pope came a good deal into collision. Addison's tragedy of Cato, for which Pope had written a prologue, had been attacked by Dennis. Pope, to defend Addison, wrote an imaginary report, pretending to be written by a notorious quack mad-doctor of the day, entitled. The Narrative of Dr. Robert Norris on the Frenz of F. D Dennis replied to it by his Character of Mr. Pope. Ultimately Pope gave him a place in his Dunciad, and wrote a prologue for his benefit.]

Prismatic glass.—A glass prism by which light is refracted, and the component rays, which are of different colors being refracted at different angles show what is called a spectrum or series of colored bars, in the order violet, indigo, blue, green, yellow, orange, red.] Sir John Denham, a poet of the time of Charles I. (1615-1668). His verse is characterized by considerable smoothness and ingenuity of rhythm, with here and there a passage of some force—Edmund Waller (1606-1687) is celebrated as one of the refiners of English poetry. His rank among English poets, however, is very subordinate.] In this passage the poet obviously intended to make "the sound seem an echo to the sense". The success of the attempt has not been very complete except in the second two lines, expressing the dash and roar of the waves, and in the last two, expressing the skimming, continuous motion of Camilla. What he refers to is the onomatopoeia of Homer and Virgil in the passages alluded to. Ajax, the son of Telamon, was, next to Achilles, the bravest of all the Greeks in the Trojan war. When the Greeks were challenged by Hector he was chosen their champion and it was in their encounter that he seized a huge stone and hurled it at Hector.

Thus rendered by Pope himself:

"Then Ajax seized the fragment of a rock
Applied each nerve, and swinging round on high,
With force tempestuous let the ruin fly
The huge stone thundering through his buckler broke."

Camilla, queen of the Volsci, was brought up in the woods, and, according to Virgil, was swifter than the winds. She led an army to assist Turnus against Aeneas.

"Dura pan, cursuque pedum praevertere ventos.
Illa vel intactae segetis per summa volaret
Gramina nec teneras cursu laesisset aristas;
Vel mare per medium fluctu suspensa tumenti,
Ferret iter, celeres nec tingeret aequore plantas."
Thus rendered by Dryden.
"Outstripped the winds in speed upon the plain,
Flew o'er the fields, nor hurt the bearded grain;
She swept the seas, and as she skimmed along,
Her flying feet unbathed on billows hung"]

This passage refers to Dryden's ode, Alexander's Feast, or The Power of Music. Timotheus, mentioned in it, was a musician of Boeotia, a favourite of Alexander's, not the great musician Timotheus, who died before Alexander was born, unless, indeed, Dryden have confused the two.

Scotists—The disciples of Duns Scotus, one of the most famous and influential of the scholastics of the fourteenth century, who was opposed to Thomas Aquinas (1224-1274), another famous scholastic, regarding the doctrines of grace and the freedom of the will, but especially the immaculate conception of the Virgin. The followers of the latter were called Thomists, between whom and the Scotists bitter controversies were carried on.

A place near Smithfield where old books were sold. The cobwebs were kindred to the works of these controversialists, because their arguments were intricate and obscure. Scotus is said to have demolished two hundred objections to the doctrine of the Immaculate Conception, and established it by a cloud of proofs.] Blackmore, Sir Richard (1652-1729), one of the court physicians and the writer of a great deal of worthless poetry. He attacked the dramatists of the time generally and Dryden individually, and is the Quack Maurus of Dryden's prologue to The Secular Masque. Millbourn, Rev. Luke, who criticised Dryden; which criticism, although sneered at by Pope, is allowed to have been judicious and decisive.

The Titans, in Greek mythology, were the children of Uranus (heaven) and Gaea (earth), and of gigantic size. They engaged in a conflict with Zeus, the king of heaven, which lasted ten years. They were completely defeated, and hurled down into a dungeon below Tartarus. Very often they are confounded with the Giants, as has apparently been done here by Pope. These were a later progeny of the same parents, and in revenge for what had been done to the Titans, conspired to dethrone Zeus. In order to scale heaven, they piled Mount Ossa upon Pelion, and would have succeeded in their attempt if Zeus had not called in the assistance of his son Hercules.

Garth, Dr., afterwards Sir Samuel (born 1660) an eminent physician and a poet of considerable reputation He is best known as the author of The Dispensary, a poetical satire on the apothecaries and physicians who opposed the project of giving medicine gratuitously to the sick poor. The poet alludes to a slander current at the time with regard to the authorship of the poem.

Longinus, a Platonic philosopher and famous rhetorician, born either in Syria or at Athens about 213 A.D., was probably the best critic of antiquity. From his immense knowledge, he was called "a living library" and "walking museum," hence the poet speaks of him as inspired by all the Nine—Muses that is. These were Clio, the muse of History, Euterpe, of Music, Thaleia, of Pastoral and Comic Poetry and Festivals, Melpomene, of Tragedy, Terpsichore, of Dancing, Erato, of Lyric and Amorous Poetry, Polyhymnia, of Rhetoric and Singing, Urania, of Astronomy, Calliope, of Eloquence and Heroic Poetry.

A powerful nation of the Germanic race, which, originally from the Baltic, first settled near the Black Sea, and then overran and took an important part in the subversion of the Roman empire. They were distinguished as Ostro Goths (Eastern Goths) on the shores of the Black Sea, the Visi Goths (Western Goths) on the Danube, and the Moeso Goths, in Moesia

Erasmus.—A Dutchman (1467-1536), and at one time a Roman Catholic priest, who acted as tutor to Alexander Stuart, a natural son of James IV. of Scotland as professor of Greek for a short time at Oxford, and was the most learned man of his time. His best known work is his Colloquia, which contains satirical onslaughts on monks, cloister life, festivals, pilgrimages etc.

Vandals.—A race of European barbarians, who first appear historically about the second century, south of the Baltic. They overran in succession Gaul, Spain, and Italy. In 455 they took and plundered Rome, and the way they mutilated and destroyed the works of art has become a proverb, hence the monks are compared to them in their ignorance of art and science.

Raphael (1483-1520), an Italian, is almost universally regarded as the greatest of painters. He received much encouragement from Leo. Vida—A poet patronised by Leo. He was the son of poor parents at Cremona, which therefore the poet says, would be next in fame to Mantua, the birthplace of Virgil as it was next to it in place.

True wit is nature to advantage dressed,
What oft was thought, but ne'er so well expressed,
Something, whose truth convinced at sight we find,

That gives us back the notion of the mind. — Alexander Pope, "An Essay On Criticism" [1711] part 2, lines 297-300

"There is, I believe, in every disposition a tendency to some particular evil, a natural defect, which not even the best education can overcome."

"And your defect is a propensity to hate everybody."

"And yours," he replied with a smile, "is willfully to misunderstand them." — Pride and Prejudice, p. 40

Among those writers most notable for their use of wit, Pope and Austen stand out as being particularly well qualified to define the term itself. The two views of wit expressed in the above quotations each in their own way address the question of its nature and appropriate use. Each provides a distinct theory, and both share distinct similarities.

Though they arise in vastly different literary contexts, the passages may be seen within the setting of the changing scientific and religious views of the eighteenth century. In addition, the reader may observe a common delicacy of balance phrase and balance that connects the two excerpts. Both passages serve as well to represent the tradition of wit that runs through English Literature.

The excerpt taken from Pope's essay on criticism presents a highly academic conception of wit and its proper function in literature. Simply and clearly stated, Pope's wit is that which immediately captures the exact essence of a subject more precisely and cleverly than any have before. His very definition captures, in its directness of expression, the nature of the subject described. In combination with the even rhythm and masculine rhyme of the neoclassical couplets, the preference for perfect clarity of statement reflects the rational bent instigated to a large degree by such major and recent scientific advances as those represented by Newton's Principia (published 1687) and the invention of the microscope.

Furthermore, the demystification of the natural world which lead to the spread of Deism can also be seen to contribute to Pope's explanation of that wit which he strives for as a poet. This factor is especially significant when one considers that he himself was a Deist, and partook of the belief that the relationship of man to God can be understood through reason.

In the quotation taken from Pride and Prejudice Austen's characterization of wit much remains the same. The clever remarks of Elizabeth and Darcy demonstrate much of that definitive quality and elegance of expression that Pope wrote of. Although she employs a prose style rather than neoclassical couplets, much of the attention to balance and symmetry remains and may be observed in the careful division of the clauses in the first sentence as well as the pleasing symmetry of the latter two lines of dialogue.

The use of wit differs, however, in that its profoundly reflective tone has lightened to one of spontaneity. Moreover, Austen depicts an increased emphasis on humour which accompanies what is perhaps the most drastic discrepancy: the movement away from solemn philosophical contemplation into the realm of social interaction.

Traces linger also of scientific and rational influence, but they are clearly not so dominant as in Pope. In conjunction with the rather Christian slant of the "natural defect, which not even the best education can overcome" (certainly much more closely connected to the concept of original sin than the Deist faith in the power of reason) the reader can detect an intentional ambiguity of meaning not present in Pope's lines. The verbal irony of the speakers leaves this passage open to interpretation regarding the extent to which the speakers intend their words to be taken seriously. Implicit in this style is the suggestion that those scientific principals and ideas that inspired such a sense of order in Pope's universe perhaps no longer command the same authority in Jane Austen's time.

Pope began to write poetry at a very early age, but even then he steeped himself in various poetic traditions. He learned Latin and Greek in childhood, and all his life wrote "imitations" and translations of classical authors such as Homer, Virgil, Horace, Quintilian and Ovid, who also provided him with the poetic genres — the epic, the georgic, the elegy and the heroic epistle — which he would employ, imitate and parody. He was also thoroughly familiar with the work of his important contemporaries: Steele and Addison, for example, demonstrated, in their Spectator papers, to which Pope himself contributed, the effect which elegant and witty remonstrance (in poetry or in prose) could have upon the morals of their society.

Later he would collaborate with Swift, who became a close friend: many of Pope's attitudes grew closer to those of Swift as they both grew older. It is interesting, however, to compare Pope's approach to Belinda's toilette in The Rape of the Lock with Swift's very different preoccupations in "A Beautiful Young Nymph Going to Bed" – or with T. S. Eliot's treatment of a similar theme in the opening of "A Game of Chess" in The Waste Land. Other contemporaries whom Pope disliked were satirized, sometimes scathingly, in his work, and he was familiar as well with the work of Neoclassical predecessors like Boileau, and with the work of the great English poets – Chaucer, Spenser, Milton, Donne, and Shakespeare, for example – who had preceded him, and whom he revered. Echoes of Milton and Shakespeare, in particular, appear frequently in his work; although, like the Augustan he was, he described Shakespeare's Plays as "an ancient majestic piece of Gothick Architecture having dark, odd, and uncouth passages."

Pope had few poetical heirs of any consequence. His popularity gradually declined after his death in 1744, as his themes and his style went gradually out of fashion. In a sense his true heirs were those who reacted against him most strongly.

Samuel Johnson noted in his Life of Pope that it would be useless to attempt to write better couplets than Pope had produced, but he suggested, too, that new poets would emphasize new images and new sentiments, and by the early nineteenth century the English Romantics, reacting against Neoclassicism and exalting Nature, had, with a few notable exceptions – Byron, for example, proclaimed his admiration of Pope's accomplishments – come to look upon him as a decorous and perhaps a brilliant artist who was also a Roman Catholic and a crabbed dwarf; as an artist whose work, unfortunately, not only reflected but examplified the deadening artificiality of his age.

He was never without adherents — Isaac D'Israeli defended The Rape of the Lock by insisting that the best poetry reflected the spirit of the age that had produced it, and that, judged by that standard, the poem was a work of genius — but his work read less and less. It was not until he had been maligned, and his work misunderstood, by increasingly vituperative Romantic, Victorian, and Edwardian critics, however (Matthew Arnold wrote that Pope's poetry lacked seriousness; Lytton Strachey called him a "fiendishly clever and spiteful monkey"; and Oscar Wilde gave it as his opinion that "There are two ways of disliking poetry. One is not to like it, and the other is to read Pope") — not, in fact, until the mid-twentieth century — that his work began to be properly appreciated once more.

In contrast, T. S. Eliot revered Pope, and paid him homage in an opening passage (written in heroic couplets) in "The Fire Sermon": Ezra Pound paid him a greater tribute still, however, when he persuaded Eliot to delete the passage from the published poem. "Pope has done this so well," Pound wrote, "that you cannot do it better; and if you mean this as a burlesque, you has better suppress it, for you cannot parody Pope unless you can write better verse than Pope — and you can't."

That it is as great a fault to judge ill as to write ill, and a more dangerous one to the public. That a true Taste is as rare to be found as a true Genius. That most men are born with some Taste, but spoiled by false education. The multitude of Critics, and causes of them. That we are to study our own Taste, and know the limits of it. Nature the best guide of judgment. Improved by Art and rules, which are but methodized Nature. Rules derived from the practice of the ancient poets. That therefore the ancients are necessary to be studied by a Critic, particularly Homer and Virgil. Of licenses, and the use of them by the ancients. Reverence due to the ancients, and praise of them.

'Tis hard to say if greater want of skill

Appear in writing or in judging ill;
But of the two less dangerous is th'offence
To tire our patience than mislead our sense:
Some few in that, but numbers err in this;
Ten censure wrong for one who writes amiss;
A fool might once himself alone expose;
Now one in verse makes many more in prose.
'Tis with our judgments as our watches, none
Go just alike, yet each believes his own.
In Poets as true Genius is but rare,
True Taste as seldom is the Critic's share;
Both must alike from Heav'n derive their light,
These born to judge, as well as those to write.
Let such teach others who themselves excel,
And censure freely who have written well;
Authors are partial to their wit, 'tis true,
But are not Critics to tneir judgment too?
Yet if we look more closely, we shall find
Most have the seeds of judgment in their mind:
Nature affords at least a glimm'ring light;
The lines, tho' touch'd but faintly, are drawn right:
But as the slightest sketch, if justly traced,
Is by ill col'ring but the more disgraced,
So by false learning is good sense defaced:
Some are bewilder'd in the maze of schools,
And some made coxcombs Nature meant but fools:
In search of wit these lose their common sense,
And then turn Critics in their own defence:
Each burns alike, who can or cannot write,
Or with a rival's or an eunuch's spite.
All fools have still an itching to deride,
And fain would be upon the laughing side.
If Mævius scribble in Apollo's spite,
There are who judge still worse than he can write.
Some have at first for Wits, then Poets pass'd;
Turn'd Critics next, and prov'd plain Fools at last.
Some neither can for Wits nor Critics pass,
As heavy mules are neither horse nor ass.

Those half-learn'd witlings, numerous in our isle,
As half-form'd insects on the banks of Nile;
Unfinish'd things, one knows not what to call,
Their generation's so equivocal;
To tell them would a hundred tongues required,
Or one vain Wit's, that might a hundred tire.
But you who seek to give and merit fame,
And justly bear a Critic's noble name,
Be sure yourself and your own reach to know,
How far your Genius, Taste, and Learning go,
Launch not beyond your depth, but be discreet,
And mark that point where Sense and Dulness meet.
Nature to all things fix'd the limits fit,
And wisely curb'd proud man's pretending wit.
As on the land while here the ocean gains,
In other parts it leaves wide sandy plains;
Thus in the soul while Memory prevails,
The solid power of Understanding fails;
Where beams of warm Imagination play,
The Memory's soft figures melt away.
One Science only will one genius fit;
So vast is Art, so narrow human wit:
Now only bounded to peculiar arts,
But oft in those confin'd to single parts.
Like Kings we lose the conquests gain'd before,
By vain ambition still to make them more:
Each might his sev'ral province well command,
Would all but stoop to what they understand.
First follow Nature, and your judgment frame
By her just standard, which is still the same;
Unerring Nature, still divinely bright,
One clear, unchanged, and universal light,
Life, force, and beauty must to all impart,
At once the source, and end, and test of Art.
Art from that fund each just supply provides,
Works without show, and without pomp presides.
In some fair body thus th'informing soul
With spirits feeds, with vigour fills the whole;

Each motion guides, and every nerve sustains,
Itself unseen, but in th' effects remains.
Some, to whom Heav'n in wit has been profuse,
Want as much more to turn it to its use;
For Wit and Judgment often are at strife
Tho' meant each other's aid, like man and wife.
'Tis more to guide than spur the Muse's steed,
Restrain his fury than provoke his speed:
The winged courser, like a gen'rous horse,
Shows most true mettel when you check his course.
Those rules of old, discover'd, not devised,
Are Nature still, but Nature methodized;
Nature, like Liberty, is but restrain'd
By the same laws which first herself ordain'd.
Hear how learn'd Greece her useful rules indites
When to repress and when indulge our flights:
High on Parnassus' top her sons she show'd,
And pointed out those arduous paths they trod;
Held from afar, aloft, th'immortal prize,
And urged the rest by equal steps to rise.
Just precepts thus from great examples giv'n,
She drew from them what they derived from Heav'n.
The gen'rous Critic fann'd the poet's fire,
And taught the world with reason to admire.
Then Criticism the Muse's handmaid prov'd,
To dress her charms, and make her more belov'd:
But following Wits from that intention stray'd:
Who could not win the mistress woo'd the maid;
Against the Poets their own arms they turn'd,
Sure to hate most the men from whom they learn'd.
So modern 'pothecaries taught the art
By doctors' bills to play the doctor's part,
Bold in the practice of mistaken rules,
Prescribe, apply, and call their masters fools.
Some on the leaves of ancient authors prey;
Nor time nor moths e'er spoil'd so much as they;
Some drily plain, without invention's aid,
Write dull receipts how poems may be made;

These leave the sense their learning to display,
And those explain the meaning quite away.
You then whose judgment the right course would steer,
Know well each ancient's proper character;
His fable, subject, scope in every page;
Religion, country, genius of his age:
Without all these at once before your eyes,
Cavil you may, but never criticise.
Be Homer's works your study and delight,
Read them by day, and meditate by night;
Thence form your judgment, thence your maxims bring,
And trace the Muses upward to their spring.
Still with itself compared, his text peruse;
And let your comment be the Mantuan Muse.
When first young Maro in his boundless mind
A work t'outlast immortal Rome design'd,
Perhaps he seem'd above the critic's law,
And but from Nature's fountains scorn'd to draw;
But when t'examine ev'ry part he came,
Nature and Homer were, he found, the same.
Convinced, amazed, he checks the bold design,
And rules as strict his labour'd work confine
As if the Stagyrite o'erlook'd each line.
Learn hence for ancient rules a just esteem;
To copy Nature is to copy them.
Some beauties yet no precepts can declare,
For there's a happiness as well as care.
Music resembles poetry; in each
Are nameless graces which no methods teach,
And which a master-hand alone can reach.
If, where the rules not far enough extend,
(Since rules were made but to promote their end)
Some lucky license answer to the full
Th'intent proposed, that license is a rule.
Thus Pegasus, a nearer way to take,
May boldly deviate from the common track.
Great Wits sometimes may gloriously offend,
And rise to faults true Critics dare not mend;

From vulgar bounds with brave disorder part,
And snatch a grace beyond the reach of Art,
Which, without passing thro' the judgment, gains
The heart, and all its end at once attains.
In prospects thus some objects please our eyes,
Which out of Nature's common order rise,
The shapeless rock, or hanging precipice.
But tho' the ancients thus their rules invade,
(As Kings dispense with laws themselves have made)
Moderns, beware! or if you must offend
Against the precept, ne'er transgress its end;
Let it be seldom, and compell'd by need;
And have at least their precedent to plead;
The Critic else proceeds without remorse,
Seizes your fame, and puts his laws in force.
I know there are to whose presumptuous thoughts
Those freer beauties, ev'n in them, seem faults.
Some figures monstrous and misshaped appear,
Consider'd singly, or beheld too near,
Which, but proportion'd to their light or place,
Due distance reconciles to form and grace.
A prudent chief not always must display
His powers in equal ranks and fair array,
But with th'occasion and the place comply,
Conceal his force, nay, seem sometimes to fly.
Those oft are stratagems which errors seem,
Nor is it Homer nods, but we that dream.
Still green with bays each ancient altar stands
Above the reach of sacrilegious hands,
Secure from flames, from Envy's fiercer rage,
Destructive war, and all-involving Age.
See from each clime the learn'd their incense bring!
Hear in all tongues consenting Paeans ring!
In praise so just let ev'ry voice be join'd,
And fill the gen'ral chorus of mankind.
Hail, Bards triumphant! born in happier days,
Immortal heirs of universal praise!
Whose honours with increase of ages grow,

As streams roll down, enlarging as they flow;
Nations unborn your mighty names shall sound,
And worlds applaud that must not yet be found!
O may some spark of your celestial fire
The last, the meanest of your sons inspire,
(That on weak wings, from far, pursues your flights,
Glows while he reads, but trembles as he writes)
To teach vain Wits a science little known,
T'admire superior sense, and doubt their own.

Causes hindering a true judgement. Pride. Imperfect learning. Judging by parts, and not by the whole. Critics in wit, language, and versification only. Being too hard to please, or too apt to admire. Partiality—too much love to a sect—to the ancients or moderns. Prejudice or prevention. Singularity. Inconstancy. Party spirit. Envy. Against envy, and in praise of good-nature. When severity is chiefly to be used by critics.

Of all the causes which conspire to blind
Man's erring judgment, and misguide the mind,
What the weak head with strongest bias rules,
Is Pride, the never failing vice of fools.
Whatever Nature has in worth denied
She gives in large recruits of needful Pride:
For as in bodies, thus in souls, we find
What wants in blood and spirits swell'd with wind:
Pride, where Wit fails, steps in to our deference,
And fills up all the mighty void of Sense:
If once right Reason drives that cloud away,
Truth breaks upon us with resistless day.
Trust not yourself; but your defects to know,
Make use of ev'ry friend—and ev'ry foe.
A little learning is a dangerous thing;
Drink deep, or taste not the Pierian spring:
There shallow draughts intoxicate the brain,
And drinking largely sobers us again.
Fired at first sight with what the Muse imparts,
In fearless youth we tempt the heights of arts,
While from the bounded level of our mind
Short views we take, nor see the lengths behind:

Bur more advanc'd, behold with strange surprise
New distant scenes of endliess science rise!
So pleas'd at first the tow'ring Alps we try,
Mount o'er the vales, and seem to tread the sky;
Th'eternal snows appear already past,
And the first clouds and mountains seem the last:
But those attain'd, we tremble to survey
The growing labours of the lengthen'd way;
Th'increasing prospect tires our wand'ring eyes,
Hills peep o'er hills, and Alps on Alps arise!
A perfect judge will read each work of wit
With the same spirit that its author writ;
Survey the whole, not seek slight faults to find
Where Nature moves, and Rapture warms the mind:
Nor lose, for that malignant dull delight,
The gen'rous pleasure to be charm'd with wit.
But in such lays as neither ebb nor flow,
Correctly cold, and regularly low,
That shunning faults one quiet tenor keep,
We cannot blame indeed—but we may sleep.
In Wit, as Nature, what affects our hearts
Is not th'exactness of peculiar parts;
'Tis not a lip or eye we beauty call,
But the joint force and full result of all.
Thus when we view some well proportion'd dome,
(The world's just wonder, and ev'n thine, O Rome!)
No single parts unequally surprise,
All comes united to th'admiring eyes;
No monstrous height, or breadth, or length, appear;
The whole at once is bold and regular.
Whoever thinks a faultless piece to see,
Thinks what n'er was, nor is, nor e'er shall be.
In every work regard the writer's end,
Since none can compass more than they intend;
And if the means be just, the conduct true,
Applause, in spite of trivial faults, is due.
As men of breeding, sometimes men of wit,
T'avoid great errors must the less commit;

Neglect the rules each verbal critic lays,
For not to know some trifles is a praise.
Most critics, fond of some subservient art,
Still make the whole depend upon a part:
They talk of Principles, but Notions prize,
And all to one lov'd folly sacrifice.
Once on a time La Mancha's Knight, they say,
A certain bard encount'ring on the way,
Discours'd in terms as just, with looks as sage,
As e'er could Dennis, of the Grecian State;
Concluding all were desperate sots and fools
Who durst depart from Aristotle's rules.
Our author, happy in a judge so nice,
Produced his play, and begged the knight's advice;
Made him observe the Subject and the Plot,
The Manners, Passions, Unities; what not?
All which exact to rule were brought about,
Were but a combat in the lists left out.
"What! leave the combat out?" exclaims the knight.
"Yes, or we must renounce the Stagyrite."
"Not so, by Heaven!, (he answers in a rage)
Knights, squires, and steeds must enter on the stage."
"So vast a throng the stage can n'er contain."
"Then build a new, or act it in a plain."
Thus critics of less judgement than caprice,
Curious, not knowing, not exact, but nice,
Form short ideas, and offend the Arts
(As most in Manners), by a love to parts.
Some to Conceit alone their taste confine,
And glitt'ring thoughts struck out at every line;
Pleas'd with a work where nothing's just or fit,
One glaring chaos and wild heap of wit.
Poets, like painters, thus unskill'd to trace
The naked nature and the living grace,
With gold and jewels cover every part,
And hide with ornaments their want of Art.
True Wit is Nature to advantage dress'd,
What oft was thought, but ne'er so well express'd;

Something whose truth convinced at sight we find,
That give us back the image of our mind.
As shades more sweetly recommend the light,
So modest plainness sets of sprightly wit:
For works may have more wit than does them good,
As bodies perish thro' excess of blood.
Others for language all their care express,
And value books, as women men, for dress:
Their praise is still—the Style is excellent;
The Sense they humbly take upon content.
Words are like leaves; and where they most abound,
Much fruit of sense beneath is rarely found.
False eloquence, like the prismatic glass,
Its gaudy colours spreads on every place;
The face of Nature we no more survey,
All glares alike, without distinction gay;
But true expression, like th'unchanging sun,
Clears and improves whate'er it shines upon;
It gilds all objects, but it alters none.
Expression is the dress of thought, and still
Appears more decent as more suitable.
A vile Conceit in pompous words express'd
Is like a clown in regal purple dress'd:
For diff'rent styles with diff'rent subjects sort,
As sev'ral garbs with country, town, and court.
Some by old words to fame have made pretence,
Ancients in phrase, mere moderns in their sense;
Such labour'd nothings, in so strange a style,
Amaze th'unlearned, and make the learned smile;
Unlucky as Fungoso in the play,
These sparks with awkward vanity display
What the fine gentleman wore yesterday;
And but so mimic ancient wits at best,
As apes our grandsires in their doublets drest.
In words as fashions the same rule will hold,
Alike fantastic if too new or old:
Be not the first by whom the new are tried,
Nor yet the last to lay the old aside.

But most by Numbers judge a poet's song,
And smooth or rough with them is right or wrong.
In the bright Muse tho' thousand charms conspire,
Her voice is all these tuneful fools admire;
Who haunt Parnassus but to please their ear,
Not mend their minds; as some to church repair,
Not for the doctrine, but the music there.
These equal syllables alone require,
Tho' oft the ear the open vowels tire,
While expletives their feeble aid to join,
And ten low words oft creep in one dull line:
While they ring round the same unvaried chimes,
With sure returns of still expected rhymes;
Where'er you find "the cooling western breeze,"
In the next line, it "whispers thro' the trees;"
If crystal streams "with pleasing murmurs creep,"
The reader's threaten'd (not in vain) with "sleep;"
Then, at the last and only couplet, fraught
With some unmeaning thing they call a thought,
A needless Alexandrine ends the song,
That, like a wounded snake, drags its slow length along.
Leave such to tune their own dull rhymes, and know
What's roundly smooth, or languishingly slow;
And praise the easy vigour of a line
Where Denham's strength and Waller's sweetness join.
True ease in writing comes from Art, not Chance,
As those move easiest who have learn'd to dance.
'Tis not enough no harshness gives offence;
The sound must seem an echo to the sense.
Soft is the strain when Zephyr gently blows,
And the smooth stream in smoother numbers flows;
But when loud surges lash the sounding shore,
The hoarse rough verse should like the torrent roar.
When Ajax strives some rock's vast weight to throw,
The line, too, labours, and the words move slow:
Not so when swift Camilla scours the plain,
Flies o'er th' unbending corn, and skims along the main.
Hear how Timotheus' varied lays surprise,

And bid alternate passions fall and rise!
While at each change the son of Libyan Jove
Now burns with glory, and then melts with love;
Now his fierce eyes with sparkling fury glow,
Now sighs steal out, and tears begin to flow:
Persians and Greeks like turns of nature found,
And the world's Victor stood subdued by sound!
The power of music all our hearts allow,
And what Timotheus was is Dryden now.
Avoid extremes, and shun the fault of such
Who still are pleas'd too little or too much.
At ev'ry trifle scorn to take offence;
That always shows great pride or little sense:
Those heads, as stomachs, are not sure the best
Which nauseate all, and nothing can digest.
Yet let not each gay turn thy rapture move;
For fools admire, but men of sense approve:
As things seem large which we thro' mist descry,
Dulness is ever apt to magnify.
Some foreign writers, some our own despise;
The ancients only, or the moderns prize.
Thus Wit, like Faith, by each man is applied
To one small sect, and all are damn'd beside.
Meanly they seek the blessing to confine,
And force that sun but on a part to shine,
Which not alone the southern wit sublimes,
But ripens spirits in cold northern climes;
Which from the first has shone on ages past,
Enligths the present, and shall warm the last;
Tho' each may feel increases and decays,
And see now clearer and now darker days,
Regard not then if wit be old or new,
But blame the False and value still the True.
Some ne'er advance a judgment of their own,
But catch the spreading notion of the town;
They reason and conclude by precedent,
And own stale nonsense which they ne'er invent.
Some judge of authors' names, not works, and then

Nor praise nor blame the writings, but the men.
Of all this servile herd, the worst is he
That in proud dulness joins with quality;
A constant critic at the great man's board,
To fetch and carry nonsense for my lord.
What woful stuff this madrigal would be
In some starv'd hackney sonneteer or me!
But let a lord once own the happy lines,
How the Wit brightens! how the Style refines!
Before his sacred name flies every fault,
And each exalted stanza teems with thought!
The vulgar thus thro' imitation err,
As oft the learn'd by being singular;
So much they scorn the crowd, that if the throng
By chance go right, they purposely go wrong.
So schismatics the plain believers quit,
And are but damn'd for having too much wit.
Some praise at morning what they blame at night,
But always think the last opinion right.
A Muse by these is like a mistress used,
This hour she's idolized, the next abused;
While their weak heads, like towns unfortified,
'Twixt sense and nonsense daily change their side.
Ask them the cause; they're wiser still they say;
And still to-morrow's wiser than to-day.
We think our fathers fools, so wise we grow;
Our wiser sons no doubt will think us so.
Once shool-divines this zealous isle o'erspread;
Who knew most sentences was deepest read.
Faith, Gospel, all seem'd made to be disputed,
And none has sense enough to be confuted.
Scotists and Thomists now in peace remain
Amidst their kindred cobwebs in Ducklane.
If Faith itself has diff'rent dresses worn,
What wonder modes in Wit should take their turn?
Oft, leaving what is natural and fit,
The current Folly proves the ready Wit;
And authors think their reputation safe,

Which lives as long as fools are pleas'd to laugh.
Some, valuing those of their own side or mind,
Still make themselves the measure of mankind:
Fondly we think we honour merit then,
When we but praise ourselves in other men.
Parties in wit attend on those of state,
And public faction doubles private hate.
Pride, Malice, Folly, against Dryden rose,
In various shapes of parsons, critics, beaux:
But sense survived when merry jests were past;
For rising merit will bouy up at last.
Might he return and bless once more our eyes,
New Blackmores and new Milbournes must arise.
Nay, should great Homer lift his awful head,
Zoilus again would start up from the dead.
Envy will Merit as its shade pursue,
But like a shadow proves the substance true;
For envied Wit, like Sol eclips'd, makes known
Th'opposing body's grossness, not its own.
When first that sun too powerful beams displays,
It draws up vapours which obscure its rays;
But ev'n those clouds at last adorn its way,
Reflect new glories, and augment the day.
Be thou the first true merit to befriend;
His praise is lost who stays till all commend.
Short is the date, alas! of modern rhymes,
And 'tis but just to let them live betimes.
No longer now that Golden Age appears,
When partiarch wits survived a thousand years:
Now length of fame (our second life) is lost,
And bare threescore is all ev'n that can boast:
Our sons their fathers' failing language see,
And such as Chaucer is shall Dryden be.
So when the faithful pencil has design'd
Some bright idea of the master's mind,
Where a new world leaps out at his command,
And ready Nature waits upon his hand;
When the ripe colours soften and unite,

And sweetly melt into just shade and light;
When mellowing years their full perfection give,
And each bold figure just begins to live,
The treach'rous colours the fair art betray,
And all the bright creations fades away!
Unhappy Wit, like most mistaken things,
Atones not for that envy which it brings:
In youth alone its empty praise we boast,
But soon the sort-lived vanity is lost;
Like some fair flower the early Spring supplies,
That gaily blooms, but ev'n in blooming dies.
What is this Wit, which must our cares employ?
The owner's wife that other men enjoy;
Then most our trouble still when most admired,
And still the more we give, the more required;
Whose fame with pains we guard, but lose with ease,
Sure some to vex, but never all to please,
'Tis what the vicious fear, the virtuous shun;
By fools 'tis hated, and by knaves undone!
If Wit so much from Ignorance undergo,
Ah, let not Learning too commence its foe!
Of old those met rewards who could excel,
And such were prais'd who but endevour'd well;
Tho' triumphs were to gen'rals only due,
Crowns were reserv'd to grace the soldiers too.
Now they who reach Parnassus' lofty crown
Employ their pains to spurn some others down;
And while self-love each jealous writer rules,
Contending wits become the sport of fools;
But still the worst with most regret commend,
For each ill author is as bad a friend.
To what base ends, and by what abject ways,
Are mortals urged thro' sacred lust of praise!
Ah, ne'er so dire a thirst of glory boast,
Nor in the critic let the man be lost!
Good nature and good sense must ever join;
To err is human, to forgive divine.
But if in noble minds some dregs remain,

Not yet purged off, of spleen and sour disdain,
Discharge that rage on more provoking crimes,
Nor fear a dearth on these flagitious times.
No pardon vile obscenity should find,
Tho' Wit and Art conspire to move your mind;
But dulness with obscenity must prove
As shameful sure as impotence in love.
In the fat age of pleasure, wealth, and ease
Sprung the rank weed, and thrived with large increase:
When love was all in easy monarch's care,
Seldom at council, never in a war;
Jilts ruled the state, and statesmen farces writ;
Nay wits had pensions, and young lords had wit;
The Fair sat panting at a courtier's play,
And not a mask went unimprov'd away;
The modest fan was lifted up no more,
And virgins smil'd at what they blush'd before.
The following license of a foreign reign
Did all the dregs of bold Socinus drain;
Then unbelieving priests reform'd the nation,
And taught more pleasant methods of salvation;
Where Heav'n's free subjects might their rights dispute,
Lest God himself should seem too absolute;
Pulpits their sacred satire learn'd to spare,
And vice admired to find a flatt'rer there!
Encouraged thus, Wit's Titans braved the skies,
And the press groan'd with licens'd blasphemies.
These monsters, Critics! with your darts engage,
Here point your thunder, and exhaust your rage!
Yet shun their fault, who, scandalously nice,
Will needs mistake an author into vice:
All seems infected that th'infected spy,
As all looks yellow to the jaundic'd eye.

Part III

Rules for the conduct and manners in a Critic. Candour. Modesty. Good breeding. Sincerity and freedom of advice. When one's counsel is to be restrained. Character of an incorrigible poet. And of an impertinent critic. Character of a good critic. The history of criticism, and characters of the best critics; Aristotle. Horace. Dionysius. Petronius. Quintiallian. Longinus. Of the decay of Criticism, and its revival. Erasmus. Vida. Boileau. Lord Roscommon, etc. Conclusion.

Learn then what morals Critics ought to show,
For 'tis but half a judge's task to know.
T'is not enough Taste, Judgment, Learning join;
In all you speak let Truth and Candour shine;
That not alone what to your Sense is due
All may allow, but seek your friendship too.
Be silent always when you doubt your Sense,
And speak, tho' sure, with seeming diffidence.
Some positive persisting fops we know,
Who if once wrong will needs be always so;
But you with pleasure own your errors past,
And make each day a critique on the last.
'Tis not enough your counsel still be true;
Blunt truths more mischief than nice falsehoods do.
Men must be taught as if you taught them not,
And things unknown proposed as things forgot.
Without good breeding truth is disapprov'd;
That only makes superior Sense belov'd.
Be niggards of advice on no pretence,
For the worst avarice is that of Sense.
With mean complacence ne'er betray your trust,
Nor be so civil as to prove unjust.
Fear not the anger of the wise to raise;
Those best can bear reproof who merit praise.
'Twere well might critics still this freedom take,
But Appius reddens at each word you speak,
And stares tremendous, with a threat'ning eye,
Like some fierce tyrant in old tapestry.
Fear most to tax an honourable fool,
Whose right it is, uncensured to be dull:
Such without Wit, are poets when they please,
As without Learning they can take degrees.
Leave dangerous truths to unsuccessful satires,
And flattery to fulsome dedicators;

Whom when the praise, the world believes no more
Than when they promise to give scribbling o'er.
'Tis best sometimes your censure to restrain,
And charitably let the dull be vain;
Your silence there is better than your spite,
For who can rail so long as they can write?
Still humming on their drowsy course they keep,
And lash'd so long, like tops, are lash'd asleep.
False steps but help them to renew the race,
As, after stumbling, jades will mend their pace.
What crowds of these, impenitently bold,
In sounds and jingling syllables grown old,
Still run on poets, in a raging vein,
Ev'n to the the dregs and squeezings of the brain,
Strain out the last dull droppings of their sense,
And rhyme with all the rage of impotence!
Such shameless bards we have; and yet 'tis true
There are as mad abandon'd critics too.
The bookful blockhead ignorantly read,
With loads of learned lumber in his head,
With his own tongue still edifies his ears,
And always list'ning to himself appears.
All books he reads, and all he reads assails,
From Dryden's Fables down to Durfey's Tales.
With him most authors steal their works, or buy;
Garth did not write his own Dispensary.
Name a new play, and he's the poet's friend;
Nay, show'd his faults—but when would poets mend?
No place so sacred from such fops is barr'd,
Nor is Paul's church more safe than Paul's churchyard:
Nay, fly to altars; there they'll talk you dead;
For fools rush in where angels fear t tread.
Distrustful sense with modest caution speaks,
It still looks home, and short excursions makes;
But rattling nonsense in full volleys breaks
And never shock'd, and never turn'd aside,
Bursts out, resistless, with a thund'ring tide.
But where's the man who counsel can bestow,

Still pleas'd to teach, and yet not proud to know?
Unbiass'd or by favour or by spite;
Not dully prepossess'd nor blindly right;
Tho' learn'd, well bred, and tho' well bred sincere;
Modestly bold, and humanly severe;
Who to a friend his faults can freely show,
And gladly praise the merit of a foe;
Bless'd with a taste exact, yet unconfin'd,
A knowledge both of books and humankind;
Gen'rous converse; a soul exempt from pride;
And love to praise, with reason on his side?
Such once were critics; such the happy few
Athens and Rome in better ages knew.
The mighty Stagyrite first left the shore,
Spread all his sails, and durst the deeps explore;
He steer'd securely, and discover'd far,
Led by the light of the Maeonian star.
Poets, a race long unconfin'd and free,
Still fond and proud of savage liberty,
Receiv'd his laws, and stood convinc'd 'twas fit
Who conquer'd Nature should preside o'er Wit.
Horace still charms with graceful negligence,
And without method talks us into sense;
Will, like a friend, familiarly convey
The truest notions in the easiest way.
He who, supreme in judgment as in wit,
Might boldly censure as he boldly writ,
Yet judg'd with coolness, though he sung with fire;
His precepts teach but what his works inspire.
Our critics take a contrary extreme,
They judge with fury, but they write with phlegm;
Nor suffers Horace more in wrong translations
By Wits, than Critics in as wrong quotations.
See Dionysius Homer's thoughts refine,
And call new beauties forth from ev'ry line!
Fancy and art in gay Petronius please,
The Scholar's learning with the courtier's ease.
In grave Quintilian's copious work we find

The justest rules and clearest method join'd.
Thus useful arms in magazines we place,
All ranged in order, and disposed with grace;
But less to please the eye than arm the hand,
Still fit for use, and ready at command.
Thee, bold Longinus! all the Nine inspire,
And bless their critic with a poet's fire:
An ardent judge, who, zealous in his trust,
With warmth gives sentence, yet is always just;
Whose own example strengthens all his laws,
And is himself that great sublime he draws.
Thus long succeeding critics justly reign'd,
License repress'd, and useful laws ordain'd:
Learning and Rome alike in empire grew,
And arts still follow'd where her eagles flew;
From the same foes at last both felt their doom,
And the same age saw learning fall and Rome.
With tyranny then superstition join'd,
As that the body, this enslaved the mind;
Much was believ'd, but little understood,
And to be dull was construed to be good;
A second deluge learning thus o'errun,
And the monks finish'd what the Goths begun.
At length Erasmus, that great injur'd name,
(The glory of the priesthood and the shame!)
Stemm'd the wild torrent of a barb'rous age,
And drove those holy Vandals off the stage.
But see! each Muse in Leo's golden days
Starts from her trance, and trims her wither'd bays.
Rome's ancient genius, o'er its ruins spread,
Shakes off the dust, and rears his rev'rend head.
Then sculpture and her sister arts revive;
Stones leap'd to form, and rocks began to live;
With sweeter notes each rising temple rung;
A Raphael painted and a Vida sung;
Immortal Vida! on whose honour'd brow
The poet's bays and critics ivy grow:
Cremona now shall ever boast they name,

As next in place to Mantua, next in fame!
But soon by impious arms from Latium chased,
Their ancient bounds the banish'd Muses pass'd;
Thence arts o'er all the northern world advance,
But critic learning flourish'd most in France;
The rules a nation born to serve obeys,
And Boileau still in right of Horace sways.
But we, brave Britons, foreign laws despised,
And kept unconquer'd and uncivilized;
Fierce for the liberties of wit, and bold,
We still defied the Romans, as of old.
Yet some there were, among the sounder few
Of those who less presumed and better knew,
Who durst assert the juster ancient cause,
And here restor'd WIt's fundamental laws.
Such was the Muse whose rules and practice tell
"Nature's chief masterpiece is writing well."
Such was Roscommon, not more learn'd than good,
With manners gen'rous as his noble blood;
To him the wit of Greece and Rome was known,
And every author's merit but his own.
Such late was Walsh—the Muse's judge and friend,
Who justly knew to blame or to commend;
To failings mild but zealous for desert,
The clearest head, and the sincerest heart.
This humble praise, lamented Shade! receive;
This praise at least a grateful Muse may give:
The Muse whose early voice you taught to sing,
Prescribed her heights, and pruned her tender wing,
(Her guide now lost), no more attempts to rise,
But in low numbers short excursions tries;
Content if hence th'unlearn'd their wants may view,
The learn'd reflect on what before they knew;
Careless of censure, nor too fond of fame;
Still pleas'd to praise, yet not afraid to blame;
Averse alike to flatter or offend;
Not free from faults, nor yet too vain to mend.

Alexander Pope amalgamates nature throughout his

Essay on Criticism in various lines to express neoclassicism. According to Albert C. Baugh, Baugh says the in Essay on Criticism pt. 1, "Pope starts with the view that as poets must by natural endowment have genius, so critics must have taste; that most men 'have the seeds of judgment in their mind,' and that this natural taste must be developed by a study of Nature (that is, of the moral system of the universe together with its manifestations) and a study of the ancients and of ancients rules...". That means that Pope has that taste that many critics wish they had in their mind. Nature is expressed by Pope as the best guide of judgment, in his Essay on Criticism, in this following stanza, "First follow Nature, and your judgment frame by her just standard, which is still the same; Unerring Nature, still divinely bright, one clear, unchanged, universal light…" (lines 68-71).

So, Pope is saying that Nature is this unchangeable source that people should follow to walk in the right path. Alexander Pope says "Those rules of old discovered, not devised, are Nature still, but Nature methodized; Nature, like liberty, is but restrained by the same laws which first herself ordained…" (lines 88-91). Pope uses this simile to describe how Nature is very similar to liberty. Harold Bloom explains that "Everything in the Essay turns on this fundamental idea of Nature, and three main principles underlie Pope's reasoning: (1) That all sound judgment and true 'wit' is founded on the observation of Nature; (2) That false 'wit' arises from a disregard of Nature and an excessive affection for the conception of the mind; (3) That the true standard for determining what is 'natural' in poetry is to be found in the best works of the ancients…".

According to Edward Niles Hooker, "A critic must understand wit if he is to talk of literature". The way that Alexander Pope coalesce wit into his work displays that Pope is indeed a poet and also a critic. Harold Bloom explains wit as "…the practice of finding resemblances in objects apparently dissimilar, as it was cultivated throughout the seventeenth century by poets like Donne, Crashaw, Quarles, and Cowley…Wit, as we see from the Essay on Criticism, was regarded in the early part of the century as a power object in poetry…".

Pope explains how authors and critics are somewhat alike in this stanza, "Authors are partial to their wit, 'tis true, but are not critics to their judgment too?" (lines 17-18). But unlike the last reference, Pope uses this stanza to explicate how searching for wit could lead to more problems, "In search of wit these lose their common sense, and then turn critics in their own defence…" (lines 28-29).

Alexander Pope elucidates genius within several lines in his Essay of Criticism. Pope explains in the following stanza that a true taste is hard to find, and that is the same for a true genius, "'Tis with out judgment as our watches, none go just alike, yet each believes his own. In poets as true genius is bur rare, true taste as seldom is the critic's share…" (lines 9-12).

In the next selected stanza, Pope explains that if you just look for fame then you just be another name, but if you reach your goal or limit its no telling how far you will go, "But you who seek to give and merit fame, and justly bear a critic's noble name, be sure yourself and your own reach to know, how far your genius, taste, and learning go…" (lines 46-49). Alexander Pope justifies in this next stanza that only one person with the right wit and imagination can understand what is going on, "One Where beam of warm imagination play, the memory's soft figures melt away. One science only will one genius fit, so vast is art, so narrow human wit…" (lines 58-61).

Chapter 15

Alexander Pope's Essay on Man

The Essay on Man is a philosophical poem, written, characteristically, in heroic couplets, and published between 1732 and 1734. Pope intended it as the centerpiece of a proposed system of ethics to be put forth in poetic form: it is in fact a fragment of a larger work which Pope planned but did not live to complete. It is an attempt to justify, as Milton had attempted to vindicate, the ways of God to Man, and a warning that man himself is not, as, in his pride, he seems to believe, the centre of all things. Though not explicitly Christian, the Essay makes the implicit assumption that man is fallen and unregenerate, and that he must seek his own salvation.

The "Essay" consists of four epistles, addressed to Lord Bolingbroke, and derived, to some extent, from some of Bolingbroke's own fragmentary philosophical writings, as well as from ideas expressed by the deistic third Earl of Shaftsbury. Pope sets out to demonstrate that no matter how imperfect, complex, inscrutable, and disturbingly full of evil the Universe may appear to be, it does function in a rational fashion, according to natural laws; and is, in fact, considered as a whole, a perfect work of God.

It appears imperfect to us only because our perceptions are limited by our feeble moral and intellectual capacity. His conclusion is that we must learn to accept our position in the Great Chain of Being — a "middle state," below that of the angels but above that of the beasts — in which we can, at least potentially, lead happy and virtuous lives.

Epistle I concerns itself with the nature of man and with his place in the universe; Epistle II, with man as an individual;

Epistle III, with man in relation to human society, to the political and social hierarchies; and Epistle IV, with man's pursuit of happiness in this world. An Essay on Man was a controversial work in Pope's day, praised by some and criticized by others, primarily because it appeared to contemporary critics that its emphasis, in spite of its themes, was primarily poetic and not, strictly speaking, philosophical in any really coherent sense: Dr. Johnson, never one to mince words, and possessed, in any case, of views upon the subject which differed materially from those which Pope had set forth, noted dryly (in what is surely one of the most back-handed literary compliments of all time) that "Never were penury of knowledge and vulgarity of sentiment so happily disguised."

It is a subtler work, however, than perhaps Johnson realized: G. Wilson Knight has made the perceptive comment that the poem is not a "static scheme" but a "living organism," (like Twickenham) and that it must be understood as such.

Considered as a whole, the Essay on Man is an affirmative poem of faith: life seems chaotic and patternless to man when he is in the midst of it, but is in fact a coherent portion of a divinely ordered plan. In Pope's world God exists, and he is benificent: his universe is an ordered place. The limited intellect of man can perceive only a tiny portion of this order, and can experience only partial truths, and hence must rely on hope, which leads to faith.

Man must be cognizant of his rather insignificant position in the grand scheme of things: those things which he covets most — riches, power, fame — prove to be worthless in the greater context of which he is only dimly aware. In his place, it is man's duty to strive to be good, even if he is doomed, because of his inherent frailty, to fail in his attempt. Do you find Pope's argument convincing? In what ways can we relate the Essay on Man to works like Swift's Gulliver's Travels, Johnson's "The Vanity of Human Wishes" (text), Tennyson's In Memoriam and Eliot's The Wasteland?

The Rape of the Lock (text) had its origins in an actual, if trivial, incident in polite society: in 1711, the twenty-one year old Robert, Lord Petre, had, at Binfield, had surreptitiously cut a lock of hair from the head of the beautiful Arabella Fermor, whom he had been courting. Arabella took offense, and a schism developed between her family and Petre's. John Caryll, a friend of both familes and an old friend of Pope's, suggested that he work up a humorous poem about the episode which would demonstrate to both sides that the whole affair had been blown out of proportion and thus effect a reconciliation between them.

Pope produced his poem, and it seemed to have achieved its purpose, though Petre never married Arabella. It became obvious over the course of time, however (especially after a revised and enlarged version of the poem, which existed at first only in manuscript copies, was published in 1714) that the poem, which Pope maintained "was intended only to divert a few young Ladies," was in fact something rather more substantial, and the Fermors again took offense — this time at Pope himself, who had to placate them with a letter, usually printed before the text, which explains that Arabella and Belinda, the heroine of the poem, are not identical.

The Rape of the Lock is the finest mock-heroic or mock-epic poem in English: written on the model of Boileau's Le Lutrin, it is an exquisitely witty and balanced burlesque displaying the literary virtuosity, the perfection of poetic "judgement," and the exquisite sense of artistic propriety, which was so sought after by Ne-classical artists. Repeatedly invoking classical epic devices to establish an ironic contrast between its structure and its content, it functions at once as a satire on the trivialities of fashionable life, as a commentary on the distorted moral values of polite society, and as an implicit indictment of human pride, and a revelation of the essentially trivial nature of many of the aspects of human existence which we tend to hold very dear.

The world of the beaux and belles of The Rape of the Lock is a an artificial one, a trivial realm of calm and decorum sustained by the strict observance of rigorous rules, a micrososm in which very real and very powerful human emotions and passions have been ignored or sublimated. The narcissistic inhabitants of this world assume that they are something more than human, but Pope shows us vulnerable, how fragile, their pretended perfection and their isolation from reality makes them. The Rape of the Lock, with all of its implicit and explicit sexual and emotional implications, shatters the calm, the order, the balance, and the decorum of their artificial world. They are undone by what Pope identifies — here, as in An Essay on Man and "An Essay on Criticism" — as their most important weakness: Pride.

A final note: it is obvious that the poem was written for a limited and very specialized audience: in Pope's day, literary art was the province of the upper classes; the domain of a culture which was pervasively literary. Contemporary readers of The Rape of the Lock would, in consequence, recognize and delight in the enormous number of literary allusions which the poem contains.

The readers of a poem so concerned with imitation ought, obviously, to be familiar with what is being imitated, and in Pope's day, if not in our own, this was largely the case. What else, though, does this pervasive emphasis on imitation, on distortion, on satire, on parody, and on irony tell us about the cultural milieu or context within which Pope created the poem, and about his relationship with the society he is reproducing in microcosm? In his postscript to his translation of the Odyssey, Pope noted that "Tis using a vast force to lift a feather": in The Rape of the Lock, however, the feather is heavier than one might suspect.

ALEXANDER POPE, SCIENCE, AND TECHNOLOGY

Pope lived during a period of intense and varied scientific activities — the development of the microscope, and Newton's formulation of a theory explaining the gravitational basis of the universe, for example — which revealed a great deal about the nature of things: for Pope, these discoveries seemed to provide scientific corroboration for a crucially important concept which he expressed in various ways, but which can be expressed as the fundamentally conservative notion that the physical universe itself, and man's place in it, are aspects of an orderly Divine scheme of things which, though it is too vast for the merely human intellect to comprehend, is nevertheless both majestic and meaningful.

Pope's acceptance of this concept, and the ways in which he managed to incorporate it into his work, are revealing: contemporary scientific discoveries, that is, seemed to him to provide acceptable answers to questions which had previously been matters of religious faith or philosophical belief. With what questions does he seem to have concerned himself most? Much more so than darker and more sceptical figures like Swift or Johnson (who were in any case much more dubious about the validity of the very notion of scientific "progress") Pope seems to have regarded contemporary scientific and technological advances — those, at any rate, which could be incorporated into his belief-system — as being somehow reassuring. Although he was clearly not a religious poet in the sense that the Herbert or Hopkins — or even poets like Donne or Tennyson or T. S. Eliot, in the latter parts of their careers — were, and though his poetry is only rarely explicitly Catholic or even overtly Christian, Pope's religion was an important factor in his life, and religious themes and imagery — sometimes employed in an ironic or satirical or disguised fashion — appear frequently in his work.

Can you detect his use of religious imagery, for example, in The Rape of the Lock? Religion played an important role in Pope's personal life from its very outset: he came of a Roman Catholic family, and he remained a Catholic, though not a particularly fervent one, when it was still decidedly disadvantageous and even dangerous to be so.

During his youth — he was born in 1688, the year of the Glorious Revolution — the Protestant hold on the throne of England was still perceived as a tenuous one, and Catholics — as Tories, as Jacobites, in league with the French, and working for the restoration of the Stuarts — were perceived as being actively or potentially treacherous. As late as 1723, in fact, Pope's edition of the Duke of Buckingham's Works was confiscated by the government upon its publication because Pope was suspected of sympathizing with the Jacobites. Many of his friends attempted to persuade him to renounce

Catholicism and become a member of the Church of England, but he refused, in a particularly polite, gentle and undogmatic fashion, to do so. In his reply, in 1717, to a letter from the Anglican Bishop Atterbury, who had written to him offering his condolences upon the death of his father, and suggesting that he might now wish to convert, Pope commented on the extent to which his religious and political beliefs were predicated upon the same principle: I'll tell you my politick and religious sentiments in a few words. In my politics, I think no further than how to preserve the peace of my life, in any government under which I live; nor in my religion, than to preserve the peace of my conscience in any Church with which I comunicate.

I hope all churches and all governments are so far of God, as they are rightly understood, and rightly administered: and where they are, or may be wrong, I leave it to God alone to mend or reform them; which, whenever he does, it must be by greater instruments than I am. Do these sentiments, in which Pope implicitly accepts traditional Christian explanations of the way the world is ordered and assumes that man must submit to God's will and trust in his benevolence, accord with the generally accepted concept of the purpose and function of the sort of Neoclassical poetry which Pope himself wrote? How does this accord with the ideas about the relationship between God and Man which Pope sets forth in "An Essay on Man"? Would Swift or Johnson agree or disagree with what Pope has to say here?

How would a proto-Romantic like Blake react to the attitudes Pope expresses here and in a work like "An Essay on Man"? What would James Thomson, the author of The City of Dreadful Night, have to say about the matter? Pope was not as philospher in any systematic sense, though he had obvious philosophical concerns, which manifested themselves most strongly in works like his An Essay on Man. He read a great deal of philosophy, but casually rather than formally: he was deeply interested in attempts to discern man's place in the universe and his relationship with God, but his interest was primarily poetic, not philosophical. Like many of his contemporaries, Pope believed in the existence of a God who had created, and who presided over, a physical Universe which functioned like a vast clockwork mechanism.

Important scientific discoveries by men like Sir Isaac Newton, who explained, in his Principia, the nature of the laws of gravitation which helped to govern that universe, were seen as corroborating that view. "Nature, and Nature's Laws lay hid in Night," Pope wrote, in a famous couplet intended as Newton's epitaph, but "God said, Let Newton be! and All was Light." This view of the universe as an ordered, structured place was an aspect of the Neoclassical emphasis on order and structure which also manifested itself in the arts, including poetry. How does An Essay on Man reflect this perspective? Remember that Pope could also portray Belinda in The Rape of the Lock in the following fashion:

"The skilful Nymph reviews her Force with Care;
Let Spades be Trumps ! she said, and Trumps they were."

Pope's work also echoes, of course, Neoclassical philosophical concerns which were intimately bound up with religious ones. Human beings were seen as imperfect creatures who occupied a middle place in the great scheme of things; in the great chain of being. What assumptions did Pope assume that man could make about his role in the universe, based upon his perception of mankind's place in it?

Pope believed, as Swift believed (it is one of the many attitudes which these two very different men shared in common) that God intended that Man should be rational, thoughtful, logical, and reasonable, but that, too often he was not; and that it was one of the poet's primary tasks to point out error, to instruct, to show the way. Pope was uniquely positioned to assume this role precisely because he maintained, all his life, (despite all of his literary feuds and squabbles) a crucial psychological distance — because he was a chronic invalid, because he was a Catholic during a period of Protestant ascendancy, because he was, physically, a dwarf — from the upper levels of English society to which his poetic genius had given him access.

Chapter 16

Quotes

- A God without dominion, providence, and final causes, is nothing else but fate and nature.
- A little learning is a dangerous thing; Drink deep, or taste not the Pierian spring.
- A man should never be ashamed to own he has been in the wrong, which is but saying, in other words, that he is wiser today than he was yesterday.
- A person who is too nice an observer of the business of the crowd, like one who is too curious in observing the labour of bees, will often be stung for his curiosity.
- A wit with dunces, and a dunce with wits.
- A work of art that contains theories is like an object on which the price tag has been left.
- Act well your part, there all the honour lies.
- All are but parts of one stupendous whole, Whose body Nature is, and God the soul.
- All nature is but art unknown to thee.
- An honest man's the noblest work of God.

  And all who told it added something new, and all who heard it, made enlargements too.
- And die of nothing but a rage to live.
- And, after all, what is a lie? 'Tis but the truth in a masquerade.
- At ev'ry word a reputation dies.
- Be not the first by whom the new are tried, Nor yet the last to lay the old aside.

- Beauties in vain their pretty eyes may roll; charms strike the sight, but merit wins the soul.
- Behold the child, by Nature's kindly law pleased with a rattle, tickled with a straw.
- Blessed is the man who expects nothing, for he shall never be disappointed was the ninth beatitude.
- But blind to former as to future fate, what mortal knows his pre-existent state?
- But Satan now is wiser than of yore, and tempts by making rich, not making poor.
- Charms strike the sight, but merit wins the soul.
- Education forms the common mind. Just as the twig is bent, the tree's inclined.
- Extremes in nature equal ends produce; In man they join to some mysterious use.
- Fondly we think we honour merit then, When we but praise ourselves in other men.
- Fools admire, but men of sense approve.
- Fools rush in where angels fear to tread.
- For fools rush in where angels fear to tread.
- For Forms of Government let fools contest; whatever is best administered is best.
- For modes of faith let graceless zealots fight, His can't be wrong whose life is in the right.
- Genius creates, and taste preserves. Taste is the good sense of genius; without taste, genius is only sublime folly.
- Gentle dullness ever loves a joke.
- Get place and wealth, if possible with grace; if not, by any means get wealth and place.
- Happy the man whose wish and care a few paternal acres bound, content to breathe his native air in his own ground.
- Health consists with temperance alone.
- Histories are more full of examples of the fidelity of dogs than of friends.
- Honour and shame from no condition rise. Act well your part: there all the honour lies.

- Hope springs eternal in the human breast: Man never is, but always To be Blest.
- Hope travels through, nor quits us when we die.
- How happy is the blameless vestal's lot? The world forgetting, by the world forgot.
- How prone to doubt, how cautious are the wise!
- How shall I lose the sin, yet keep the sense, and love the offender, yet detest the offence?
- I find myself hoping a total end of all the unhappy divisions of mankind by party-spirit, which at best is but the madness of many for the gain of a few.
- If a man's character is to be abused there's nobody like a relative to do the business.
- In words, as fashions, the same rule will hold; Alike fantastic, if too new, or old: Be not the first by whom the new are tried, Nor yet the last to lay the old aside.
- Is pride, the never-failing vice of fools.
- Know then this truth, enough for man to know virtue alone is happiness below.
- Know then thyself, presume not God to scan; The proper study of mankind is man.
- Like Cato, give his little senate laws, and sit attentive to his own applause.
- Lo, what huge heaps of littleness around!
- Lo! The poor Indian, whose untutored mind sees God in clouds, or hears him in the wind.
- Lulled in the countless chambers of the brain, our thoughts are linked by many a hidden chain; awake but one, and in, what myriads rise!
- Man never thinks himself happy, but when he enjoys those things which others want or desire.
- Many men have been capable of doing a wise thing, more a cunning thing, but very few a generous thing.
- Men dream of courtship, but in wedlock wake.
- Men must be taught as if you taught them not, and things unknown proposed as things forgot.
- Men would be angels, angels would be gods.

- Nature and nature's laws lay hid in the night. God said, Let Newton be! and all was light!
- Never elated when someone's oppressed, never dejected when another one's blessed.
- Never find fault with the absent.
- Never was it given to mortal man - To lie so boldly as we women can.
- Nc one should be ashamed to admit they are wrong, which is but saying, in other words, that they are wiser today than they were yesterday.
- No woman ever hates a man for being in love with her, but many a woman hate a man for being a friend to her.
- Not always actions show the man; we find who does a kindness is not therefore kind.
- Not to go back is somewhat to advance, and men must walk, at least, before they dance.
- Of Manners gentle, of Affections mild; In Wit a man; Simplicity, a child.
- On life's vast ocean diversely we sail. Reasons the card, but passion the gale.
- On wrongs swift vengeance waits.
- One science only will one genius fit; so vast is art, so narrow human wit.
- Order is heaven's first law.
- Our passions are like convulsion fits, which, though they make us stronger for a time, leave us the weaker ever after.
- Party-spirit at best is but the madness of many for the gain of a few.
- Passions are the gales of life.
- Praise undeserved, is satire in disguise.
- Pride is still aiming at the best houses: Men would be angels, angels would be gods. Aspiring to be gods, if angels fell; aspiring to be angels men rebel.
- Remembrance and reflection how allied. What thin partitions divides sense from thought.

- Satan is wiser now than before, and tempts by making rich instead of poor.
- Slave to no sect, who takes no private road, But looks through Nature up to Nature's God.
- So vast is art, so narrow human wit.
- Some old men, continually praise the time of their youth. In fact, you would almost think that there were no fools in their days, but unluckily they themselves are left as an example.
- Some people will never learn anything, for this reason, because they understand everything too soon.
- Teach me to feel another's woe, to hide the fault I see, that mercy I to others show, that mercy show to me.
- The bookful blockhead, ignorantly read With loads of learned lumber in his head.
- The difference is too nice - Where ends the virtue or begins the vice.
- The greatest magnifying glasses in the world are a man's own eyes when they look upon his own person.
- The hungry judges soon the sentence sign, and wretches hang that jurymen may dine.
- The learned is happy, nature to explore; The fool is happy, that he knows no more.
- The most positive men are the most credulous.
- The proper study of Mankind is Man.
- The ruling passion, be it what it will. The ruling passion conquers reason still.
- The same ambition can destroy or save, and make a patriot as it makes a knave.
- The vulgar boil, the learned roast, an egg.
- The way of the Creative works through change and transformation, so that each thing receives its true nature and destiny and comes into permanent accord with the Great Harmony: this is what furthers and what perseveres.
- The world forgetting, by the world forgot.

- The worst of madmen is a saint run mad.
- There is a certain majesty in simplicity which is far above all the quaintness of wit.
- They dream in courtship, but in wedlock wake.
- Those move easiest who have learn'd to dance.
- Tis but a part we see, and not a whole.
- 'Tis education forms the common mind; just as the twig is bent the tree's inclined.
- 'Tis not enough your counsel still be true; Blunt truths more mischief than nice falsehoods do.
- To be angry is to revenge the faults of others on ourselves.
- To err is human; to forgive, divine.
- To observations which ourselves we make, we grow more partial for th' observer's sake.
- True ease in writing comes from art, not chance, as those who move easiest have learned to dance.
- True politeness consists in being easy one's self, and in making every one about one as easy as one can.
- Trust not yourself, but your defects to know, make use of every friend and every foe.
- Virtue she finds too painful an endeavour, content to dwell in decencies for ever.
- What some call health, if purchased by perpetual anxiety about diet, isn't much better than tedious disease.
- Who shall decide when doctors disagree, And soundest casuists doubt, like you and me?
- Whoever thinks a faultless piece to see, Thinks what ne'er was, nor is, nor e'er shall be.
- Wit is the lowest form of humour.
- Woman's at best a contradiction still.

Bibliography

Morris R. Brownell, *Alexander Pope and the Arts of Georgian England* (Oxford: Clarendon Press, 1978). An account of Pope's "*virtuosoship,*" his role as a critic and arbiter of taste in the arts of painting, landscape gardening, architecture, and sculpture.

Carole Fabricant, "'*Binding and Dressing Nature's Loose Tresses': The Ideology of Augustan Landscape Design,*" *Studies in Eighteenth-Century Culture* 8 (1979): 109-35.

Jean H. Hagstrum, *The Sister Arts: The Tradition of Literary Pictorialism and English Poetry from Dryden to Gray* (Chicago: Univ. of Chicago Press, 1958).

John Dixon Hunt, *The Figure in the Landscape: Poetry, Painting, and Gardening during the Eighteenth Century* (Baltimore and London: Johns Hopkins Univ. Press, 1976). Discusses Pope on pp. 58-104.

James Lee-Milne, *Earls of Creation: Five Great Patrons of Eighteenth-Century Art* (London: Hamish Hamilton, 1972). The five earls (Bathurst, Pembroke, Burlington, Oxford, Leicester) whose lives, houses, and gardens form the focus of this study influenced Pope in his ideas on architecture and gardening, and were, in turn, influenced by him.

Peter Martin, *Pursuing Innocent Pleasures: The Gardening World of Alexander Pope* (Hamden, Conn.: Archon Books, 1984). A biographical approach to Pope's life-long interest in landscape gardening, including the gardens of his friends and contemporaries.

Carole Fabricant, "'*Binding and Dressing Nature's Loose Tresses': The Ideology of Augustan Landscape Design,*" *Studies in Eighteenth-Century Culture* 8 (1979): 109-35.

Christa Knellwolf, *A Contradiction Still: Representations of Women in the Poetry of Alexander Pope* (Manchester and New York: Manchester Univ. Press, 1998).

Felicity Nussbaum, *"The Brink of All We Hate": English Satires on Women 1660-1750* (Lexington: Kentucky Univ. Press, 1984). Places Pope's *Epistle to a Lady* in a tradition of anti-feminist satire that was very much alive in the Restoration and early eighteenth century.

Ellen Pollak, *The Poetics of Sexual Myth: Gender and Ideology in the Verse of Swift and Pope* (Chicago and London: Univ. of Chicago Press, 1985). This book explores some important eighteenth-century cultural myths about gender (such as the "*myth of passive womanhood*") and then applies this contextual perspective, in Pope's case, to new readings of *The Rape of the Lock* and *Epistle to a Lady*.

Valerie Rumbold, *Woman's Place in Pope's World* (Cambridge: Cambridge Univ. Press, 1991). An approach to Pope through some of the important women in his life, including his mother, the Blount sisters, and Lady Mary Wortley Montagu.

Claudia N. Thomas, *Alexander Pope and His Eighteenth-Century Women Readers* (Carbondale and Edwardsville: Southern Illinois Univ. Press, 1994). Chronicles the complex response of eighteenth-century women readers and writers to Pope's poetry. His work furnished a model to be imitated, appropriated, critiqued, and sometimes repudiated.

Carolyn D. Williams, *Pope, Homer, and Manliness: Some Aspects of Eighteenth-Century Classical Learning* (London and New York: Routledge, 1993). The general focus of this study is on constructions of gender in the context of eighteenth-century readings of the classics, though, as Williams notes, her book also "*has much to say, directly and implicitly, about women*" (p. 3). An illuminating analysis of gender issues in Pope's work.

Douglas Brooks-Davies, *Pope's "Dunciad" and the Queen of the Night: A Study of Emotional Jacobitism* (Manchester: Manchester Univ. Press, 1985). Raises the controversial question of Pope's Jacobite sympathies in relation to *The Dunciad*. Suggests that Jacobitism is "*an ultimate clue*" to the poem. A highly speculative study that invokes some esoteric contexts for the *Dunciad,* including the mysteries of Isis and alchemy.

Howard Erskine-Hill, *Pope: "The Dunciad"* (London: Arnold, 1972). A helpful introductory study of the poem.

Emrys Jones, *"Pope and Dulness," Proceedings of the British Academy* 54 (1968): 231-63. An important study that argues for Pope's fascination with the anarchic energy of the dunces and their world, despite his professed repudiation of them.

John E. Sitter, *The Poetry of Pope's "Dunciad"* (Minneapolis: Univ. of Minnesota Press, 1971).

Aubrey Williams, *Pope's "Dunciad": A Study of Its Meaning* (1955). An influential study that establishes the spatial grounding of the poem in the cities of London and Westminster. Argues that the poem must be read as a serious critique of cultural decay in Pope's time. Explores Pope's allusions in the poem to Virgil and Milton, which have the effect, in Williams's view, of heightening the poem's seriousness.

Gillian Beer, *"'Our Unnatural No-voice': The Heroic Epistle, Pope, and Women's Gothic," Yearbook of English Studies* 12 (1982): 125-51.

Susan Manning, *"Eloisa's Abandonment," Cambridge Quarterly* 22 (1993): 231-40.

Peter Dixon, *The World of Pope's Satires: An Introduction to the Epistles and Imitations of Horace* (London: Methuen, 1968).

Miriam Leranbaum, *Alexander Pope's "Opus Magnum," 1729-1744* (Oxford: Clarendon Press, 1977). See above, under *Essay on Man.*

Robert W. Rogers, *The Major Satires of Alexander Pope* (Urbana: Univ. of Illinois Press, 1955).

Earl Wasserman, *Pope's "Epistle to Bathurst": A Critical Reading with an Edition of the Manuscripts.*

David Morris has an excellent essay on this poem in *Alexander Pope: The Genius of Sense* (Cambridge, Mass.: Harvard Univ. Press, 1984).

William Empson, "Wit in the *Essay on Criticism," Hudson Review* 2 (1950): 559-77.

Martin Kallich, *Heav'n's First Law: Rhetoric and Order in Pope's "Essay on Man"* (De Kalb: Northern Illionois Univ. Press, 1967).

Miriam Leranbaum, *Alexander Pope's "Opus Magnum," 1729-1744* (Oxford: Clarendon Press, 1977). A study of the "ethic scheme" or "*opus magnum*" projected by Pope as the grand poetic work of his maturity. Only *An Essay on Man* and the four *Epistles to Several Persons* were actually completed. Gathers together evidence relating to Pope's plan and suggests that our understanding of the existing poems can be enriched by an awareness of the larger scheme.

A. D. Nuttall, *Pope's "Essay on Man"* (Unwin Critical Library) (London and Boston: George Allen & Unwin, 1984).

Martin Price, *To the Palace of Wisdom* (Garden City, New York: Doubleday, 1964), pp. 129-42. Price, like Maynard Mack, is a perceptive and sympathetic reader of the *Essay*. For Mack's views, see his Introduction to volume 3.1 of the Twickenham edition (listed above).

Harry M. Solomon, *The Rape of the Text: Reading and Misreading Pope's "Essay on Man"* (Tuscaloosa and London: Univ. of Alabama Press, 1993). Argues that Pope's *Essay*, widely praised in his own time as a masterpiece of didactic poetry, has been "*systematically misread*" and "*trivialized*" in the twentieth century. Argues that the fault lies not with Pope but with our habits of reading: we need to learn anew how "*to take philosophical poetry seriously as a genre.*"

Douglas H. White, *Pope and the Context of Controversy: The Manipulation of Ideas in "An Essay on Man"* (Chicago and London: Univ. of Chicago Press, 1970). Places the poem in the context of philosophical and theological controversies of the early eighteenth century. Fleshes out the contemporary intellectual context of the poem.

Peter Dixon, *The World of Pope's Satires: An Introduction to the "Epistles" and "Imitations of Horace"* (London: Methuen, 1968).

Jacob Fuchs, *Reading Pope's "Imitations of Horace"* (Lewisburg: Bucknell Univ. Press, 1989).

T. E. Maresca, *Pope's Horatian Poems* (Columbus: Ohio State Univ. Press, 1966).

Robert W. Rogers, *The Major Satires of Alexander Pope* (Urbana: Univ. of Illinois Press, 1955).

F. Stack, *Pope and Horace: Studies in Imitation* (Cambridge: Cambridge Univ. Press, 1985). Pope published his Horatian imitations alongside the original Latin poems of Horace. Stack explores in detail the complex intertextual relation between Horace's originals and Pope's imitations.

Richard Steiger, *The English and Latin Texts of Pope's "Imitations of Horace,"* Garland Publications in English and American Literature (New York and London: Garland, 1988).

Harold Bloom, ed., *Modern Critical Interpretations: "The Rape of the Lock"* (New York: Chelsea House, 1988). A handy collection of essays on the poem.

J. S. Cunningham, *Pope: "The Rape of the Lock,"* Studies in English Literature No 2 (London: Edward Arnold, 1961).

Robert Halsband, *"The Rape of the Lock" and Its Illustrations, 1714-1896* (Oxford: Clarendon Press, 1980). A study of the rich legacy of illustrations of the poem, which themselves constitute a set of readings or critical commentaries of the poem.

John Dixon Hunt, ed., *Pope: "The Rape of the Lock," A Casebook* (London: Macmillan, 1968). An earlier, but still useful, compilation of essays.

The Rape of the Lock, Contexts 2, ed. William Kinsley (Hamden, Conn.: Archon, 1979). A collection of literary and historical documents from Pope's time and earlier that furnish a literary context for Pope's poem. A more recent collection of such documents is to be found in Cynthia Wall's 1998 edition of the poem.

Louis A. Landa, "Pope's Belinda, the General Emporie of the World, and the Wondrous Worm," *South Atlantic Quarterly* 70 (1971): 215-35.

G. S. Rousseau, ed., *Twentieth-Century Interpretations of "The Rape of the Lock"* (Englewood Cliffs, NJ: Prentice-Hall, 1969). Essays and commentary from the mid twentieth century.